DECISIONS, DECISIONS

More Praise for *Decisions, Decisions*

"Drawing on history, philosophy, and psychology, Welch's ground-breaking writing provides advice of practical value to every kind of decision maker. Home purchasers, gamblers, risk analysts, and international negotiators among others will all benefit from this entertaining and erudite guide to the high art of decision making. An enjoyable and highly instructive read for business people, students, and diplomats alike."
—Anthony Campbell, Former Director of the
Privy Council Office Intelligence Secretariat, Canada

"Using engaging examples and a lively style, Professor David Welch adroitly translates the lessons of political decision analysis into a guide for decision making in everyday life."
—Sherry Glied, Associate Professor and Head,
Division of Health Policy and Management, Columbia University

"*Decisions, Decisions* should be required reading for anyone working in financial markets. Professor Welch provides a link between how financial analysts expect people to make decisions and how those decisions are actually made."
—Arthur M. Heinmaa, Managing Partner,
Toron Capital Markets Inc.

"Professor Welch has provided a compelling book that experts will credit as reliable and everyone will credit as helpful. More than a few of us will see our foibles played out in the engaging anecdotes Welch uses to illustrate his points."
—Peter D. Feaver, Associate Professor,
Political Science, Duke University

"A readable, thought-provoking book that helps us reexamine our own decision-making processes. Welch describes basic principles in a variety of disciplines, from philosophy to economics to probability, and entertainingly shows how they can offer concrete advice for personal decision making in everyday situations."
—Neal Madras, Professor, Mathematics and Statistics,
York University

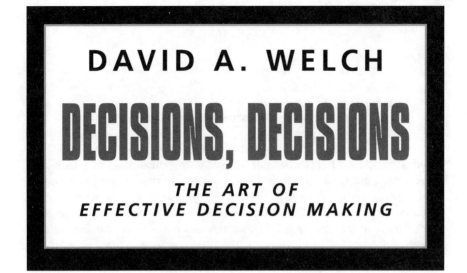

DAVID A. WELCH

DECISIONS, DECISIONS

THE ART OF
EFFECTIVE DECISION MAKING

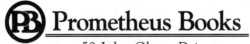

Prometheus Books

59 John Glenn Drive
Amherst, New York 14228-2197

Published 2002 by Prometheus Books

Inquiries should be addressed to
Prometheus Books
59 John Glenn Drive
Amherst, New York 14228–2197
VOICE: 716–691–0133, ext. 207
FAX: 716–564–2711
WWW.PROMETHEUSBOOKS.COM

06 05 04 03 02   5 4 3 2

Library of Congress Cataloging-in-Publication Data

Welch, David A.
    Decisions, decisions : the art of effective decision making / David A. Welch.
        p. cm.
    Includes bibliographical references and index.
    ISBN 1–57392–934–4 (pbk. : alk. paper)
    1. Decision making. I. Title.

BF448 .W45 2001
153.8'3—dc21   2001041871

Printed in the United States of America on acid-free paper

For Melissa and Nathaniel

CONTENTS

ACKNOWLEDGMENTS

Many people helped make this book possible in various ways, large and small. Some read the complete manuscript. Some read specific parts. Some allowed me to pick their brains on minor points when they could supply expertise that I lacked. Some consented to my telling anecdotes involving them (anonymously, of course). So many helped me in so many ways that were I to try to thank everyone by name, I would surely fail, inadvertently leaving someone off the list. I hope I will be forgiven for acknowledging them all with an enormous collective "thank you." You know who you are, even if I can't quite remember.

That said, I would particularly like to thank Jim Blight, Richard Burgess, Walter Daschko, Virgil Duff, David Dyzenhaus, Peter Feaver, David Fott, Sherry Glied, Jody Joseph, Juris Jurjevics, Veronica Jarek-Prinz, Victoria Kamsler, Nancy Kokaz, janet Lang, Cathy Lu, Neal Madras, Cheryl Misak, Sean Mulrooney, Mark Nickel, Louis Pauly, Tim Prinz, Julie Schnaithmann, Debora Spar, Janice Gross Stein, Douglas Welch, Stephen Welch, Bruce Westwood, and Griffin Williams for their especially valuable aid. My agent, Lisa Adams of the Garamond Agency, and my editor at Prometheus Books, Linda Regan, also greatly helped me improve the manuscript.

The greatest debt of all I owe (as usual) to my wife, Melissa Williams, who read everything in draft many times, and who provided a wealth of valuable feedback. The muffled chuckles that came from the next room as she read provided just the gauge I needed to know that I was striking the right tone. It is to her, and to our six-year-old son, Nathaniel—who wonders that his parents write books without pictures—that I dedicate this volume.

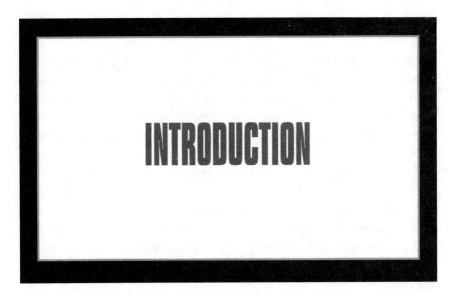

INTRODUCTION

As soon as questions of will or decision or reason or choice of action arise, human science is at a loss.
—Noam Chomsky, television interview, March 30, 1978

That's nonsense.

You make thousands of decisions every day. Most of them are trivial. Do you watch the news or the football game? Do you run for the bus, or walk and catch the next one? Coke or Pepsi? These decisions are usually pretty easy. If you have trouble making decisions like these, you desperately need this book.

You typically make several important decisions every day, too. By "important," I mean decisions with potentially significant costs or gains. Do you sell your shares in Microsoft, or hang onto them? Do you stop, or try to run the yellow light? Do you eat last week's egg salad, or throw it away? While many of us make decisions like these without much effort, they are not trivially easy. They require a little thought—preferably, in advance. If decisions like these cause you a certain amount of anxiety, you are perfectly normal, and this book can help you.

Once in a while you make a decision that is likely to have a profound effect on the course of your life. Do you go to medical school, or do you get a job? Do you buy a house, or continue to rent? Do you have a child? Do you cheat on your spouse? Most people find these decisions very difficult. A few people can make them quickly and confidently—and some of *those* folks always seem to make the right decision. If you are one of them, consider yourself blessed and put down this book, for it has nothing to offer you. Whatever you're doing, you're doing it right, so just keep doing it. But if you are not one of those people, read on: for, despite Mr. Chomsky's eloquent aphorism, there is a great deal that human science has to say about decision making, and the odds are that it can help you make better decisions—both major ones and minor ones.

If you have trouble making decisions, or if the decisions you make just don't seem to work out, you probably think it is because you are not smart enough, or because you are unlucky. (Psychological research shows that if you think the reason is that you are not smart enough, you are probably a woman, and if you think it is because you are unlucky, you are probably a man.) Frankly, I doubt that your problem is lack of brains. You do not have to be a rocket scientist to be a good decision maker. Some of the most effective decision makers are people of just average intelligence. In fact, there is some evidence to suggest that people of unusually high intelligence have *more* trouble making decisions. They tend to be more "cognitively complex," meaning they take a larger number of considerations into account than does the average person when trying to make a decision. This can lead to paralysis. In terms of raw intellect, Jimmy Carter probably ranks among the smartest presidents the United States ever had. But he was a notoriously bad decision maker. He craved detail. He looked at things from every possible angle. He got so bogged down in the complexities of things that he had trouble seeing the forest for the trees. If this sounds like you, your problem may simply be that you are quite literally too smart for your own good.

Whether you are too smart, not smart enough, or just plain unlucky, the single most likely cause of your grief is that you aren't quite sure *how* to make a decision. Effective decision makers are not simply lucky: they know how to go about making the choices that they have to make. They cultivate certain skills and habits that help them to make better decisions over the long run, and to do so more quickly and with less effort. No matter how smart you are, you can learn *how* to go about making better decisions, and you can cultivate the necessary skills and habits. You can become an effective decision maker, too.

Effective decision making is not *perfect* decision making. We all make mistakes once in a while. Sometimes fate steps in to thwart us. "The best laid schemes o' mice an' men gang aft a-gley," as Robbie Burns put it. Anyone who has seen *Dial M for Murder* knows this. But effective decision makers are good at making decisions that control for downside risks. They understand how and why things can go wrong, and they position themselves to deal with the consequences if they do. The end result is that, while good decision makers will make mistakes, or will sometimes be unlucky, they will tend to do much better than the average person over the long run. The principles and practices covered in this book explain how to do that.

THE PLAN OF THE BOOK

There are two crucial things you need to know in order to become an effective decision maker. First, you need to know how someone would make a decision in the ideal world. Second, you have to appreciate that in *this* world, there are very few situations where you can actually do that. Thus you need to know how to make decisions in circumstances where you do not have and cannot get all of the information you would like to have, or where you could not process that information even if you had it. You make most of your interesting and important decisions in a context of uncertainty. How you handle uncertainty is the best predictor of your success.

Chapter 1 introduces you to the ideal. It describes and explains the logic of a model of choice, which, in the academic world, goes by the ten-dollar name of "subjective expected utility maximization" (or SEU, for short). In this chapter, you will discover that there are only a few situations in which you can actually apply the model directly. Using a variety of everyday examples, I explore the nature of the constraints under which we typically have to make choices, and discuss how and when to approximate an SEU choice within them. The key is to follow what I call the "nine steps to effective decision making," and chapter 1 introduces them to you.

Whenever we make a decision, we do so according to a *strategy*, whether we are conscious of this or not. Effective decision makers understand the strategies available to them, and know which ones to invoke in any given case. Chapter 2 explores a rich repertoire of decision-making strategies, and discusses in depth the circumstances under which each is appropriate—again making liberal use of everyday examples. By the end of chapter 2, you will have a good grasp of how to go about making decisions in a general, abstract sense, and in most of the rest of the book you can concentrate on matters of execution.

Many decisions involve numbers, or have important quantifiable elements. Decisions involving money obviously fall into this category. So too do decisions that involve elements of random chance. Chapter 3 is designed to help you better understand numbers. This is not a chapter about mathematics, nor about finance. It presumes nothing more than basic arithmetical skill and a passing familiarity with money. It does not burden you with equations or formulae. However, it explores in some detail several important things most people do not appreciate about money, probability, and how we deal with numbers psychologically. Many of the mistakes people make in decisions involving money or chance can be traced directly to misconceptions about these issues.

Chapter 4 delves into the psychology of perception, judgment, and choice, and also explores how emotions affect decision making. It is a chapter, in short, about human nature. Some of the important differences between how an ideal decision maker would make a choice in an ideal world, and how real people make choices in the real world, have their roots not in the circumstances of choice, but simply in the fact that we are human. In this chapter, you will discover both how and why human nature leads people to make a number of common decision-making errors. Knowing a bit about these can help you make better choices, muster more persuasive arguments, and do better in negotiations with others (in effect, taking advantage of *their* tendencies to make certain kinds of mistakes). It is not possible, of course, to eliminate these errors from your decision making entirely. That would be a superhuman feat. But being aware of them can help you avoid a few, minimize their dangers, or understand other people better—all of which can help you make more effective decisions.

Chapter 5 discusses moral decision making. Most of the interesting decisions we make in life have some moral component to them. The overwhelming majority of us take moral considerations seriously. Yet very few of us have any formal training in moral reasoning. In this chapter, I provide an overview of some of the more important philosophical issues, and I discuss different ways of tackling moral problems. I argue that it is possible to approach moral decisions much as you would approach nonmoral ones. My hope is that you will find this discussion congenial to your own moral commitments, whatever they may be, and helpful as you tackle the moral dilemmas that arise in your own life.

Chapter 6 delves into the turbulent waters of sex, gender, and decision making. There is a widespread popular belief that men and women make decisions very differently. According to the stereotypes, men make decisions "rationally" and cool-headedly, while women make decisions "intuitively" and emotionally. There is also a widely held view that women tend to be less decisive than men, and that in comparison to men they take relatively greater pleasure from the process of choosing than from the outcome of the choice itself. There is also a popular view that women and men tend to value fundamentally different things. For all of these reasons, decision making commonly provides a superb field of battle for the sexes. In this chapter, I explore the claim that men and women make choices differently, arguing that the variation in decision-making styles *within* the sexes is more striking than variation *between* them. But there are indeed socialization pressures acting upon men and women that can lead them to make decisions somewhat differently. I also try to argue, however, that "masculine" and "feminine" decision-making styles are both flawed as ideals, and that effective decision making is essentially gender-neutral. In any given case it may be difficult for either a man or a woman to change old patterns of decision making, but there is nothing in human biology or sociology that makes this impossible in principle.

Finally, the book concludes with a discussion of decision-making habits. Habits are the secret to efficiency, and cultivating good habits is an investment of time and energy that pays off over and over again. It is by cultivating certain habits that effective decision making becomes second nature. If you are indecisive or chronically unfortunate, developing effective decision-making habits is the surest cure for what ails you.

SOME BACKGROUND

When people ask me, "What is your area of expertise?" I always answer that my specialty is why people screw up so badly so often. More specifically, I spend most of my time studying how national leaders make decisions about national and international security.

Like most people, I suspect, I grew up with the naive and comfortable belief that "they"—the people in charge—knew what they were doing. I thought we could trust them to make the right decisions for our welfare and security. The Vietnam War shattered that faith, as it did for so many others of my generation. My college years were among the darkest and most dangerous of the Cold War. I studied international relations and philosophy to try to understand better the dimensions and dynamics of that protean ideological struggle. My motive was fear: fear of World War III. I did not so much fear that World War III would come about as the result of the deliberate choices of evil people, as had World War II, but rather as the result of mistakes, misperception, and accidents, as had World War I (and, I would argue, Vietnam). In short, I feared the human fallibility of national leaders on both sides of the Iron Curtain.

In graduate school, I was fortunate enough to participate in the Project on Avoiding Nuclear War at Harvard University's Center for Science and International Affairs, funded by the Carnegie Corporation of New York. The multiyear mandate of the ANW Project was to identify the most likely causes of nuclear war, and ways of minimizing the dangers.[1] We quickly reached the conclusion that a nuclear war was unlikely to begin out of the blue. Instead, it was most likely to grow out of an international crisis. Nuclear crises were fairly rare events (fortunately); but in order to understand their dangers, it was absolutely necessary to study one in intimate detail—to try to get into the heads of decision makers, in effect, and to understand the pressures and constraints under which they operated as they felt and understood them at the time. The obvious crisis to study was the Cuban missile crisis of 1962—the event most people identify as the single most dangerous episode of the Cold War. The Cuban missile crisis was comparatively well documented, and, most importantly, several senior members of the Kennedy administration were still alive and willing to tell their tale. Thus began a ten-year study that eventually expanded to include Soviet and Cuban decision makers right up to the highest level.[2]

Time and time again, our intensive study of the Cuban missile crisis revealed that the primary source of nuclear danger was human fallibility. In 1962, perfectly normal people making perfectly normal decisions brought the world to the brink of nuclear destruction through a series of misjudgments, misperception, and mistakes. "They," in short, were the problem. Fortunately, two of them found a solution. We can justly criticize U.S. President John F. Kennedy and Soviet Premier Nikita Khrushchev for bringing the world to the nuclear precipice, but, to their great credit, they managed to step back from it gracefully and creatively. I was (and remain) struck by the contrast between the quality of their decision making before the crisis, and the quality of their decision making during the crisis. The event poignantly demonstrated how dangerous faulty decision making can be, but it also showed how quickly well-motivated men of roughly average intelligence can learn from their mistakes and recover, even under almost unimaginable pressure.

Looking at the Cuban missile crisis through a decision-making lens was enormously helpful. It threw into sharp relief issues typically ignored by foreign policy "experts," who tend to be preoccupied by strategic and political considerations, and who tend to assume that decision making is unproblematic and can be ignored. Over the years, I have looked closely into a number of international conflicts involving states large and small all over the globe, and I am convinced that the *best* way to explain what happens is to look inside the decision-making process. We learn relatively little from strategic or political context. If you want to know why people do what they do, you need to try to understand what they want and how they see the world.[3] If you can put yourself in someone else's shoes, you can make much better decisions yourself.

"I've met and worked with a good many people whose names are in the history books or in the headlines," former Secretary of State Dean Rusk once told me, "[and] I have never met a demigod or a superman. I have only seen relatively ordinary men and women groping to deal with the problems with which they are faced."[4] Yet for some strange reason, the popular imagination has it that national leaders are coolly rational beings who are less prone to mistakes than the rest of us, who are somehow immune to emotion, who have their eyes firmly on "the national interest" (whatever that means), and who care nothing for right or justice. In my experience, even national leaders believe it—of others, if not of themselves. They may understand that their own decisions reflect sincere moral impulses; they may feel the force of their own passions; they may even appreciate that their own decision making is flawed—but they assume that their enemies are not similarly constrained. Time and time again this fundamental misunderstanding has led to disastrous misjudgments and mistakes.[5]

Fortunately, social scientists in disciplines such as psychology, sociology, and economics have made great strides in understanding decision-making processes. There are now rich bodies of research upon which to draw, and in recent years my colleagues in political science have made great progress redressing the neglect of decision making in the study of international relations.

In my own work, two things have repeatedly struck me, however. First, insights from the study of decision making can be readily applied to everyday choice situations people face, not merely to relatively narrow (if important) topics such as national or international security decision making—and yet the academic community has made little effort to explore or to communicate their practical applications. Second, most of the relevant research is inaccessible even to those who might seek it out. Academic work tends to be laden with jargon; presented in a dry, technical style; and buried in obscure, difficult-to-find journals.

My aim in this book is to redress those two unfortunate facts by making this fascinating and important material generally accessible. I aim to demonstrate the practical application of the science of decision by drawing examples and illustrations not only from international politics, but from everyday choice situations. I will do so with a minimum of jargon. Throughout, I will provide in notes references to some of the more interesting and more important academic work that informs my presentation, but there is no sense in which I will presume familiarity with any of it—nor, except to satisfy curiosity, need readers bother with any of it further.

One final introductory caveat is in order: while I believe it is helpful to approach decision making methodically, I do not mean to communicate that I think decision making can be reduced to a mechanical exercise. At bottom, decision making is what the ancient Greeks would have called *technê*: an art *informed by* science. It is not a narrowly technical skill. It more closely resembles music than typing.[6] This is not, therefore, a typical "how-to" book. It is, instead, a resource. As decision makers, people have different strengths and weaknesses. To adapt the insights in this book to your own peculiar circumstances, it is important for you to appreciate your own strengths and weaknesses, and, in an imaginative way, to apply those insights creatively to the sometimes unique situations that you face. This is simply another way of saying that an effective decision maker is self-reflective. This is a theme that runs throughout the book.

And on that note, we can begin.

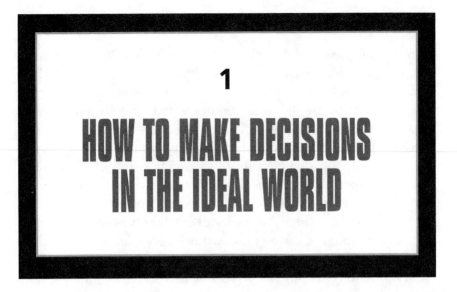

1

HOW TO MAKE DECISIONS IN THE IDEAL WORLD

In theory there is nothing to hinder our following what we are taught; but in life there are many things to draw us aside.
—Epictetus, *Discourses*, chap. 26

All decisions have three parts: (1) you identify your goal; (2) you identify your options; and (3) you choose from among your options. Even the most trivial choice you make fits this pattern. Suppose it is a hot day, and you are thirsty. You crave lemonade. You walk into a convenience store, pluck a bottle out of the refrigerator case, pay the clerk a dollar, and take a nice, long, gratifying swig. You probably do this without giving the process much thought. But, in fact, if this is what you have done, you have made a decision with all three parts: (1) you have identified your goal (to quench your thirst); (2) you have identified lemonade as an option; and (3) you have chosen that option.

Now, suppose you walk into the convenience store, and you discover that they are out of lemonade. This is a great shame, because you *really* crave lemonade. Nevertheless, you are still thirsty; your goal has not changed. You survey the vast expanse of sodas, fruit juices, punches, bottled waters, flavored iced teas, and dairy products in the refrigerator case before you, skipping no can, bottle, jug, or carton. You are identifying your options. As you look at each, you imagine how it would feel to drink it. You are lactose-intolerant, so the dairy products are out. You hate iced tea. The bottled water would do, but there must be something better. Punches are too sweet. So are the sodas. Somewhere in the deep recesses of your body's biochemistry, a plaintive voice cries out for moderate sweetness, mild acidity, and electrolytes to replenish the supply in your bloodstream depleted by the scorching sun. Of everything you see, grapefruit juice tastes best on your mind's palate—but the store has only large bottles that cost three dollars each. A small bottle will do, and there are plenty of small bottles of orange juice for only a dollar. Orange juice would taste almost as good as grapefruit juice. You choose it.

Who among us has not lived out this scenario, and yet how many of us have been conscious of the fact that in so doing, we have gone through a specific kind of decision-making process which was only one of several available to us? How many of us are aware at the time that the outcome of our decision might well have been different had we chosen to make our choice in a different way? In this case, you took the time and the trouble to identify and consider every kind of drink the convenience store had in stock. That probably took a whole minute of your precious time. It might have been much quicker simply to start at one end of the refrigerator case and stop looking when you found something that would have been *good enough.* Instead, you tried to find the *best available* drink. In fact, though you found the best available drink (grapefruit juice), you did not buy it. You bought the second-best available drink. This is because you took the trouble not only to think about how satisfying each drink might be, but also about how much each one cost. You did not have to do that. You chose to do that.

THE SEU IDEAL

The decision process you went through that led you to choose orange juice was a typical real-world approximation of a *subjective expected utility maximization* (SEU) process. "Utility" is a technical term economists and philosophers use to designate happiness, pleasure, or satisfaction. "Subjective utility" is *your own* happiness, pleasure, or satisfaction as *you* perceive and experience it—not someone else's, nor society's as a whole (economists and philosophers call that "social utility"). "Expected utility" is happiness, pleasure, or satisfaction that you don't yet have, but that you hope to get—though you might not get it if you are unlucky or something unexpected happens. As a model of choice, SEU maximization represents an ideal, because if you consistently seek to maximize subjective expected utility, then, everything else being equal, you will be better off over the long run than if you make decisions in any other way.

You may be wondering why anyone bothers with a word like "utility" when we have perfectly good everyday words to describe what it means: happiness, pleasure, satisfaction. The word "utility" allows economists and philosophers to convince themselves that this is something truly quantifiable. As I explain in more detail later, sometimes it makes sense to think of utility as something quantifiable, and sometimes it does not. But one reason why it is useful to think of utility as something quantifiable is that the very concept of SEU maximization makes most sense when you think about it numerically. Let's go back to the convenience store to see why this is so.

We begin by scoring on a scale from zero to ten how satisfying each of the available drinks would be on a hot day. We will score *your* satisfaction, not mine or someone else's (my scores would be quite different, since I like sodas and iced tea):

TABLE 1. SATISFACTION SCORES

Drink	Score
Grapefruit juice	9
Orange juice	8
Bottled water	5
Punch	2
Soda	2
Iced tea	0
Milk	0

Remember that you are not indifferent to cost. In fact, you care about cost just as much as you care about quenching your thirst. Here is what each drink costs:

TABLE 2. PRICE

Drink	Price
Grapefruit juice	$3.00
Orange juice	$1.00
Bottled water	$1.50
Punch	$0.85
Soda	$0.80
Iced tea	$1.00
Milk	$1.75

In this case, the *subjective utility* of each drink will be a function of its satisfaction score and its price, since both of those considerations are important to you. (This is why it is useful to have a single abstract concept such as "utility": it allows us to combine into one measure more than one thing of value.) Now, since you care equally about taste and price, what you really want to do is to find the most "cost-effective" drink, where by "effective" you mean "thirst-quenching." Put another way, you want the drink with the best "bang for the buck." Dividing each drink's price into its satisfaction score gives us this number. Think of it as "units of satisfaction per dollar":

TABLE 3. SUBJECTIVE UTILITY

Drink	Satisfaction score	Price	Subjective Utility
Grapefruit juice	9	$3.00	9/3 = 3
Orange juice	8	$1.00	8/1 = 8
Bottled water	5	$1.50	5/1.5 = 3.33
Punch	2	$0.85	2/.85 = 2.35
Soda	2	$0.80	2/.8 = 2.5
Iced tea	0	$1.00	0/1 = 0
Milk	0	$1.75	0/1.75 = 0

Here is how the drinks rank now:

1. Orange juice (8)
2. Bottled water (3.33)
3. Grapefruit juice (3)
4. Soda (2.5)
5. Punch (2.35)
6. Iced tea and Milk (0 each)

As you can see, orange juice is indeed your utility-maximizing choice. You did as well as you could possibly have done by choosing it. Its subjective utility score of "8" is by far the highest. (Note, by the way, that if you didn't care about cost—if you were extremely rich, for instance—each drink's subjective utility would simply be the same as its satisfaction score. You wouldn't have factored in price. Subjective utility depends upon what you care about, and how much you care about it.)

Now, technically, we forgot the "expected" part. A true SEU calculation must take into account the likelihood that you will actually get the satisfaction that you hope for. There is some chance that you won't get the satisfaction you think you'll get. The orange juice may have gone bad, for instance. Or perhaps it was made from inferior fruit. You might have a heart attack on the way to the cash register. The clerk may be insane and may refuse to sell it to you. An airplane may crash into the convenience store. All kinds of things could happen. But never mind. You have no reason to suspect any of these things. Nor is there any reason to think that you are less likely to get the satisfaction you expect out of orange juice than out of one of the other drinks (no matter which drink you choose, you won't enjoy it if you drop dead of heart failure before you have a chance to open it). So you might as well assume that the satisfaction you think you'll get is a sure thing. Probabilities range from zero (no chance) to one (sure thing), and if you multiply the subjective utility of each drink by 1, you change neither the scores nor the rankings. (Throughout the book, by the way, we will use an italic, lowercase p to mean "probability"; stay tuned.)

Now, I described the decision-making process you went through at the beginning of the chapter as *a typical real-world approximation* of an SEU process. You identified *all* of your options, and you considered how satisfying each and every one would be. You also took cost into account. These are all things one would do if one were trying to maximize SEU in this situation. Strictly speaking, though, you did not meet all of the very stringent conditions of a true SEU calculation. First—and least importantly—you did not take probabilities into consideration. Why bother? You knew intuitively that you were virtually certain to get the satisfaction each drink promised if you bought it. You would have been wasting your time giving the concept of probability a moment's thought. Second, and more importantly, you did not actually score the satisfaction you would get from each drink numerically. You assessed this very impressionistically. As a result, you could not figure out each drink's "bang for the buck." Instead, you eliminated all options but two (grapefruit juice and orange juice) on the basis of promised satisfaction, and, very imprecisely, you factored in their relative cost in order to choose between them. That was a shortcut.

Quite frankly, in this case you would have been wasting your time had you done otherwise. The decision just wasn't important enough to put more effort into it. Had you stood there punching numbers into a pocket calculator, the clerk might even have called the police. As things turned out, you chose the drink with the highest SEU anyway. But notice that if you had attempted a real SEU calculation, you would have discovered that grapefruit juice was *not*, in fact, your second-best choice. Bottled water was. You were choosing between the wrong two contenders. Only a true SEU calculation lets you see this.

The convenience store scenario is a good illustration of a case where it is technically possible to make a high-quality SEU calculation. All of the information you needed was there. The arithmetic was simple. In the ideal world, that is exactly what you should have done. If you can do it, an SEU calculation will, over the long run, maximize your satisfaction—*guaranteed*. But we do not live in the ideal world. We live in a world where there are constraints on our time and energy. We live in a world where delays in decisions are sometimes themselves very costly. Not every decision where an SEU calculation is possible is worth the investment of time and energy that it would require. In this case, it certainly was not.

What are the circumstances in which you can, and should, make SEU calculations? You *can* make SEU calculations whenever you can quantify the costs, benefits, and probabilities of your options. You *should* make SEU calculations whenever you can if the calculation is easy, or—if the calculation is difficult—when the decision is very important.

You are on a long road trip, and you need to fill your car with gas. You pull off the highway and notice four gas stations, one at each corner, with different brands and prices, and three grades of gasoline each. If you watch a lot of television, you may think you face a hard choice between twelve options, because oil companies claim that their gasoline is better than their competitors' and that higher-octane fuels, while more expensive, improve your engine's performance, keep its fuel-injectors cleaner, and make it last longer. Any good mechanic will tell you that this is baloney. Unless you drive an expensive car whose engine is specifically tuned for high-octane fuel (check your owner's manual!), there are no bene-fits to buying premium gas, and no meaningful differences between brands. In fact, the odds are pretty good that the gasoline at each of the four stations came from exactly the same storage tank at the nearest major port. Very likely, all the oil companies did was mix in their own package of chemical additives. Your engine can't tell one additive package from another. So an SEU calculation would tell you to fill up at whichever station had the cheapest reg-ular unleaded gasoline. You simply choose between four options on the basis of price. SEU calculations get no easier than this.

Sometimes the SEU calculation is harder, but worth the time and trouble to go through carefully because so much is at stake. Let's look at an example, in contrast to the last one, where proba-bilities are key.

You are the manager of the Chicago Cubs, and it is the bottom of the ninth inning in game seven of the World Series against the

Boston Red Sox. Your team is at bat, down by a run, and the bases are loaded, with two outs. The Red Sox bring in their last decent pitcher—a right-hander—to face your right-handed batting slugger. You have a left-handed pinch hitter available on the bench. All other things being equal, left-handed batters tend to do better against right-handed pitchers than do right-handed batters. Do you let your slugger bat, or do you pinch-hit?

This is certainly a case where you can play the percentages, and baseball is a statistician's paradise.*

Let's suppose your hitters have all faced this particular pitcher many times before (he used to be the closer for the Cincinnati Reds, another National League team, until the former owner chased him out of town for reasons unrelated to his talent). Here is how your hitters have done against him in the past:

TABLE 4. PERCENTAGES

	Slugger	Pinch hitter	On-deck hitter
Singles	.095	.154	.146
Doubles	.032	.026	.000
Triples	.000	.013	.021
Home runs	.063	.051	.042
Hit-by-pitch	.032	.000	.000
Walks	.116	.013	.167
Strikeouts	.253	.154	.292

Since the bases are loaded and there are two outs, a base hit will almost certainly win the game for you. Adding up the probabilities of singles, doubles, triples, and home runs, you discover that the probability of your slugger getting a hit against this particular pitcher is .189,† and the probability of your pinch hitter getting a hit is .244. At this point you are tempted to pull your slugger for the pinch hitter. If you did this, the color commentator up in the

---

*See appendix 1 for a detailed analysis of this example.

†The percentages in table 4 actually add up to .190, but as appendix 1 shows, .189 is the more accurate figure. Rounding accounts for the difference.

broadcast booth would almost certainly praise you for "playing the percentages," noting that this was a particularly sound decision on your part, because your slugger is far more likely to strike out against this pitcher than is your pinch hitter (p ["probability"; remember?] =.253 vs. .154).

But wait! This may not, in fact, be the expected-utility maximizing choice. If the only way for you to win the game were for the current batter to get a hit, you should definitely pinch-hit. But you have more than one way to win the game. Another is for your current batter to draw a walk or get hit by a pitch (scoring the tying run), and then for your on-deck batter to get on base, either by getting a hit, drawing a walk, or getting hit by a pitch (scoring the winning run). Even if your on-deck batter made the final out of the inning, you would still have a chance of winning the game in extra innings. Since your two teams have each won three games in the series and the score is virtually tied in the bottom of the ninth inning of the seventh game, you can assume that your teams are fairly evenly matched, and that the odds of your winning the game if it goes into extra innings are roughly fifty-fifty. (In fact, they are probably a little better than that, since you have home-field advantage.)

Because your slugger draws walks against this pitcher much more frequently than does your pinch hitter, and because he is more likely to get hit by a pitch, he has a much higher on-base percentage, even though his batting average is lower, and even though he is more likely to strike out. If you combine the probabilities of winning the game in this appearance, of the on-deck batter winning the game for you this inning, and of winning the game in extra innings, you discover that you are more likely to win one way or another if you let your slugger hit (.290 to .253), and that is what you should do. Of course, no matter what you decide, if it works, they will call you a genius, and if it doesn't, they will call you an idiot. Sadly, the odds are better than 70 percent (1.000 − .290) that you are going to lose no matter what you do. Dust off that résumé.

You may object that it's unreasonable to expect even a major-league manager to make these calculations in such a pressure-packed situation. You are probably right. My point here is simply that all of the relevant information is available should a manager choose to do so, and that this is a case where it would definitely be worthwhile crunching the numbers. But an intelligent and experienced manager will already know that in this kind of situation the most important consideration is a hitter's on-base percentage. As long as he knows (or can figure out) this statistic, the rest of the arithmetic is unnecessary. As I explore in more detail in chapter 2, sometimes there are decent shortcuts to SEU-maximizing choices, and this is a case in point.

There aren't many situations where such high-quality SEU calculations are possible. Often the information you would need is unavailable, or the calculations would be too hard even if you had it. Take, for example, a predicament I faced a few years ago.

One Tuesday morning in December, I had to give a midterm exam to a large undergraduate course at 9:00 A.M. sharp. I left the house at 8:10 to catch the subway, with 250 test papers safely tucked under my arm. The subway arrived at 8:25, as usual. Normally, it would take ten minutes to get to campus, six stops away—in plenty of time for the exam. But as soon as the train pulled into the next station, the lights went out and the ceiling fans stopped. I waited nervously to see if the power would come back on. Nothing happened.

I faced a dilemma. If I stayed on the train and the power did not come back on within ten minutes, I would be late. I could run upstairs and jump into a taxi, which would get me to campus on time for sure, but at an additional cost of roughly ten dollars. As I was thinking, I noticed a few people in business suits with briefcases starting to leave the train. I knew there were only so many cabs in the area. If I wanted to catch one, I had to act quickly.

How likely was it that the power would come back on in time for me to get to the exam hall by 9:00? It would be a disaster if I didn't. I would have to reschedule the exam. My students would be furious. There would be dozens of complaints against this thoughtless professor who couldn't even be bothered to make it to his own exam on time when they had put their whole lives on hold literally for *weeks* to prepare. At the end of the year there would be endless appeals of final grades because of the disruption. My chair would call me into his office and dress me down. My teaching evaluations would tank. My reputation would be ruined. I might have to resign in disgrace. I absolutely *had* to get there in time. I dashed out the door, ran upstairs, and grabbed a cab. Fifteen minutes later, I arrived on campus, in time for the exam, ten dollars poorer.

In this case, I was not in a position to make an SEU calculation, because I had no way of estimating how long it would be before the power came back on. I knew that power outages happened in the subway from time to time, though I had never experienced one myself. But when they happened, how long did they tend to last? I had no idea. Unless I knew the length of the average power outage, and how much they tended to vary in length, I couldn't compare the SEU of staying on the train and rushing to get a cab. I had to choose some other principle of choice to make my decision. I simply chose the option that, as far as I could tell, carried the smallest possibility of disaster.*

Later, I learned that the power came back on almost as soon as I had left the train. If I had stuck it out, I would have saved myself ten dollars, and I probably would have arrived at my destination even earlier than I did (since the subway is generally faster than traffic during rush hour). If you judge by the outcome, clearly I made the wrong decision.

Someone also told me later that the average length of a power outage on the subway is two-and-a-half minutes. I never did find any information on how much the lengths of power outages varied, but even if I had had all that information at the time, I doubt I would have been able to figure out the probability that the

---

*In case you are curious, what I technically needed to know in this case was (a) the average length of power outages, and (b) their standard deviation. Standard deviation is a measure of dispersion in a frequency distribution, and it is equal to the square root of the mean of the squares of the deviations from the average. A low standard deviation would have indicated that most power outages tended to last a similar length of time. A high standard deviation would have indicated that the length of power outages varied considerably. If the mean length of power outages was low (say, two minutes), and the standard deviation was also low (say, one minute), then it would have been highly likely that the power would come back on within ten minutes, and an SEU calculation probably would have told me to save my ten dollars and stay on the train.

power would come back on within ten minutes. That's a tough calculation, and I am no math genius.

Although I would have been better off staying on the train, I think I made a sensible decision, even in hindsight. Jumping off the train and grabbing a cab gave me a very high likelihood of an acceptable outcome. To me, that's generally the mark of a decent option. While the alternative—staying on the train—might have had a higher expected utility, I could not know this. Clearly, in the real world we need to have alternative *ways* of making decisions when SEU calculations are impossible or inappropriate.

THE NINE STEPS TO EFFECTIVE DECISION MAKING

Think of decisions as investments. You put time and energy into them—and sometimes money, too. The more you invest in making a decision, the more likely it is that you will make the best possible decision. But sometimes the difference between the best possible decision and the worst possible decision is not very great, or the stakes in the decision are not very high. In such a case, you certainly do not want to invest much in the choice. The nine steps to effective decision making are designed to help you make good decisions *no matter what your investment may be*. They are practical guidelines to help you navigate the three phases of any decision-making problem: identifying goals; identifying options; and choosing from among your options.

1. Identify your objective

All decisions are goal-oriented. Whenever you make a decision, there is something specific that you wish to achieve. In the examples I have used thus far, it is easy to identify the goals:

- Convenience store (quench thirst)
- Road trip (fill gas tank)

- World Series (win)
- Subway dilemma (arrive on time)

But while knowing your objective is absolutely necessary, for all but the simplest decisions, *it is not enough*. Your decisions generally affect more than one thing you care about. The more important your decision, the more care you need to take in identifying the stakes. The stakes, however, may depend upon the options before you. Toward the beginning of your decision-making process, then—before you actually consider the costs and benefits of your options—you need to identify your main alternatives and consider what things you value that they might affect.

2. Do a preliminary survey of your options

Let's say that you have an important final examination coming up, and you set as your objective getting a grade of A. You are a hard-working student, but you find the material very difficult. What are the various ways in which you might get an A?

One way would be to study hard. There are many different ways of studying for an exam, so, in fact, you have many "study hard" options. You could design a rigid review schedule. You could write mock exams. You could form a study group with some friends. You could try a combination of these things. It may be worth thinking in detail about the advantages and disadvantages of these various options later, but not quite yet. First, you want to determine whether there are any other *kinds* of options available to you, because they may have implications for things you care about.

You could cheat. You have a good friend—a genius, in fact—who, for a couple of hundred dollars, would probably be willing to write the exam for you. As luck would have it, he is out on probation right now and is available. Alternatively, you might try to hack into the grades database and falsify your transcript. Or, you could try to bribe the grader. Again, there may be advantages and disadvantages to these various options worth thinking about in detail later, but in your preliminary survey, you simply want to identify cheating as an option.

After not much time and effort, you decide that these are your two main avenues. You can work hard and hope for the best; or you can cheat. Nothing else comes to mind.

3. Identify the implicated values

In easy or unimportant decisions, you normally do not need to ask yourself why you have any particular objective. If you spend a moment's time and energy pondering the question, "Why do I want to quench my thirst?" then you belong on a mountaintop in Tibet, not in a convenience store. Nevertheless, you do realize that quenching your thirst is not the *only* thing that you care about: you also care about money. Your decision about which drink to buy implicates your wealth as well as your physical comfort.

Your deliberation about your looming final exam is more important, because a great deal more is at stake. This is a case where it is worth asking yourself why you want to get an A so badly. Let us suppose the answer—as is almost always the case, in my experience—is that you want to get into law school, and you need an A to have any chance. Fair enough. But the desire to quench a thirst is a natural human impulse that speaks for itself. Why on Earth would anyone want to get into law school? Let's suppose that, as you think about it, you realize that the answer is because you want to be rich.

You are now in a position to identify the values implicated in your decision. You know your objective; you have a broad sense of your options; and you can identify the various things you care about that your decision will affect. One of these is wealth. If you get an A on this exam, you stand a decent chance of getting rich. If you do not, you can look forward to a life of only modest material comforts. At least one of your options, moreover, may require you to spend some money.

You are, however, by nature and by upbringing an honest person. Without question, if you were to cheat, you would feel terrible. You would lose sleep. You would become depressed. You would have a sick feeling in the pit of your stomach. In short, you would hate yourself. Your self-respect, then, is also at stake here.

Wealth and self-respect are two things that can affect your life profoundly. The more money you have, the more options you have before you. Almost everyone prefers having more money to less. It may seem odd to think of self-respect as analogous to money, but in this sense it is. They are both things that are useful to you no matter what your other goals in life may be. (Philosophers some-times call wealth and self-respect "primary goods," because no matter what other things you value, it is better to have more wealth and self-respect than to have less.[1]) When you make a decision that affects your self-respect, it reverberates through your entire life and can affect other important decisions that you have to make. If you make a long string of decisions that so erode your self-respect that you eventually decide you are a worthless human being, you will make choices—consciously or unconsciously—that will reinforce your sense of worthlessness. You will live up (or down) to your own expectations, and to those of others. You can kiss long-term satisfaction good-bye. On the other hand, if you make decisions that constantly reinforce your self-respect, you build the foundation for ever-higher levels of (nonmaterial) satisfaction.

Some decisions, however, affect things you care about only slightly, or do so only briefly. Physical pleasure is generally a good example of a value implicated in a lot of decisions, but the degree of physical pleasure you experience at any given time is unlikely to have a profound effect on your life. When you are thirsty, grape-fruit juice might taste great, but the next morning your life will not have changed one whit if you drink orange juice or water instead. Not all decisions affecting your wealth have earth-shattering implications, either. Whether you become a lawyer or hamburger flipper will have a profound effect on your life choices, but the two dollars you save by buying orange juice rather than grapefruit juice will not. I don't mean to suggest that you shouldn't care about the two dollars—I simply want to make the obvious point that, while wealth is something that is often at stake in our choices, not all decisions involving money are equally important.

4. Assess the importance of the decision

You need to assess the importance of a decision in order to determine how much to invest in it. You don't want to spend a lot of time and energy making trivial choices; you don't want to make life-altering decisions blithely. *You judge the importance of a decision by examining the implicated values.* A decision that could profoundly affect your life prospects and your future decisions is an important one. A decision that only briefly or only marginally affects things you care about is an unimportant one.

To assess the importance of a decision, you may have to put it into context. What may be a minor decision in most contexts may, in fact, be an extremely important one for *you*.

Suppose you are at a party and someone offers you a drink. You have to decide whether to accept or decline. If you are like most people, a drink gives you a certain amount of pleasure. If the drink is free, the decision will not even implicate your wealth. In most contexts, this is an unimportant decision and an easy choice. Bottoms up!

Suppose now that someone offers you a drink in one of the following contexts:

- You are a recovering alcoholic, and you have not had a drink in six months. By joining Alcoholics Anonymous, you have finally managed to put your life back together. Your marriage is on the mend. Your job is safe. Things are looking up at last.
- You have just had four drinks in the past hour and a half. You have no way to get home other than to drive yourself. If you have one more drink, you will not be sober enough to drive yourself home when you have to leave.
- According to your religious faith, drinking is a sin.
- You have liver disease. You are at a party your friends threw for you to celebrate the news that they have finally found a transplant donor and have scheduled your surgery for the following day.

In each of these contexts, the implicated values are profound—your life, your health, your marriage, your job, your self-esteem, and so on. Deciding whether to accept or to decline the drink is an important one in each of these contexts. (As Nancy Reagan might say: "Just say no.")

It is also possible to imagine contexts where what might be an important decision for most people would be an unimportant decision for you: for example, deciding whether to buy a Mercedes (if you are a multimillionaire), whether to start taking heroin (if you are terminally ill and have three weeks to live), or whether to fire on American airplanes (if you are Saddam Hussein).

While you can usually know that a decision is important, it is sometimes difficult to know that a decision is *not* important. Every once in a while what seems like an innocuous choice will turn out to have significant implications for our lives. When someone offers you your first cigarette at age fourteen, you may not realize that one puff will rapidly develop into a physical and psychological dependency that will ultimately lead to lung cancer and death at age fifty. Or, when someone offers you pot, you may not realize that in thirty years someone will use your decision to accept it as evidence against your fitness for high (pardon the pun) political office. Bill Clinton had *amazing* foresight to realize that he shouldn't inhale.

You should also be aware that there is no necessary correlation between the importance of a decision and its difficulty. Important decisions can be very easy; unimportant decisions can be hard. A decision whether to play Russian roulette would be an important one, but it ought to be easy (though there are circumstances in which it may be very hard—for example, if you are young and under enormous peer pressure). On the other hand, some people are paralyzed by a simple choice between Coke and Pepsi. Generally speaking, you should take more care making more important decisions, but you should be able to make easy decisions quickly no matter how important they may be.

5. *Budget your time and energy*

Once you have identified your main alternatives and the implicated values, you should decide how much time and energy (and, if necessary, how much money) to spend making the decision itself. Budget more time and energy for more important decisions; strictly limit your investment for unimportant ones. The reason you want to do this is that your time and energy are valuable to you, and you may therefore justly think of them as elements of your "utility." The ideal is to maximize your utility, yet it is difficult to quantify your time and energy. The next best thing, as a practical matter, is to budget them. This makes it unlikely that you will squander them on decisions that are unimportant, decisions that are easy, and choices between alternatives with almost indistinguishable outcomes. It also makes it unlikely that you will make a poor high-stakes decision because you put inadequate effort into it.

When you budget your time and energy for a decision, take into account situational constraints. You may be thinking of buying a new house in the indefinite future, but have not yet laid the groundwork for a careful deliberation about which house, if any, to buy. (To do this, you would need to get an appraisal of the value of your current house, if you own one; identify your financing options; decide how much you can afford to spend; work out the timing for a careful home search; identify a workable time frame for closing a deal and arranging to move; and so forth and on.) On the way home from work one day, you discover a "For Sale" sign on the front lawn of your dream home. It is a seller's market, and you know that the house will sell within a few days. If you want it, you will have to act quickly. This is a case where you have an important decision to make—one for which you would normally budget weeks of your time and energy—but the circumstances do not allow you to spend more than a few days. You will either have to pass up the opportunity, or do the best you can in the time available (something that may well constrain your choice of *strategy*, which is coming up in step 6).

The amount of time and energy you spend on a decision also

depends upon you. If you are a very busy person, or a nervous wreck, you can't afford to invest as much in a decision as someone who is relaxed and who has time on her hands. All other things being equal, busy people and nervous wrecks will make worse decisions. You can increase the chances of making good decisions if you can find better ways of managing your time and your stress in general. Cultivating good decision-making habits can help, but may not be enough. You might benefit (for instance) from the services of a behavioral or clinical psychologist. For many people, whether or not to seek professional help is a good example of an important decision.

6. Choose a decision-making strategy

The time and energy you can devote to making a decision will affect the strategy you choose. A strategy is a plan of action, a scheme for getting-where-you-want-to-go or getting-what-you-want-to-get. While we are not always conscious of it, we always do use some strategy or other when we make a decision. Some strategies are good, and some are bad. Some are good in one context, and bad in another. All things considered, it is generally better to choose a strategy consciously, and to tailor the strategy to the choice that you have to make.

Because the strategy you choose can have such a profound effect on the decision you make, you want to be very careful not to choose an inappropriate one. To help you avoid that important pitfall, chapter 2 examines decision-making strategies in detail. This is not the time to get too deeply into the subject. But in case you are wondering what a decision-making strategy *is*, here are a few run-of-the mill illustrations:

- You are late for the theater and are looking for a parking meter. As you get close, you have to decide whether to grab the first acceptable spot you find, or to try to identify the available spot closest to the theater.
- You are at dinner after the show. You are torn between the

beef and the lamb. You can ask the waiter which he recommends, or you can just pick one at random.

- The sommelier asks you, as host, which wine you would like to order. You can play the wine snob and make the decision yourself, or you can engage the entire table in the decision jointly.
- You opt for deliberation and it yields no consensus. You take matters into your own hands. You can choose the cheapest appropriate wine, the best available wine, the wine that looks like the best bargain, or a wine you already know.
- Dinner is over and it was awful, except for the wine, which was superb. You drank a lot of it. You are not quite sure whether you can drive home safely. You are at a nice restaurant, not a dive, so there is no coin-operated breathalyzer machine near the front door. You can wander around the neighborhood looking for one, or for a police car to flag down, hoping they might have one; you can try to determine whether you feel alert enough to drive by trying to walk a straight line with your eyes closed; or you can just play it safe and invoke the "When in doubt, take a cab" rule.

In each case, your choice of decision-making strategy may have an effect on the outcome of your choice. In a sense, therefore, your choice of strategy is *part of* the decision you make, even before you make it.

At this point you may be asking yourself, "If the choice of a decision-making strategy is an important choice, how do I decide which strategy to choose?" There is great danger here of infinite regress. How do you choose a strategy for choosing a strategy for making a decision? How do you choose a strategy for choosing that strategy? And so forth and so on. These kinds of questions keep philosophers awake at night, but not the rest of us. As I said in the introduction, decision making has elements of art. It cannot be reduced to a simple technical exercise. Once you have identified the importance of a decision and how much time and energy you should invest in it, you will have a sense of the range of strategies open to you that you can, in fact, carry through, as it were, "on budget." You will find that you are relatively good at some decision-making strategies, and relatively poor at others. With practice, you will develop a repertoire of preferred strategies, and will eventually map the contours of a comfort zone. Who is to say that, over time, you will do any better by doing things any other way? Who is in a position to second-guess the considered practices that you cultivate? One thing we know for sure is that if we spend all of our time and energy thinking about designing our decision-making processes, we will never make decisions. One hardly needs to say that this is no recipe for satisfaction.

7. Identify your options

At this point, you are ready to start considering your alternatives. Now, you already have a rough sense of at least the *kinds* of choices available to you. You had to consider those when you assessed the importance of the decision you are about to make. It is possible that as you now begin to examine your options in more detail, you may discover new options with different implicated values. You may also discover that the values implicated by the broad options you identified way back at step 2 are more (or less) weighty than you thought. Occasionally, in the interest of making a sound decision, you may have to jump back and revise your estimates of the parameters of your decision (steps 3–5) and your decision-making strategy (step 6). As you become a more effective decision maker, you should have to do this less and less often.

It is nice when your options present themselves to you, as was the case in the convenience store, road trip, and World Series examples. Given where you were, what you were doing, and what your objectives were, it took no great effort to figure out the set of things from among which you had to choose. (In my subway dilemma, there was at least one option I did not consider: hitchhiking. Under the time pressure of the moment, it simply didn't occur to me. The oversight shows that we do not always manage to identify the full slate of possible options.) In more interesting decisions—though not necessarily more important ones—we have to roll up our sleeves and do some digging to determine our options. In *really* interesting decisions, our options change as we deliberate. Buying a house in a seller's market is a particularly good example of a really interesting, generally important decision: there may be dozens or even hundreds of properties on the market at any given time that are within your price range and satisfy whatever other minimal requirements you may have. Every day some new ones come on the market; every day some come off the market. As buyers bid (or fail to bid) on houses, the prices change. Some houses that you thought were unaffordable may all of a sudden become affordable; fierce competition may bid the price of other houses out of range. Your future house may be a moving target. In that case, it really pays to organize your choice as much as you can in advance of having to make it, so that you can evaluate your options quickly and accurately.

I once did a close study of Israeli decision making during the 1991 Gulf War.[2] Israeli leaders faced a very important decision: whether to respond to Iraqi Scud missile attacks with military strikes of their own. Well before the war broke out, Israeli leaders had an inkling that Iraq would try to draw Israel into a war so as to split the American-led coalition that was trying to drive Iraqi forces out of Kuwait. The coalition included a number of Arab countries deeply hostile to Israel, and it stood to reason that if Saddam could provoke Israel into attacking Iraq, some important Arab countries might switch sides, or at least stand down. Israeli leaders knew that they would face political pressure from the United States (and others) not to respond, because this would play directly into Saddam's hands. There was a great deal of uncertainty about how much damage Iraq could inflict; whether Iraq would attack merely with conventional weapons, or with chemical or biological weapons; and what the consequences would be for Israel, and for the coalition, if Israel did or did not retaliate. It is difficult to imagine a harder decision to make. Yet Israeli leaders made the decision just about as easy as it could possibly be (though it was *still* hard) by doing a good job of advanced preparation. Before Iraq launched its very first Scud missile, Israeli leaders had identified their objectives, surveyed their broad options, debated the implicated values, assessed the importance of the decision (this was especially easy!), agreed on a decision-making strategy, and set up a broad range of military and nonmilitary options. In the heat of battle, Israel had to modify some of its options, and put back on the table certain options that it had provisionally ruled out earlier in the crisis (most notably, accepting American offers to deploy U.S.-manned Patriot antiballistic missile batteries on Israeli soil)—but for the most part, the only thing Israeli leaders had to concern themselves with during the war itself was following through on the decision-making strategy they had chosen in advance.

In the Gulf War case, Israeli leaders did not merely *identify available* options; they *created* some. The Israel Defense Forces (IDF) had no preexisting plans (for instance) for pinpointing mobile Scud launchers in the western desert of Iraq, quickly landing special forces, and engaging Iraqi crews in firefights. This was an option the IDF put together as a result of creative thinking about how to deal with a problem that, just a few months earlier, no military planner would have considered likely. It was able to do this because it had the resources and procedures in place to do so before the contingency arose. You may not always be in a position to create options, but, as the Israeli example shows, if you find yourself in a position where you would like to be able to choose from as wide a set of options as possible, it is nice to be able to do so.

There may be options that you *should* consider, but that, for one reason or another, you are unlikely to identify yourself. The odds are that there is someone out there who can help you identify them. Tax planners and investment counselors, for example, have specialized knowledge and can draw to your attention ways of managing your money that you may not even imagine. They can also tell you whether some of the things you *can* imagine are, in fact, legal.

8. Evaluate your options

When you choose a decision-making strategy, you also choose a way of evaluating your options. Now is the time to do that.

The simplest evaluations require you merely to judge an option on one dimension (for example, on price, if you are filling up with gas). Some strategies require you to evaluate options on more than one dimension (for example, if you are buying a house, on price, location, size, condition, amenities, property taxes, and so on). Some strategies require you only to evaluate as many options as it takes to find an acceptable choice; some require you to wait until you have evaluated *all* of your options. A few strategies get you off the hook of having to evaluate options at all. The best example of this is a random toss of a coin.

Interesting decisions can involve fairly elaborate evaluations. Again, there are many cases when you will want to enlist outside help to evaluate your options properly. Unless you are yourself expert, it is almost always a good idea to have a qualified financial consultant help you work through your retirement savings options, for example. You may also benefit from investment advice, tax planning, and moral or spiritual guidance. For almost any kind of decision you might wish to make, there is someone out there who is expert at helping you evaluate your options. Deciding whether to seek advice on a difficult decision is often easier (and more fruitful) than making the decision on your own.

9. Make your choice—on time, on budget

As soon as you have finished all of the evaluation your strategy requires—and *only as much* as it requires—you make your choice. Some people have difficulty making a choice, even when they have all of the information that they need. Often this is because they fear the consequences of choosing badly.

A colleague of mine had to choose between offers of admission from Harvard and the University of Chicago. "Relax," said her mentor. "No matter which you choose, you will regret it." There is timeless wisdom in that comment. It is almost always possible to regret our choices, because we do not have to live with the consequences of the alternatives we pass by. We can easily convince ourselves that we would have been better off if we had chosen differently. In most cases, though, there is no good reason to believe that.

If you design your decision-making process well, you run the lowest possible risk of choosing badly, and any additional time and energy you spend fretting about your decision simply adds to its cost. There is no point in making decisions more expensive than they are worth. If you rigidly stick to your schedule and your budget, you will find that you will eventually tame the demon of regret. Rest assured, though, that you will still make lousy choices once in a while. This is inevitable, no matter what you do.

SELF-KNOWLEDGE: A CRUCIAL ASSET

The nine steps to effective decision making are not inherently onerous. For the vast majority of decisions you have to make, you will find them easy to follow, and not especially trying. Before long, they will become second nature.

Since the nine steps help you organize deliberations that you would go through haphazardly in any case, it is useful to think of them not as additional *overhead*, but as *capital*. If you make the investment of training yourself into working through them reflexively, they will almost certainly boost the effectiveness of your decision making. Nevertheless, there are circumstances in which following these steps scrupulously will be draining, both emotionally and intellectually. The first few times you use them to help you make an important and difficult decision, you will find that they force you to think about a number of things that, in the ordinary course of events, probably would not break the surface of your subconscious, and which have the potential to disturb you. They may make you think explicitly about the things you value, about the kind of person you are, and about the kind of person you would like to become. They may force into the open the stark con-

flicts you feel (say) between your desires and your moral sensibilities. If cheating is the only way you can possibly get an A on your
final exam, and if you desperately need an A to get into law school,
you will find it psychically painful to admit to yourself that you
know cheating is wrong. As I discuss in more detail in chapter 4,
you will naturally want to avoid, not to confront, the fact that if
you cheat, your self-esteem will suffer a serious blow. You will not
want to acknowledge that you must either relinquish your cher-
ished goal or become a small, pathetic, miserable person who will
never be able to claim that you deserve the rewards you seek. It is
much less painful to try to ignore this and to rationalize your conduct—to convince yourself that the blow to your self-respect will
be temporary; to chant the mantra that if a Kennedy can do it, so
can you; to tell yourself over and over again the bald-faced lie that
everyone cheats to get into law school, until you finally believe it;
to make yourself the empty promise that you will atone by doing
more than your share of pro bono work once firmly established;
and so forth and so on.

A painful decision such as this will be much easier if you bring
to it the degree of self-knowledge that you might otherwise seek to
avoid if you were to begin your deliberations unreflectively. The
better you know what you want in life, the more clearly you
understand what you value, and the better sense you have of your
own strengths and weaknesses as a decision-maker, the more
easily you can handle decisions, painful or otherwise. When stated
this way, the point seems so obvious that it almost amounts to a
platitude. Yet how many of us take the time and trouble to reflect
deeply on these things? How many of us have discovered important facts about ourselves in the course of making a hard decision
when we ought to have known them before we even began?

My brother, an astrophysicist, came home from work one day
to discover a note in his mailbox scrawled in an eight-year-old's
hand that read, "If you're so smart how come you ain't rich?" The
youngster who wrote that note is in the process of being trained by
his parents, by his peers, by the television he watches, by the bill-
boards he sees, and by the thousands of cues and signals society

gives him every year, to think of wealth as the primary yardstick of success in life. I am astounded at the proportion of my students who tell me frankly that they want to become lawyers or stock-brokers so that they can enjoy the lifestyle of the rich and famous. (Usually this comes up in the context of a discussion spurred by the question: "What can I do with a degree in political science?") I ask each and every one whether they consider a six-figure income worth a mind-numbingly boring career, a seventy-hour work-week, ulcers, and hypertension. I ask them what the point of wealth is when they will have no time to enjoy it. I am always astonished to discover that these are issues most of them have never even thought about.

We in the liberal, individualistic West like to think that we allow people more space for self-knowledge than do other soci-eties and cultures, because we stoutly defend individual rights and freedoms, and we pay lip service to tolerating diversity. And per-haps this is so. But in our society, we certainly do not actively encourage people to think deeply about what they value, what kind of person they are, what kind of person they would like to be, and what would truly make them happy. We supply images and ideals, and put enormous pressure on people to conform to them. We train people first and foremost to be materialistic consumers.

It is, in fact, impossible to value wealth for its own sake. It is only possible to value wealth for what it can bring you. Some people value the material comforts wealth affords; others value the social status, or the recognition they and others bestow upon people who are financially successful. You may be someone who values wealth highly for one or both of those reasons. So be it. You are who you are. It is not my purpose to lobby you to try to become someone else. If you value wealth highly, and if you are clear in your mind about *why* you do so, you are in a position to make more effective decisions—decisions that will tend to improve your wealth—simply by virtue of the fact that you understand this important fact about *you*. Self-knowledge will help you achieve your goals, whatever those goals may be.

You may be someone who does not value what most others

value, but who feels that this is evidence of some deficiency in you. You may feel constrained to try to make other people's values your own. You may strive to become someone society will better understand and approve. Every year I meet a number of students who would really like to study philosophy, but who study commerce instead, because their friends and relatives measure their worth strictly in financial terms. I try to encourage them to think long and hard about whether they can be truly happy trying to become someone other than who they really are.

A lot of people *think* they would be happy if they struck it rich, but discover otherwise. Consider the case of Micheline Gravel, an interior decorator and costume designer who in 1985 won a $4 million lottery jackpot. She split her winnings with her husband, and together they built a $400,000 new home, bought two new cars, and gave some of their fortune to their relatives. Then the phone calls started. Long-lost relatives, people she barely knew, and charity pit-bulls began harassing her for cash. "You don't change, but everyone around you does," she later reflected. "When you win enormous sums like this, people around you think there's no end to your money." Her marriage soured over money issues, and finally ended in divorce. She lost her fortune to bad advice and lawyer's fees. Ultimately, she declared bankruptcy, and, in a fit of despair, attempted suicide.

Her story may be a little extreme, but it is not unusual. Fifteen other jackpot winners she contacted in the course of writing a recently published autobiography all reported being less happy after their winnings than before—mostly because of the disruption of their lives and relationships. "People initially think, 'I'm going to be happy now,'" she says, "But money doesn't usually bring happiness in itself. People want to please everybody, so they become generous. But after a while they ask themselves, 'What am I, a bank?' "[3]

Money may be a good thing, but experiences such as these suggest that for some people, at least, it is certainly possible to have too much of it. If you are not the kind of person who values wealth above all else, you should reflect on what you *do* value highly. It may be love. It may be family. It may be friends. It may be community. It may be faith. It may be a social or political cause. It may be excitement. It may be adventure. It may be physical pleasure. It may be power. It may be any number of things, singly or in combination. The more you know about yourself, the more likely it is that you can make the decisions that will promote your "utility." The more you know about yourself *in advance* of making important decisions, the easier those decisions will be. Self-knowledge is truly a crucial decision-making asset.

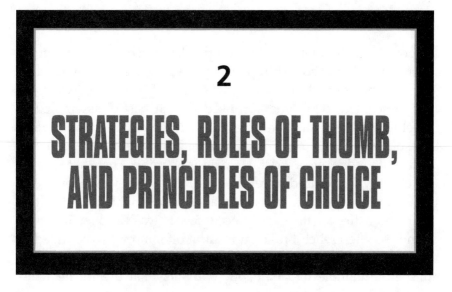

2

STRATEGIES, RULES OF THUMB, AND PRINCIPLES OF CHOICE

[T]here is such a choice of difficulties that I own myself at a loss how to determine.
— James Wolfe, Dispatch to Pitt, 2 September 1759

For two months Major General James Wolfe gazed at the fortress of Québec from the south shore of the St. Lawrence River, scratching his head, trying to figure out how to dislodge the well-entrenched French defenders on the north shore. A bungled frontal assault on July 31 failed utterly. There was no way to outflank them. Operating in hostile territory, he could not starve them out. Time was against him. His fleet would have to retire to Halifax before the autumn storms, and his army with it. He fell sick. The weather soured. His generals mocked him. He sank into depression.

Finally, on September 12, 1759, exasperated and desperate, Wolfe led 3,600 men fourteen miles downriver in the dead of night, in a difficult and complicated maneuver wholly dependent upon precise timing, at the mercy of the weather and the tides, and in danger of challenge and discovery at any moment. His target was a small cove at the base of a cliff—easily missed in the darkness— a stone's throw from the city itself and right between the main French concentrations. Somehow, most of his boats found the spot.

Exposed and vulnerable, his troops clambered up, praying the French would not sound the alarm before daybreak. They reached the top and formed in lines on the Plains of Abraham, exhausted but unscathed, while the surprised French hastily assembled to meet them. Wolfe strutted up and down the ranks, trying to raise his soldiers' spirits. The French marched forward, firing. A musket ball shattered Wolfe's wrist. He paid it no mind. For what seemed an eternity, he refused to return fire. Finally, with the French but forty yards away, he gave the signal, and the double line of British marksmen fired with deadly accuracy. It was all over in a few minutes. The French broke and ran. Wolfe, mortally wounded in the lungs and stomach, survived just long enough to learn that his desperate gamble had paid off. With his final breath, he whispered: "Now I can die—content."

For sheer recklessness, Wolfe has few equals. None of his generals had confidence in his plan. Even senior officers known for their daring considered it somewhere between "highly unlikely to succeed" and "impossible." To those who knew him well, however, it was entirely in character. He was reputed to be kind, considerate, gentle, soft-spoken—but slightly crazy. "Mad, is he?" King George II is alleged to have said to the Duke of Newcastle. "Then I wish he would bite some of my other generals."[1]

We celebrate Wolfe as a hero and praise his daring (if we aren't French, that is) because he won. Had he lost, we would surely ridicule his stupidity. It is hard to describe Wolfe's decision-making process as brilliant, but there is no disputing the result. The case usefully demonstrates the point that there is no necessary relationship between the quality of a decision-making process and its outcome. It may even be that, in certain circumstances, a "high-quality" decision-making process is likely to lead to a worse outcome than a decision-making process that seems far less impressive in a strictly technical sense. This is an important point to which I shall return. But I do not wish to suggest that just any decision-making process will do. If there were no way of systematically improving your chances of a good outcome, then there would be no point in my writing this book. What I wish to suggest is that it is at least as useful to know how and when to deviate from the ideal as it is to understand the ideal itself, and also that a single unexpected success or failure provides no basis whatsoever for judging the quality of a decision-making process. You win some, and you lose some.

Since it is rarely possible (or desirable) to attempt a true exercise in SEU-maximization, we must often decide how we are going to decide. There are many different kinds of decision-making strategies, each of which represents either an approximation of, or an explicit deviation from, the SEU ideal. Knowing which strategy to use in which context is an important decision-making skill, and the first goal of this chapter is to give you a sense of the possibilities and the contexts under which each is more (or less) suitable.

Having chosen a strategy, you must then evaluate your options and choose from among them. Evaluating options can be a difficult and time-consuming task, and it is often very helpful to make use of shortcuts such as "rules of thumb." The second goal of this chapter is to help you tell the good rules of thumb from the bad and the ugly.

Finally, once you have evaluated your options, you must choose among them. To do this, you invoke one of a large number of available principles of choice or decision rules (the terms are interchangeable). A principle of choice is a criterion you invoke for choosing between a known set of options with at least some number of known possible outcomes. This is the last thing you do before you make a decision. The final goal of this chapter is to show you a menu of decision rules.

STRATEGIES AND CHOICES
IN THE REAL WORLD

Suppose you and your coworkers decide one night to go to Chinatown for dinner. You start talking about where you might like to eat. You have a bewildering array of choices. There are dozens of restaurants stretched along the main drag and dozens more tucked away on narrow side streets and alleys. Each of you likes certain dishes, and each of you is on a budget. What do you do?

In the ideal world, you would *optimize*: you would seek the *best possible* restaurant. It is never possible to know that you have found the best possible restaurant, however, unless you have checked them all out. If you want to make an optimal choice, then, you had better bring a thick notebook and plenty of pencils. Bring your calculator, too, because you have an enormous amount of arithmetic ahead of you. You should probably also bring something to eat, because it is going to take you a very long time to survey every single menu in Chinatown. In fact, you are not likely to finish before closing time. Here is a situation where an attempt to find the best possible option would be self-defeating.

Alternatively, you and your coworkers could agree to *satisfice*: that is, to look for the *first acceptable restaurant* instead of the best possible restaurant. This is much easier. All you have to do is agree where to start looking and which route to take. You look at each menu and simply stop when you find a restaurant that has a dish everyone in your group finds appealing at an acceptable price. This strategy holds out the prospect that you will actually find a place to eat before you die of starvation.

There are intermediate options, too. For example, you could agree to survey all of the restaurants on a particular block, or as many as you could check out thoroughly in fifteen minutes, and choose the best of those. This is not pure optimization, because you have no way of knowing whether the best restaurant in Chinatown falls within your limited search area. Nor is it really satisficing, because you may come across several perfectly acceptable restaurants during your limited search. It is instead an arbitrarily *constrained optimization*. The constraint you choose is arbitrary because there is no meaningful difference between one block and a block and a half, between this block and that block, or between fifteen minutes and sixteen minutes. "Arbitrary" here does not mean "stupid," however. After all, you do need to eat.

Satisficing and constrained optimization are reasonable decision-making strategies for groups in search of Chinese food. Optimizing is not—at least, not if there are more restaurants than you could check out in a short period of time. The whole point of the expedition is to enjoy good food and good company; pure optimization when there are so many alternatives from which to choose would be a recipe for no food and grumpy company. Most people who go to Chinatown for dinner are smart enough to know this.

Now, the above discussion is misleading in one important respect. What I have described as "optimization" is actually optimization on only two dimensions: selection and price. If you truly wanted to find the best possible restaurant, you would seek to optimize on *quality* of food, too. This is hard to do, because the restaurants you survey are unlikely to let you sample the food without insisting that you buy it. Even if they did let you sample their food, you would certainly be full long before you covered every restaurant. Is there any way to improve your chances of getting good food without actually tasting it?

Sure there is. Having had a good meal somewhere yourself in the not-too-distant past is one good reason to expect a decent meal there again. So is the recommendation of a friend whose judgment you trust. So also is a positive restaurant review by a critic who has steered you right in the past. Now, if you choose on the basis of prior experience or a recommendation, you do stand a chance of being disappointed, whereas if you sample the food yourself each time before you commit, you do not. But that's impractical anyway.

Quality of food is not the only additional thing you care about, however. To some extent, you might also care about novelty. All other things being equal, you might prefer to eat somewhere you have never eaten before (though McDonald's and Burger King have made a fortune on precisely the opposite assumption). You might also care about décor: all other things being equal, you would rather eat in a well-lit-but-not-too-bright, colorful, comfortable room, where the future lobster dinners do not stare at you reproachfully from a huge, overpopulated aquarium. You certainly care a great deal about your time, your physical comfort, and your stress level. Looking for somewhere to eat can implicate all of these. It is mainly because the optimizing strategy I described involves such a high cost on these dimensions that people are unwilling to use it if there are more than just a few alternatives from which to choose.

It is fairly easy in theory to try to optimize on selection and price alone. It is hard to know how to optimize on selection, price, quality, novelty, décor, time, physical comfort, and stress. This is because the last three of these are costs associated with the decision-making process itself. The longer and more careful your search, the larger the price you have to pay on these three dimensions. At some point the aggravation ceases being worth it. If you can know in advance that a thorough search of all of your available options is going to take a long time, make you hungry, and stress you out, you can also know in advance that a strategy of optimizing on a limited number of dimensions is, in fact, *suboptimal* when you look at the full range of implicated values. It will leave you less happy than you otherwise might be.

What do you do when a careful, rigorous attempt to find the best possible option proves to be self-defeating? I present to you an Act in Three Parts:

Scene 1: 6:00 P.M., at the water cooler

YOU: What's the matter?

FRIEND 1: Did you see that e-mail about "misuse of office computers"? It's like all of a sudden playing solitaire is a criminal offense! I get all my work done by lunch. What am I supposed to do the rest of the day?

FRIEND 2: Do what I do. Surf "eBay."

YOU: Hey, it's quittin' time; whaddaya say we go to Chinatown?

FRIEND 1: Great idea! I'm hungry. You like Szechuan?

YOU: As long as they have mild stuff, too.

FRIEND 2: I'm into Moo Shoo in the biggest possible way.

FRIEND 1: Where do you want to go?

YOU: I'd like to go somewhere new. I'm getting tired of the usual places.

FRIEND 2: Fine by me, as long as they have Moo Shoo.

FRIEND 1: And not too steep; I only have fifteen bucks.

YOU: I have more work to do tonight, so I don't want to be out too late. We can get to Chinatown by 7:00; let's make sure we're seated by 7:15, okay?

FRIEND 2: Fine by me, as long as they have Moo Shoo. Anywhere you want to try that you've heard about?

FRIEND 1: Taiwan-On got a great review in the paper yesterday; let's try that.

YOU, FRIEND 2 (in unison): Okay.

(Exeunt)

Now, you will notice that this was a complete decision-making process. We can see this if we break it down and look at in the light of the nine steps to effective decision making:

- *Identify your objective:* You and your friends all want to eat authentic, high-quality Chinese food at a reasonable price, and to enjoy each other's company in pleasant surroundings, preferably somewhere new.
- *Do a preliminary survey of your options:* All of the restaurants in Chinatown. This was implied in the discussion.
- *Identify the implicated values:* You and your friends clearly care about gratifying the palate; social interaction; money; time; physical comfort; and novelty. Later we will discover that you also care about aesthetics, although no one mentioned it here (that fact doesn't imply that you *don't* care about this, it simply means that so far no one made that implicated value clear).
- *Assess the importance of the decision:* None of you thinks that the decision is very important in the grand scheme of things. Picking a restaurant never is, unless you are hosting a visiting head of state. You did not discuss this explicitly, but it goes without saying.
- *Budget your time and energy:* Since deciding where to eat is not very important, you proposed to the group that you spend no more than fifteen minutes looking for a restaurant. No one objected. Silence implies consent.
- *Choose a decision-making strategy:* The strategies we have

already discussed include optimizing, satisficing, and constrained optimization. You opted for none of these. Instead, you decided to cut right to the chase and choose on the basis of a restaurant review. You could also have chosen simply to go somewhere you already knew, or somewhere someone you knew recommended to you. These are three varieties of a strategy we will call *preselection*. In essence, it is a way of choosing that enables you to avoid surveying alternatives, evaluating them, and choosing from among them. Preselection is an extremely efficient decision-making strategy. It does not always work, as we will see shortly—but there are times when this is the best decision-making strategy.

There is one other strategy that you might have chosen and which is neither optimization, satisficing, constrained optimization, nor preselection: namely, *randomization*. This strategy enables you to avoid evaluating your alternatives, but it does not get you off the hook of identifying them.

Notice that you did not deliberate about your decision-making strategy. The first strategy mentioned—preselection—was acceptable to all. It would be correct, if pedantic, to point out that your implicit strategy-for-choosing-a-strategy was satisficing. A strategy-for-choosing-a-strategy is a "metastrategy"; a strategy-for-choosing-a-metastrategy would be a "meta-metastrategy," and so forth. As I mentioned in the previous chapter, this road leads to infinite regress, and we will block the temptation to travel down it further. It is worth noting, however, that satisficing is a good metastrategy for unimportant decisions. Important decisions warrant a more explicit survey of your available strategies, and a more careful comparison of the prospects that they might help you make a good choice at the end of the day.

- *Identify your options:* This is moot; your strategy narrowed your options to one.
- *Evaluate your options:* This is moot, too.
- *Make your choice—on time, and on budget:* You already have. In fact, the whole process from start to finish took under a minute; you came in fourteen minutes under budget!

Now, this decision-making process involved no heavy lifting. You may be suspicious of a claim that it is worthy of emulation. After all, you did not compare any of your alternatives, and you did no math whatsoever! All of the action took place at the strategy-choosing stage, and it had a kind of "How about this?"— "Whatever" character to it. No one even mentioned optimizing, satisficing, constrained optimization, or choosing randomly as available strategies. And yet if we compare the strategies explicitly, we can see that such a discussion would have been unnecessary overhead. You and your friends are quite a skillful decision-making group. Your genius lay in your recognition early on that your choice was unimportant, and not worth much of your time.

Why should we not fault you for failing to examine more closely the other available strategies? You are smart enough to know in advance that an optimizing strategy is not feasible in the time available. No one ever picks a restaurant randomly right off the bat. Experience tells us that there are too many lousy restaurants for this to be a good gamble, and in any case, if you thought about it, you would discover that engineering a mechanism for choosing randomly between dozens of options—many of which you have not even identified yet—would be a difficult and time-consuming problem in and of itself. As I mentioned earlier, satisficing and constrained optimization are reasonable strategies for restaurant hunters, but you all knew in advance that these would involve a commitment of time and effort that you could simply avoid through preselection. You also knew intuitively in advance that there was no reason to expect either of these strategies to yield a better choice than a reliable restaurant review. If you had discussed the full range of strategies explicitly, the odds are that you would have decided very quickly as a group that preselection was the best strategy available.

We can see this if we examine the choice of strategies explicitly ourselves. Let's start with rough estimates of how you would have done on each of the dimensions you care about if you had adopted each available strategy. Table 5 gives the results.

TABLE 5. LIKELY OUTCOMES BY STRATEGY

Strategy	Selection at chosen restaurant	Price of chosen restaurant	Novelty value of chosen restaurant	Aesthetic value of chosen restaurant	Cost in time, effort, hunger, frustration
Optimize	Excellent for sure	Excellent for sure	Probably high	Probably high	Extremely high
	1	1	1	1	7
Satisfice	Adequate for sure, possibly good or excellent	Adequate for sure, possibly good or excellent	Probably high	Probably moderate or high	Probably low
	6	6	1	5	4
Constrained optimization	Good for sure, possibly excellent	Good for sure, possibly excellent	Probably high	Probably moderate or high	Low to moderate
	2	2	1	5	5
Preselect on prior experience	Good for sure, possibly excellent	Good for sure, possibly excellent	None	Probably high	None
	2	2	7	2	1
Preselect on recommendation	Good for sure, possibly excellent	Good for sure, possibly excellent	Probably high	Probably high	None
	2	2	1	2	1
Preselect on restaurant review	Good for sure, possibly excellent	Good for sure, possibly excellent	Probably high	Probably high	None
	2	2	1	2	1
Randomize	No guarantees	No guarantees	Probably high	No guarantees	Moderate to high
	7	7	1	7	5

Now, this table is wordy, and it isn't easy to see right off the bat which strategies are promising and which are not. So to make things a little clearer, I have ranked each strategy from 1 (best) to 7 (worst) on each dimension listed in the top row, with ties sharing a ranking, and I have put this number in the bottom right-hand corner of each cell.

Rankings such as these—"ordinal" measures—do not capture the magnitudes of costs and benefits. Scores, on the other hand— "cardinal" measures—not only order alternatives, but also give us a sense of how much better or worse each alternative is compared to all of the others. Where they are possible and meaningful, cardinal measures are almost always more useful than ordinal ones— but let us put that aside for the moment. What jumps right out of the rankings in table 5 is the fact that preselecting a restaurant on the basis of a recommendation or review ranks first or second on every dimension. Randomizing, on the other hand, is dead-last on three out of five. Satisficing, constrained optimization, and preselecting on prior experience have middling rankings, but you can see that, unless you put great weight on novelty value, preselecting on prior experience beats the other two hands down. Optimizing looks great, until you look at the last-place ranking on the thing you care most about (cost in time, effort, hunger, and frustration). Without doing any math whatsoever, we have grounds for suspecting that the best strategy for choosing a Chinese restaurant is to follow someone's recommendation.

Let's push this just one unnecessary step further and see what happens if we put in scores (i.e., cardinal measures) instead of just rankings. This is unnecessary because we already have pretty strong reasons for thinking that choosing on the basis of a recommendation is the way to go. But the exercise is still useful, for two reasons. First, it shows you one way of handling a decision where you don't care equally about everything at stake (we'll get into that a bit more later). Second, it demonstrates that there is sometimes no payoff whatsoever to putting more effort into a decision. Effective decision makers are great at knowing just how much to invest. Plugging in scores helps us also see why optimizing isn't such a great strategy here, even though it has a lot of first-place rankings in table 5.

TABLE 6. CARDINAL ESTIMATES AND WEIGHTS

Strategy	Selection at chosen restaurant (50)	Price of chosen restaurant (25)	Novelty value of chosen restaurant (10)	Aesthetic value of chosen restaurant (10)	Cost in time, effort, hunger, frustration (−200)
Optimize	50	25	10	10	−200
Satisfice	30	15	10	5	−15
Constrained optimization	40	20	10	5	−20
Preselect on prior experience	40	20	0	8	0
Preselect on recom- mendation	40	20	10	8	0
Preselect on restaurant review	40	20	10	8	0
Randomize	25	12.5	10	5	−80

For the sake of argument, let's assume that table 6 accurately reflects your values and estimated scores (your friends' might be a little bit different, but never mind that). The numbers in parentheses in the top row reflect how much weight you give each particular consideration, thus providing a rough measure of what you care about (positive numbers indicate benefit, and negative numbers indicate cost). The numbers in the cells of the table reflect your considered judgment of the likely payoff on each dimension for each strategy you might choose. If we add up the scores in each row, we can rank the strategies quite precisely (higher scores are better):

1. Preselect on restaurant review (78)
2. Preselect on recommendation (78)
3. Preselect on prior experience (68)
4. Constrained optimization (55)

5. Satisfice (45)
6. Randomize (–27.5)
7. Optimize (–105)

Lo! and behold, our impressionistic rankings were right. There was no alternative strategy with a better prospect of yielding an SEU-maximizing choice than preselecting a restaurant on the basis of a trustworthy review—although a friend's recommendation would have been just as good.

Scene 2: 7:00 P.M., in Chinatown, at the Taiwan-On restaurant

YOU: Well, here we are. There's the review in the window. Four stars!

FRIEND 1: I can't wait; I'm starving!

FRIEND 2: Hold on a minute. Look at this menu. No Moo Shoo.

FRIEND 1: Do you have to have Moo Shoo? There's lots of other stuff here.

FRIEND 2: I'm sorry, but I really had my heart set on Moo Shoo. There must be a good restaurant with Moo Shoo around here.

FRIEND 1: I don't know, I've never been in this part of China-town before. Let's just eat here.

FRIEND 2: Excuse me, but if you recall, I said very clearly that I wanted Moo Shoo. This place has no Moo Shoo. I'm not eating here.

FRIEND 1: Okay, okay, don't make a federal case out of it. We'll eat somewhere else. Whaddaya want to do?

YOU: It's 7:00 o'clock; how about we see which restaurants have Moo Shoo on this block, and we'll pick one of those?

FRIEND 1: Fine. God, I'm hungry. [Pause] Picky, picky . . .

FRIEND 2: Get off my back.

The strategy failed. You were thwarted by the fact that the review did not mention that the restaurant had no Moo Shoo. This failure was not the result of your decision-making process; these things just happen.

You returned to step 6 and chose constrained optimization. There was very little discussion of this choice, and rapid—if grudging—agreement. Full optimization is still a nonstarter, as is randomizing (what if you randomly chose a place with no Moo Shoo?). You had no information on the basis of which to preselect in the area, and all of you knew without having to discuss it that the unimportance of the decision, and the premium on time, militated against going very far to a restaurant you already knew. Satisficing would probably have been a perfectly acceptable strategy, and would probably have led to an acceptable choice; but time is not so short that you cannot afford the luxury of spending a few minutes canvassing the full range of options on the block to see if you can find something better than just "adequate." Remember that constrained optimization beat satisficing in our ranking of your available strategies.

Scene 3: 7:12 P.M., down the block from the Taiwan-On

YOU: Okay, we've checked out all six restaurants on this block. Four have Moo Shoo.

FRIEND 1: The one with the linen tablecloths is not in my budget.

YOU: The first one was empty, too; that's a bad sign.

FRIEND 1: That leaves two.

FRIEND 2: Let's eat at the one with the pink wallpaper.

FRIEND 1: C'mon, man, that place was tacky. They had one of those big aquariums.

FRIEND 2: What's wrong with that?

FRIEND 1: I'd rather eat at the third one.

FRIEND 2: No way, they had fluorescent lights.

YOU: Look, I don't care which we choose. Let's just eat.

FRIEND 2: I vote for the pink wallpaper.

FRIEND 1: I vote for the third one.

YOU: How about we just go to McDonald's?

FRIEND 2: I'll eat at either one; I'd just prefer the one with the pink wallpaper, that's all.

YOU: Let's toss a coin.

FRIENDS 1 AND 2 (in unison): Fine.

YOU (pulling a coin out of your pocket): Heads it's the pink wallpaper, tails the fluorescent lights.

[Flip]

FRIEND 2: It's heads. Let's go.

FRIEND 1: I'm sitting with my back to the aquarium.

You identified your options (step 7) by eliminating all that had no Moo Shoo or were too expensive. You then proceeded to evaluate the remaining three (step 8).

Remember that you still care more about the quality and authenticity of the food than either a restaurant's novelty value or its décor. Yet you have no information about the quality of the food at any of the remaining three restaurants, and you are not about to ask if you can sample their wares. Is there any other way to estimate these? Yes indeed—imperfectly. You ranked the empty restaurant last, invoking the "rule of thumb" that a restaurant that is empty at a busy time of day must have lousy food.

Webster's gives two definitions for a "rule of thumb": (1) "a general or approximate principle, procedure, or rule based on experience or practice rather than on scientific knowledge"; and (2) "a rough, practical method of procedure."[2] There is a popular myth that the term comes from an old English common law tradition that a man could beat his wife without fear of prosecution so long as he did not use a stick wider than his thumb. The true origin, however, appears to be more prosaic: seventeenth-century English woodworkers simply used their thumbs to make quick rough measurements.[3] Certainly this explanation fits the meaning of the term better. For most jobs, a seventeenth-century woodworker could tolerate some measurement error without hurting the function or form of his product. An experienced woodworker would be able to measure quite accurately with his thumb in any case. Why be more precise than you need to be, especially since, while rulers are always hiding somewhere in the clutter, your thumb is always handy (so to speak)?

The rule of thumb that an empty restaurant has lousy food makes sense, on the fair assumption that people generally tend to prefer good food to bad food. Another common rule of thumb is that a restaurant full of ethnic Chinese is more likely to have authentic food than a restaurant full of people with names like Tex, Jethro, and Charlene. These rules of thumb will steer you wrong only in certain unlikely cases. The one may cause you to pass up an excellent restaurant that has been open only a very short time and that no one has yet discovered. The other may mislead you in a true melting-pot community where patrons of all ethnic backgrounds are equally clueless about authenticity.

The remaining two restaurants are almost full, and the clientele seems more or less indistinguishable. They both have adequate variety and novelty value, and are both affordable. The only basis for choosing between them is aesthetic. You are indifferent; your friends have different tastes, but preferences of approximately similar intensity. When looked at from the perspective of the subjective expected utility of the group as a whole, these two restaurants are tied. This is a perfect example of a case where a random toss of a coin is as good a way of making the final decision as any other, and this was the decision rule you proposed. Your friends readily agreed. As a result, you made your choice on time and on budget (step 9).

We are done with Chinese restaurants now, and I will try not to mention them again in this book—but I do wish to point out several important things before we move along. First, the relative unimportance of the decision shaped the parameters of the decision-making process, and despite the failure of the group to reach consensus at the end of the day, no one had an interest in making the decision-making process itself more expensive in time, effort, stress, or bad feeling than the choice at hand warranted. Second, to make a choice here ultimately required backtracking a few steps once new information became available. This is common both for important decisions and for trivial ones. Third, when it was appropriate to do so, the group changed its decision-making strategy. It was appropriate in this case because the context of the decision changed. At the water cooler, the group had not yet invested any time and effort in traveling to any particular part of Chinatown. But once there, having discovered that the chosen option was, unfortunately, unacceptable, there was little time left in the decision-making budget, which forced the group to eliminate a number of remaining possible strategies. Constrained optimization was the best one remaining. Fourth, the group made use of a reasonable rule of thumb when attempting to identify the best remaining choice. The empty restaurant might have been empty because it was new, not because its food was bad; but still, over the long run, following the rule of thumb that "an empty restaurant has lousy food" will lead to greater satisfaction than ignoring it, and this was a case where the decision itself was not so important, and the available alternatives were not so lousy, as to justify abandoning it. Fifth, when an evaluation of the remaining options demonstrated both that consensus was impossible and that the group as a whole was indifferent to two acceptable alternatives, the group invoked a principle of choice—random chance—that was perfectly suitable here, but that would have been utterly inappropriate in many other circumstances.*

KNOWING WHEN TO CHOOSE HOW

Obviously, whenever you make a choice, you also make a series of choices about how to choose. You may do this explicitly or implicitly, but it is unavoidable. How do you know when to choose one way rather than another?

It is useful to be aware that different decision-making strategies have different strengths and weaknesses. What will be a virtue of a decision-making strategy in one context may be a vice in another. It is therefore a good idea to become familiar with various decision-making strategies' comparative strengths and weaknesses and to reflect upon the circumstances in which each is likely

---

*Note that *random choice* can be either a strategy for making a choice prior to the evaluation of options—in fact, it is a strategy that allows one to *skip* a detailed evaluation of options—and a principle for choosing among options already evaluated. It is, of course, appropriate in the latter case only under a condition of true indifference.

to perform well. It is crucially important to note, however, that the strengths and weaknesses of decision-making strategies in the abstract must always be interpreted in the light of the individual decision maker's idiosyncratic temperament and skills. Some strategies, for example, require an enormous investment in time to perform well. An individual who values time highly will consider this much more of a weakness than will someone else who likes never to be rushed. Other strategies reveal to the decision maker less information about the alternatives that one is likely to pass up. Someone whose psychological comfort requires a very high degree of confidence that they are doing the best possible thing will consider this a serious weakness, whereas someone prone to value efficiency, and not particularly inclined to feel regret, will not. If you are someone who both *values* time highly *and* is tormented by doubt and regret, you are snookered. Read on, though.

Having chosen a strategy, you may be required to evaluate alternatives about which you know far less than you would like. Almost any interesting decision will present this predicament. This is where rules of thumb become very handy. You may be lucky enough to have an adequate stock of rules of thumb available to you from folk wisdom, but even so, some of these may be likely to mislead you. In many cases folk wisdom will come up dry. When that happens, an imaginative decision maker may be able to deduce some on the fly. This is one of those elements of decision making that involves at least as much art as science, and it is impossible to be formulaic in one's approach. Nevertheless, it is possible to learn some tips and tricks from interesting examples.

When at last you know what your alternatives are, and when you have finally gauged some of their crucial characteristics, you must choose among them. Here, it is possible to be formulaic. If you are familiar with a decent menu of choices of decision rules, you will have a much better sense of which characteristics of your alternatives are particularly important to you and which are not. Knowing this helps you zero in on the appropriate choice.

In the remainder of this chapter I would like to try to answer three questions: (1) How do you know which decision-making strategy to pursue in any given case? (2) How do you know which rules of thumb are appropriate in any given case, and which are not? (3) How do you choose a principle of choice? I will finish the chapter, as I began it, with a detailed look at a particular decision. This time, however, the decision will be important, and it will require close attention to strategy. It is an example of the kind of decision many people have to make it least once in their lives, and it usefully demonstrates how a combination of imagination and technical skill can make a tough decision much, much easier.

How do I know which decision-making strategy to pursue in any given case?

There are five broad types of decision-making strategies: optimization, constrained optimization, satisficing, preselection, and randomization. Three of these are "pure type" strategies, meaning that there is really only one way to do them properly: optimization, satisficing, and randomization only come in plain vanilla. There are many different ways of constraining an optimization, however. One could set the constraints fairly tightly, seeking to optimize over only a very small set of alternatives, or loosely, requiring a much more expansive search and evaluation. Normally, one would also have considerable leeway in deciding exactly how to set the constraint. Depending upon the choice at hand, one could limit one's search and evaluation to a specific period of time, to a specific geographic area, to a particular name brand or set of name brands, and so forth. It is also possible to set multiple constraints. Not surprisingly, constrained optimization is a common decision-making strategy, because it can suit so many different kinds of choice problems. Knowing how to set the constraints in any given case is a great skill to cultivate.

One can preselect on the basis of many different considerations as well—for example, on the basis of prior experience, recommendation, moral or religious injunction, or customary practice. Doctors often invoke preselection as a decision-making strategy because there is such a premium on their time, and in the medical community, customary practice often serves as a preselection criterion. This explains why circumcisions were routine in many English-speaking countries from 1875 to 1950 (and are still very common in the United States), and also why people of different age groups have wildly different likelihoods of having had their tonsils removed.[4]

The reason why it is important to do a preliminary survey of your options before you choose a strategy is that your choice of strategy is likely to depend very heavily upon the number and the nature of alternatives you might consider. If you have only two choices, optimization may be a viable strategy, whereas if you have hundreds, it may not. If evaluating the alternatives is straightforward, you can afford to examine more of them than you could if it were a complicated, time-consuming process. If you can tell from your preliminary survey of options that a preselection strategy will not identify a single alternative, then you will be forced to use some other strategy anyway, so you might as well choose that strategy at the outset. It is simply not possible to choose a strategy sensibly without some rough idea of what it is that the strategy will help you choose among.

The crucial advantage of optimization is that it will help you find the best possible alternative. It works well when you have a relatively small number of alternatives to choose from, and/or when the full set of alternatives is relatively easy to identify and evaluate. Optimization almost always takes more time than any other strategy, and generally requires the most information about the largest number of options. The more time and energy you have available for making a decision, and the more important the decision, the more attractive optimization becomes. For unimportant decisions, optimization is overkill unless the identification and evaluation of alternatives is trivially easy.

Satisficing is the strategy of choice when you have to choose among a large number of alternatives about which you know virtually nothing in advance, and when every little extra bit of time and energy you would have to spend to identify a better alternative would swamp the benefit you would reap (or, as the economists would say, when the "marginal cost" exceeds the "marginal gain"). It is rarely appropriate for important decisions—the exception being a choice among alternatives that are functionally identical. In a tightly regulated auto insurance market, for example, where the state controls both rates and service, satisficing is just as good as optimizing, and much quicker. There is no benefit to looking past the first broker you encounter. Satisficing is usually efficient, but it is not always significantly more efficient than an alternative strategy likely to help you make a better choice. If you need to fill your car with gas, for example, you should satisfice when service stations are few and far between, but optimize—or pursue a constrained optimization—when they are clustered close together and post their prices prominently.

It is useful to think of constrained optimizations as on a sliding scale. The more important the decision, the more time you have, and/or the easier it is to find and evaluate alternatives, the less constrained your optimization should be. Cast your net widely. A tightly constrained optimization is perfect for a fairly unimportant choice that you have to make quickly (but not immediately) between alternatives that require moderate effort to evaluate properly.

Preselection is the most efficient strategy of all. It is the only strategy that enables you to skip the search and evaluation phases of the decision-making process. However, it does carry its risks. It can commit you to a course of action whose flaws you will only later discover, by which time the costs of changing your mind may have increased dramatically. Once your tonsils are out, there is no putting them back. It is easy to see also how preselection can lead you to miss an available alternative that you would have greatly preferred had you taken the time and trouble to explore it. Preselection is therefore a good strategy to follow for unimportant decisions, or for important decisions where your preselection criterion carries so much weight with you that it is possible for you to know, and to feel, that the choice it will point you toward is the only choice you could live with. If you are a devout conservative Catholic, for example, and you find yourself unexpectedly pregnant, you may know in advance that if there are no complications with your pregnancy, there is no point in exploring any of your options other than carrying your fetus to term.

There are very few circumstances where randomization is a good decision strategy. On the one hand, it does commit you to collecting a full set of alternatives. This will ordinarily take some effort. In most circumstances, satisficing, constrained optimization, or preselection hold out the promise of at least as good an outcome at a far lower cost of time and effort—plus they give you the psychic satisfaction of knowing that your choice is based upon some knowledge of the alternatives, not a shot in the dark. As I will discuss shortly, randomization is an excellent *decision rule* to invoke when you have to choose among known alternatives about which you are completely indifferent, and it is therefore a useful arrow to have in your quiver at the end of the decision-making process. But it is not very useful as a *strategy* closer to the beginning. The chief exceptions to this generalization are choices that you must make solely on the basis of fairness. For example, if it is your job to run a raffle, you must design the process of choosing a winner in such a way that you can draw at random from among some utterly unknown number of entries, and from among entrants whose identities you also do not know in advance. No judge is likely to be persuaded by your argument that you were maximizing social utility by looking over all the entries and choosing your cousin Fred's because he has an exceptional capacity for joie de vivre and would enjoy the winnings more than anybody else.

How do I know which rules of thumb are appropriate in any given case, and which are not?

If you have chosen a strategy that requires you to identify and evaluate alternatives, you may find yourself in a situation where good information about crucial aspects of your options is hard to come by. In some cases, if you spent enough time and effort, you could get that information, and in other cases the information would simply be unavailable to you. Commonly, though, you will find that your time and energy budget will not allow you to dig very deeply. This is when you will want to resort to rules of thumb.

We all use rules of thumb, consciously or not. You are out for a stroll late at night in a park and approach a fork in the path. You see a tall, ugly male walking toward you from the left, and a petite, beautiful woman with a dog on a leash coming toward you from the right. You instinctively judge that it is more dangerous to go left. Little do you know that the man is a priest and the woman a psychotic killer who has just escaped from a maximum security prison. And her dog is a rabid Rottweiler. How could you know that? You could try to get more information before you got too close. You could shout: "Excuse me, but does either of you have a record of violent assault? And, ma'am, does your dog bite?" But that would be a very odd thing for you to do. *They* would probably think *you* were the sick one. Besides, even if the woman's dog *did* bite, she probably wouldn't answer truthfully. Pet owners—especially psychotic convict pet owners—never admit that their dogs are dangerous. So you just follow your instincts. In any case, by the time you got close enough to conduct an interview, it would be too late.

Later, while they stitch you up in the emergency room, you can take some comfort in the fact that you had no alternative here but to rely on a rule of thumb, and that the rule of thumb you invoked —"A man is more likely to attack a stranger than is a woman"— was a perfectly good one. Statistics confirm this.[5] It is also extremely rare for leashed dogs to attack nonthreatening passersby. You can also console yourself with the knowledge that the universe is not perfect. You win some and you lose some.

Had you looked more closely, however—or if the light had been brighter—you would have noticed the man's clerical collar, and you would have observed the Rottweiler foaming at the mouth. You would then have had more information about your two alternatives, and it would no longer have been appropriate to rely solely on the rule of thumb that men are more violent toward strangers than are women. You would now rely upon the rule of thumb that a Rottweiler foaming at the mouth is more likely to attack you than is a priest.

Now, the quality of this rule of thumb is harder to evaluate. No one keeps statistics on the proportion of leashed Rottweilers that lunge at strangers. Certainly breeders and owners would insist that Rottweilers have an undeserved reputation, and that relatively few of them are aggressive. In any case, the chief cause of foaming at the mouth among all dogs, Rottweilers included, is strenuous exercise, not rabies, and the most likely explanation for the foam is certainly that this particular dog has simply just had a good run. In principle, you could estimate the proportion of priests who randomly attack strangers in parks. People do keep records both of the number of priests and of violent assaults. (Strictly speaking, you would also want information on the number of people who impersonate priests.) But it would take you five or six months of full-time work to gather all that information, and you have at most three seconds in which to decide—and in any case, that information would be useless to you without analogous information about Rottweilers against which to compare it. You have certainly heard more stories about people being attacked by Rottweilers than by priests, however, and as we shall see in the next chapter, it would be normal for you to allow your relative ease of recall on this point to influence your estimates of danger.

While you did not see the man's clerical collar or the Rottweiler foaming at the mouth, you *did* notice that the man was ugly and the woman beautiful. This reinforced your decision to choose the right-hand path. You unthinkingly invoked the rule of thumb that physically ugly people are more dangerous than physically beautiful people. This is not a particularly good rule of thumb, and you probably would not have leaned on it very heavily if you had seen *The Elephant Man*. There is no logical relationship between physical beauty and propensity toward violence.

"Ah!" you might object. "Sadly, there *is* such a relationship. It is natural to judge people on the basis of their looks, to react with aversion to physical ugliness, and to reward people for their physical beauty. Psychologists call this the 'beauty-is-good' effect, or the 'beauty-goodness stereotype.' As a result of it, beautiful people sometimes have opportunities in life that ugly people do not have.

In addition, poor folks cannot afford weight-control programs, gym memberships, fancy skin creams, spa treatments, and cosmetic surgery. Hence poor people are more likely on balance to be ugly than are rich people.* And we all know that violence correlates with poverty. On top of that, violent people often bear scars that make them even uglier than they were to begin with. So, all things considered, there probably is a correlation between physical ugliness and violence, and this rule of thumb is perfectly warranted in this case!"

This is a clever if tasteless retort, and it indicates that you probably did well in your sociology and psychology courses in college. But the relationship between ugliness and violence, whatever it is—as far as I know, nobody keeps statistics on this—must be weak, because plenty of ugly people are born into wealthy circumstances full of opportunity, plenty of good-looking people are born into deprivation, and we all know that the circumstances of your birth strongly predict your life prospects. In any case, studies indicate that the strength of the beauty-is-good effect depends heavily upon the presence or absence of other information about people.[6] If you show the subjects of a psychology experiment photographs of an ugly person and a beautiful person and ask them which is more likely to be a convicted felon, of course people will point to the ugly one. But if the ugly one has a clerical collar and the beautiful one a Rottweiler, all bets are off.

Finally, as the morphine begins to take effect, you console yourself with your grandmother's last words as she lay dying from her injuries. "Never forget," she said. "The left-hand of a fork is *always* the dangerous one!" She should know, you tell yourself. It was the left-hand of a fork that did her in. She never saw the One-Way—Do Not Enter sign.

What we have here, then, are examples of (1) a good rule of thumb; (2) a rule of thumb whose value is difficult to estimate; (3)

---

*On the basis of my own anecdotal observations, I am personally skeptical of this. I teach on two different campuses, and the students at the suburban campus, while significantly disadvantaged vis-à-vis their counterparts downtown economically, clearly spend a great deal more time, effort, and money attempting to maintain a standard of physical beauty. I have often wondered whether this reflects a conscious or unconscious attempt to capitalize upon the beauty-is-good effect in pursuit of upward socioeconomic mobility.

a rule of thumb of dubious value; and (4) a truly awful rule of thumb. A good rule of thumb has a sound basis in empirical fact, and/or expresses the true conclusion of a valid logical inference. A bad rule of thumb has no basis in fact or is utterly illogical (your grandmother was generalizing from a single case—always a mistake). The second and third rules of thumb are more interesting. They are both perfectly understandable psychologically, even if they are difficult to justify logically or empirically. In principle you could have known this if you had had much more time to reflect upon them critically than you actually had available in the park. This is a common problem. We often make judgments (especially under severe time pressure) that critical reflection would not endorse, and, as I discuss in chapter 4 at greater length, there is no way to eliminate this source of error completely. However, you can practice critical reflection on the rules of thumb you invoke. You can train yourself to be suspicious of rules of thumb that are founded on myths, stereotypes, prejudices, biases, logical fallacies, small numbers of cases, misunderstandings of probability, and natural but insupportable assumptions about the goals, intentions, or beliefs of others. We will come back to these themes.

How do I choose a principle of choice?

If you choose a satisficing strategy, your principle of choice is straightforward: you will select the first option you encounter that is satisfactory on whatever dimension(s) you care about. The number of relevant dimensions can be as few as one, or as many as you like. Obviously, the more things you care about, the longer you can expect to look before finding a satisfactory option—but the decision rule itself is uncomplicated.

The flip side of choosing the first *satisfactory* option is rejecting any *unsatisfactory* options you encounter first. Something about them just isn't good enough for you. The technical term for this weeding-out-unsatisfactory-options decision rule is *elimination by aspect*. This is what you *always* do when you satisfice; but very often it will be your first-stage decision rule even in cases where you will not ultimately make your choice by satisficing. Suppose you need to get to Chicago from New York and have to choose between flying, taking the bus, renting a car, taking the train, or hitchhiking. If you must absolutely get there by the next day and have only $100 to your name, you have to rule out flying because it is too expensive, and hitchhiking because you cannot guarantee to get there in time. This is elimination by aspect. Ultimately you will choose between taking the bus, renting a car, and taking the train. Since this is not a complicated choice, the odds are that you will probably pursue an optimizing strategy to make it. But before you try to optimize, you first narrow your options through elimination by aspect.

Sometimes it is not possible to weed out any options through elimination by aspect, and very often, even if you do, you will still be left with two or more to pick from. Whenever you wind up having ultimately to compare and choose between two or more options, you will need to invoke another decision rule. In fact, as our restaurant example illustrated, you may have to try several decision rules in succession. If you choose an optimizing strategy, you have already committed the time and resources to try to find the best possible option, and so it would seem natural that once you have identified your options and closely examined their possible costs and benefits, you would choose among them by asking which of them had the highest SEU. However, where your attempt to optimize leads to the conclusion that two or more alternatives have the same SEU, SEU-maximization will not help you choose between them. You need to try something else, and random choice often fits the bill.

You have quite a wide range of possible criteria to use when making a final choice. For example, you may opt for a choice with a certain minimum payoff. You may opt for a choice that involves a very limited degree of risk. You may do your best to avoid a loss, even at the cost of foregoing a significant possible gain. Or, if you are a thrill seeker, you may even opt for a choice with a minimally *high* degree of risk. A dedicated mountaineer, for example, might prefer tackling the sheer face of a mountain to hiking up a gently sloping trail, even though the odds of returning alive are certainly much worse.

Here are some of the more common principles of choice:

- *SEU Maximization:* "Choose the alternative with the highest subjective expected utility." This is what I have described as optimization, and what we normally mean by "rational" choice in the social sciences when we use that word as a *mot d'art*.
- *Minimax:* "Choose the alternative with the best worst outcome."*
- *Maximax:* "Choose the alternative with the best possible outcome."
- *Disaster Avoidance Principle:* "Choose the alternative with the smallest chance of disaster."
- *Risk Minimization Principle:* "Choose the alternative with the highest chance of an acceptable outcome."
- *Loss Avoidance Principle:* "Choose the alternative with the lowest likelihood of loss."
- *Random choice:* "Choose any of your options randomly."

Very often, several of these decision rules would point you toward the same choice. For instance, if you have $1,000 extra cash that you will not need for a month, you have a choice between stuffing it in your mattress, putting it in a savings account, buying some stock, buying a bond, or investing in a mutual fund. You could actually wind up losing money in the stock, bond, or mutual fund markets, especially if you have to pay loads or commissions—so in this case Minimax, the Disaster Avoidance Principle, and the Risk Minimization Principle will all rule these out. Maximax would tell you to invest in a penny stock, where a small upward movement in the absolute price of the stock could see your $1,000 double or

---

*Some would prefer that I use "Maximin" instead of "Minimax." Technically, Minimax seeks to minimize the largest possible loss (*mini*mizing a *maxi*mum), while Maximin seeks to maximize the smallest possible gain (*maxi*mizing a *mini*mum). Both prescribe choosing the option with the best worst outcome, however, and we can use them interchangeably in this sense.

triple in a very short period of time—but if the price drops, you could lose it all.

Occasionally, you will find yourself in a position where *all* principles of choice point you toward one and only one option. This is nice when it happens, but the universe is not so neatly ordered that it happens every day. The technical term for the favored option here is a *dominant choice.* A dominant choice is one that is at least as good as all the other alternatives on every dimension, and better than all the others on at least one. In my opinion, the local grocery store's no-name brand ultra-low-fat whipped salad dressing dominates all the name brand whipped dressings and mayonnaises. It's cheaper, and tastes just as good or better. It has the lowest fat and fewest calories, too. It wins or ties on every important dimension. Putting $1,000 into a savings account also dominates stuffing it into your mattress. Your money is at least as safe in a bank, and your mattress pays no interest.[7]

Very rarely, each decision rule would point you toward a *different* choice. This is where it pays to think very hard about the decision rule you want to invoke. Real-world examples are hard to come by and are bound to invite debate about their interpretation, so for the sake of clarity, I will illustrate the point with an entirely contrived example made up off the top of my head.

Suppose you are forced to appear on a Kafkaesque game show in which you are told that you must play one of six games (you can choose which). You will roll a pair of dice, and table 7 tells you what you will win or lose, depending upon which game you choose to play. If you are like most people (as I will explain in chapter 4), you will look at what might happen to you if you roll high numbers, and you will try to beg off. "Thanks anyway, I'd rather not play," you will say, whereupon the sadistic authoritarian game-show host will point a gun to your head and tell you to choose a game or else.

Let's assume, for the sake of argument, that you would be perfectly happy to get away from the ordeal with only a small monetary loss—say, ten dollars. If you don't do worse than that, you will consider yourself lucky. So a loss of ten dollars defines the low end

TABLE 7. "LET'S MAKE A DEAL WHETHER YOU LIKE IT OR NOT"

Roll	Game A	Game B	Game C	Game D	Game E	Game F
2	$1,000,000	$50	$2,000,000	$1,000	$40	$50
3	$100,000	$25	$0	$100	$35	$40
4	$10,000	$10	$0	–$10	$30	$30
5	$1,000	$5	$0	–$25	$25	$20
6	$100	$0	$0	–$50	$20	$10
7	$10	–$2	$0	–$100	$15	$0
8	–$10	–$5	–$100	–$200	–$5	$0
9	–$100	–$10	–$1,000	–$300	–$5	$0
10	–$1,000	–$25	–$10,000	–$400	–$5	–$100
11	–$10,000	–$1,500	–$100,000	–$500	–$2,000	–$1,500
12	–$100,000	–$2,000	–$1,000,000	–$3,000	–$2,500	–$3,500

of what you would consider an acceptable outcome. You could win as much as $2 million—needless to say, *that* would be an acceptable outcome, too! Your finances are quite precarious, though, and if you were to lose $1,000 or more, that would be disastrous. You might have to run off and join the French Foreign Legion.

Your choice of which game to play would depend upon the decision rule you chose:

- Game A is the expected-utility maximizing choice. Remember that utility is the product of a payoff (or loss) and its probability. If you multiply all of the probabilities of rolling any particular number by the appropriate payoff or loss, and then add these up, you will discover that game A has an overall expected value of $30,864.17—which is not bad at all. Of course, if you roll a 9, you will be unhappy, and if you roll a 10, 11, or 12, you are toast. But still, overall this game has the highest expected utility. (The only other game with a positive expected value is game C: $21,263.89. The other four games all have negative expected values in the range of $100 to $200 losses.)*

---

*See appendix 2 for the detailed analysis of all six games. We will cover probability and gambling in more detail in the next chapter.

Here and elsewhere in the book I do not ordinarily bother distinguishing between "expected utility" and "expected value." From an economist's perspective this is a technical

- Game B has the best worst outcome, and is therefore the Minimax choice. The worst you can do here is lose $2,000. All of the other games have higher possible losses.
- Game C has the best possible payoff, and is therefore the Maximax choice. You are *really* gutsy if you choose game C, because you have only a 1-in-36 chance of rolling a 2. But if you get a real thrill out of a small chance of a windfall, coupled with a bigger chance of disaster, then this is the game for you! Presumably, this is the game General Wolfe would have chosen.
- Game D carries the smallest chance of disaster, so it satisfies the Disaster Avoidance Principle. Only by rolling a 12 can you lose $1,000 or more, and the chance of this is only 1-in-36.
- Game E gives you the best chance of an acceptable outcome, and is therefore the risk-minimizing choice. Only by rolling 11 or 12 will you lose more than ten dollars in this game, whereas in the next best game (game F) you will lose more than ten dollars if you roll 10, 11, or 12.
- Game F is the game that carries the least risk of a loss. In all the other games, you will lose money if you roll 8 or higher. Only by rolling 10 or higher can you lose money here.

Of course, you could also choose which game to play randomly. You could ask the game-show host to lend you one die and let you roll to see which game to play: for example, you will play game A if you roll a 1, game B if you roll a 2, and so on. Interestingly, this choice has a positive expected value: $8,573.69—the average of the

---

mistake because the "utility" of each dollar gained or lost can vary (a $100 jump in income usually brings much more happiness or satisfaction to someone whose monthly pay is $1,000 than to someone whose monthly pay is $10,000, and the first $100 jump in income would usually be worth more to both of them than would a second $100 jump). Also, someone who gets a thrill from risk might be attracted to a gamble that someone who dreads risk would shun, and hence the gamble would technically have different "utilities" for these two people even though it had the same expected value. I leave this distinction aside for two reasons. First, I do not wish this book to start sounding like a microeconomics text. Second, "rational-choice" explanations of behavior are trivially true if we use an expansive understanding of "utility," and something that explains everything explains nothing. But I thank Sherry Glied for encouraging me to be up front about the issue here. If I don't always distinguish these concepts clearly, I will at least try not to confuse them perniciously.

expected values of the six individual games. You *really* enjoy gambling if this is the decision rule you choose!

The important point to note here is that the decision rule you choose will depend entirely upon your level of comfort with risk. This varies from person to person, and there is no single "rational" choice of decision rule.

Now, there are those who would say that only the first is a "rational" principle of choice. It is the only one that makes sense if your goal is to maximize your wealth. But this does not take into account the psychological stress of playing the game itself. Many of the games with lower expected values actually give you a better chance of walking away with no loss at all, or a much smaller loss, than does game A. Stress represents a cost—something most of us like to avoid—and so it bears on our overall happiness, too. Second, there are certain goods that we need in minimal quantity just to get by and keep on living. Money is one; oxygen is another; so are food and water. It is crucially important that we always have some minimum amount of these things. It therefore makes perfect sense to choose those options that give us a higher probability of securing a vital minimum. You would never choose which airplane to fly by comparing average cruising altitudes: you would always choose the airplane with the best chance of staying airborne. People who don't like risks will therefore not choose game A. They are more likely to choose game B, D, E, or F. And who is to say that they are "irrational"?

It is for this reason that it is a mistake to confuse a "high-quality" decision-making process with a well-executed SEU maximization—although some well-executed SEU maximizations would certainly count as high-quality decision-making processes. Many have praised President John F. Kennedy's handling of the Cuban missile crisis, for example, on the grounds that he chose his response to the Soviet Union's secret deployment of missiles to Cuba only after a very careful consideration of the costs and benefits of all of his available options. But in fact, this is not what President Kennedy did. He and his advisers carefully considered only a small number of options. Very quickly, they eliminated several by aspect (for instance, simply accepting the Soviet fait accompli, or immediately going to war). They kept on the table only those options that did not immediately commit the United States to military action, and that carried a low risk of provoking an aggressive response from the Soviet Union. Throughout the Cuban missile crisis, Kennedy took guidance from the Disaster Avoidance Principle. He was aware of his minimal tolerance for risk, and chose accordingly. To my mind, the quality of his decision making was very high. It was not, however, "rational" in a narrow technical sense.[8]

In order to be an effective decision maker, then, you must reflect upon your comfort level with risk. Very often this will determine your choice of decision rule. Be very careful not to let regret confuse you on this point. If you are a risk-averse person, for example, you will inevitably find that sometimes you would have been better off had you made a riskier choice. Sometimes the horse you bet to show actually wins. It would be normal for you to feel some regret at not having been bolder. But you would be making a grave mistake if you let this regret systematically alter the way you made decisions unless you truly do believe that you are a pathologically mousy person. In the population as a whole, the normal range for risk tolerance is quite broad. If you fall within it, you have nothing to apologize for, and you do yourself no service by berating yourself for being someone other than who you are.

WHICH HOUSE TO BUY?

Let's tie all of this together by having a careful look at an important decision many of us make at least once in the course of our lives: namely, buying a house.

Suppose you and your spouse have just taken new jobs in a large metropolitan city with a tight rental market. In any case, the two of you have a strong preference for owning rather than renting, both because you want the equity and because you want to feel as though you are the masters of your own premises. You also hate moving—it is expensive, time-consuming, and aggravating. You therefore set as your objective buying a house that you can be comfortable in for a long time. You find a real-estate agent who helps you do a preliminary survey of your options. She explains that there are several vibrant neighborhoods downtown, some of which are not far from where you will work, some of which are close to where your spouse will work, and a few of which are in between. There are also many suburban bedroom communities roughly within a forty-five-minute to one-hour commute. You begin to think about the implicated values. One, of course, is money. You have a very good idea of the maximum that you can spend. Another is quality of life. This has many dimensions, and it is obvious from your preliminary survey of options that you will have to make trade-offs between them. If you live in the suburbs, you will be able to afford a nicer house, and a bigger one. You will have a larger yard. Your children will be able to play in the streets with minimal supervision and with a lower risk of being run over by cars. If you live downtown, however, you will be able to get by with only one car; you will be able to walk to shops and restaurants; and you will have at most a short subway ride to work. Your community will also be more diverse ethnically (for the sake of civil peace, let's hope you consider this a good thing). Your children are still in school, too. You want them to have a good education. The suburban schools are newer, larger, and flashier. The downtown schools are more diverse, less plastic, and offer better life lessons. But of course, individual schools vary quite considerably in their quality, both downtown and in the suburbs.

Obviously, this is a very important decision. Consequently, you and your spouse decide to budget considerable time and energy for making it. You decide to fly in for ten days, stay at a hotel, prearrange a mortgage, and spend as much time as you have available making your choice. Your intention is to leave ten days later having successfully bid on a house, preferably the house of your dreams.

Since this is a very important decision, and since you have a reasonable amount of time available, you decide to try to optimize. If you only had a day or two, you might satisfice. But here you think you can do better than that. Of course, you will not attempt to consider every available house in the city. Instead, you will concentrate all of your energies on houses in two or three neighborhoods. In other words, you will attempt a constrained optimization. So your first task is to choose which neighborhoods to look at closely. This may strongly affect the final outcome of your expedition, but it is useful to think of it as a separate, prior choice.

Here is where things start to get a bit complicated. There are plenty of neighborhoods you might look at. There are many things you want in a neighborhood. It is unlikely that one neighborhood will dominate all the rest (remember: a dominant choice is one that is at least as good as all the others on every dimension, and better than all the rest on at least one). There's no way you can do a simple "bang for the buck" calculation of the kind you could have done in the convenience store way back in chapter 1. What, then, can you do?

There are different ways of designing a decision such as this, but the one we will walk through is a fairly standard version of a *multi-attribute* optimization. All this means is that you want to do the best you can possibly do taking into account everything you really care about, and (roughly) how much you care about them. It's possible to do this strictly qualitatively—for example, just keeping a list of each neighborhood's pros and cons and knocking them off one by one. This is what most people would do. And often it works just fine. But there is a better way: going through a numerical exercise. This has two crucial advantages over the old-fashioned eyeballing-a-list-of-pros-and-cons approach. First, you can handle a whole lot more information more rigorously. Second, you are less likely to goof up. Numbers never lie.

To help you work through this decision (and any other you might make where a multi-attribute optimization would be the appropriate way to go), you can visit the companion Web site for this book at http://www.decisionhelper.com. There you will find a multi-attribute utility maximization tool that lets you set up your own decision problem and handles all of the math for you. You will also find some ready-made templates (for example, for buying a house, buying a car, and choosing a job), which you can use on-line or download in spreadsheet form. It's fun, it's handy, and, best of all, it's free. To make good use of these resources, though, it will help to work through this example here.

End of advertisement.

You are now at the seventh step of your decision-making process: identifying your options. You will first go through steps 7 through 9 for neighborhoods, and then repeat steps 7 through 9 for individual houses.

The first thing you do is come up with a list of everything you care about in a neighborhood, in no particular order. You and your spouse first draw up your own lists, and then collate them. You then have a discussion together to try to decide whether you left anything important off your lists. Let's suppose that your final list looks like this:

- Size of house
- Size of yard
- Quality of amenities in the house
- Quiet street
- Kid-friendliness of neighborhood
- Access to a place of worship (or to a community center)
- Access to parks and playgrounds
- Quality of local schools
- Convenience of your commute
- Convenience of your spouse's commute
- Convenience of amenities
- Diversity

You and your spouse then decide how important each of these is to you. You could try just ranking them, but it would be even more helpful if you could assign each a weight on a scale (say) from 1 to 10, where 10 is something you care about intensely, and 1 is something that would merely be nice. It makes no difference what scale you use; 1 to 100 or 1 to 500 would work just as well—you simply need enough space in the scale to capture the order of your preferences on each dimension, and to provide room for some rough comparisons of the kind, "I like this option ten times better than that one." This is something a scale of 1 to 3, for instance, could not provide—unless you're happy working with a lot of decimals, which I personally consider a pain in the neck.

Let's suppose your weights look like this:

TABLE 8. WEIGHTS

	Your weights	Your spouse's weights
Size of house	5	4
Size of yard	3	3
Quality of amenities in the house	6	6
Quiet street	4	6
Kid-friendliness of neighborhood	7	7
Access to place of worship or community center	6	6
Access to parks and playgrounds	8	7
Quality of local schools	10	10
Convenience of your commute	8	
Convenience of your spouse's commute		6
Convenience of amenities	5	8
Diversity	4	2

You talk about these and probe each other's weights, happy to discover that although some of them are a little different, on balance you have compatible values and probably did not make a huge mistake marrying each other. You decide that your weights should count equally, so where they differ you will just average them.

You now gather as much information as you can about the neighborhoods that your realtor recommends you explore. We will call them S_1 through S_4 (for the suburban neighborhoods) and D_1 through D_5 (for the downtown neighborhoods). For each thing you care about, you and your wife decide to estimate together how well that neighborhood scores on a scale from 0 to 10, multiply each score by the appropriate weight, and sum the total weighted score for each neighborhood. This will not take a very long time; your realtor knows these neighborhoods pretty well. (You could have scored these separately and averaged the scores, but you prefer to do the scoring jointly. This is fine; whether you do it separately or together is a matter of taste.) Let's suppose table 9 gives what you come up with.

TABLE 9. EVALUATING NEIGHBORHOODS

	Average weight	S_1	S_2	S_3	S_4	D_1	D_2	D_3	D_4	D_5
Size of house	4.5	9	10	10	9	5	6	6	5	4
Size of yard	3	10	10	9	9	4	5	5	5	4
Quality of amenities in the house	6	8	9	8	7	7	6	7	7	5
Quiet street	5	10	10	10	10	6	6	5	5	6
Kid-friendliness of neighborhood	7	10	10	10	10	4	5	4	5	2
Access to place of worship or community center	6	8	7	7	5	5	6	6	7	5
Access to parks and playgrounds	7.5	6	5	5	5	7	9	9	8	7
Quality of local schools	10	9	7	3	8	7	9	8	9	8
Convenience of your commute	8	0	0	1	0	8	9	9	8	6
Convenience of your spouse's commute	6	0	0	0	1	6	8	9	9	10
Convenience of amenities	6.5	3	2	2	3	10	10	9	10	9
Diversity	3	0	1	0	1	8	8	7	9	9
Total Score		441	414.5	370.5	405.5	476	545.5	526	541.5	460

You and your spouse have a clear preference for downtown neighborhoods. Quite possibly, you knew that without having to go through this exercise. But in any case, what jumps out from this is the finding that downtown neighborhoods 2, 3, and 4 score well above all the others. D_2 is the best. You are optimizing, so you decide to start your search there. You do not need a huge selection of acceptable houses to choose from, so you will only look in D_4 or D_3 if you do not find enough homes in D_2 that fit your bill.

Now you go back to step 7, this time looking for houses, not neighborhoods. Your realtor tells you that there are forty-eight houses for sale in D_2, thirty-six in D_4, and fifty-seven in D_3. You begin eliminating houses by aspect. First, you will not look at houses listed over a certain fixed price. Second, you will not look at houses that have fewer than three bedrooms and two bathrooms. Third, you will not look at houses that do not have off-street parking. Within those parameters, you are willing to consider anything. Your realtor has access to the full database of listings on the Multiple Listing Service, and discovers that you have eliminated all but eight houses in D_2, ten in D_4, and fifteen in D_3. She gives you copies of the listings for each, and you prepare to go hunting.

You now draw up your lists of everything you care about in a house, just as you did for neighborhoods, and assign them weights. The list includes everything on your neighborhoods list (since you still care about those things), plus things specific to individual houses. Armed with this list, you hit the road. You discover that two of the houses in D_2 have just sold, leaving six. Four of those are in such horrible shape that they would need extensive renovations just to be habitable—something for which you have neither the time nor the money. You want to consider more than just two houses, though, and as you are only on your fourth day in town, you decide you can expand your search into D_4 and spend a couple of more days looking there. Of the ten houses in D_4, eight are still on the market, and three of those are in reasonably good shape. Your realtor informs you that one of the houses in D_2 has just sold, but another one has come on the market that falls within your parameters. You check it out and decide that it is in the running.

After a few days' house hunting, you have five houses to choose from. You and your spouse score each, and average the scores. In the course of so doing, you rely upon what you have seen, as well as on a number of rules of thumb for things you cannot see (for example, that houses built in certain decades were built more solidly and with better materials than others; that one-way streets are quieter than two-way streets; etc.). After scoring the houses and doing some math, you rank them. Table 10 gives your final score sheet.

TABLE 10. FINAL HOUSE RANKINGS

	Weight (your average score)	D_2 House A	D_2 House B	D_4 House A	D_4 House B	D_4 House C
Size of house	4.5	6	5	5	6	7
Size of yard	3	5	5	4	4	5
Quality of amenities in the house	6	6	9	5	8	7
Quiet street	5	6	5	5	5	4
Kid-friendliness of neighborhood	7	5	5	5	5	5
Access to place of worship or community center	6	6	6	6	7	7
Access to parks and playgrounds	7.5	9	9	8	8	9
Quality of local schools	10	9	9	7	9	7
Convenience of your commute	8	9	9	7	8	8
Convenience of your spouse's commute	6	7	8	9	9	9
Convenience of neighborhood amenities	6.5	10	10	10	9	10
Neighborhood diversity	3	8	8	9	9	9
Quality of construction	10	8	7	7	5	7
Quality of kitchen	7.5	10	5	6	4	8
Entertainment space	4.5	8	8	7	7	8
Play room/family room	7	4	8	4	5	6
Updated mechanics	8	9	8	10	5	6
Heating and air conditioning	7.5	9	4	10	5	5
Fireplace	3	0	8	8	0	10
Floors and carpets	4	4	6	4	6	6
Light	4.5	9	8	9	7	9
Storage space	4	7	7	2	8	5
High ceilings	3	10	8	8	7	8
Convenience of laundry	4.5	6	2	6	8	8
Garden	5.5	9	6	9	6	7
Deck	4	10	5	2	8	5
TOTAL SCORE		1129	1045.5	1019	976	1059.5
RANK		1	3	4	5	2

Your first choice is house A in neighborhood D_2, and your second choice is house C in neighborhood D_4. You decide to put a bid in on the former, letting your realtor know that you have other fish to fry—a piece of intelligence that should encourage the vendor to make a deal.*

This is really quite a good example of a constrained optimization. Most people who buy houses do not take the time and trouble to work through the problem so systematically. Many people buy houses impressionistically. Now, it may be that some people have such a good intuitive sense of what they are looking for in a house that they really do not need such a carefully planned decision. It may be that if they were to go through a decision-making process like this, it would point them toward the exact choice they would make intuitively in any case. But for many people, it is helpful to think through explicitly what it is that they want, and it is useful to impose the artificial discipline of a little arithmetic. Among other things, the exercise can generate a useful rank ordering of preferences that can help discipline buyers when they get into the bidding. It may even result in a few surprises. First impressions are often accurate, but it may be that explicit reflection upon the full range of things one cares about in a house reveals that your true preferences are not, in fact, what you originally suspected them to be.

Buying a house is not a science, however, and there are several things worth noting about this exercise. First, the longer you make your list of things you value, the greater the danger of diluting the numerical weight of the things you care about most. If the quality of the neighborhood schools is your number one concern, it can make a big difference whether you list four additional values or nine: ten points out of fifty carries greater weight than ten points out of one hundred. Of course, you can correct for this if you are disciplined about the weights you give to other considerations. The more things you add to your list, therefore, the more careful

---

*Many people who buy houses work within a budget and seek to find the best house they can afford. They do not bother to calculate a "bang for the buck." There is nothing wrong with this approach; but if you *did* wish to calculate a "bang for the buck," you could divide the overall score of each home by its price. In table 10, your second-ranked house would have to cost 94 percent (or less) of your first-ranked house to have a higher "bang for the buck."

you have to be to keep their weights down relative to the things you *really* care about intensely. For things you really feel intensely about, consider making them a criterion for elimination by aspect.

Second, be aware that your scores are bound to be imprecise. This means that small differences in overall scores are really negligible analytically. Do not be lulled into a false sense of precision. If your second-ranked choice scores very close to your first-ranked choice, you are probably indifferent as between the two.

Third, you may find that after you go through an exercise such as this, your gut tells you that you have made the wrong choice. Listen to your gut. If it is telling you this because you are the kind of person who is indecisive and tends to feel regret intensely, then the odds are pretty good that your gut would tell you the same thing no matter what you chose, and you should probably try to convince yourself to ignore it. But if you do the thought experiment of imagining how you would feel if you had chosen differently, and if your gut tells you that you would have been happier, take notice. This is a warning sign that you did not do a very good job of identifying the things that are important to you, or of assigning the appropriate weight to give to each. You need to work on your introspection skills.

Fourth, human nature is such that most of us cannot make important decisions comfortably without some minimal degree of angst and solemnity. There is a danger that if you treat an important decision as a technical exercise involving only cognitive resources and arithmetical skills, you may experience a debilitating sense of psychic dissatisfaction—even if you make the right decision.

Some friends of mine recently faced a choice between taking jobs on the West Coast and on the East Coast. Pretty soon it became clear that he wanted to go west, and she wanted to go east. Each had a strong preference, and their preferences were equally intense. They both have strong personalities, and they are both liberal, so there was no possibility of him deciding and her simply complying.

On the verge of divorce, they explained their predicament to me, knowing that I had an interest in decision making. After some probing into matters that were really none of my business, I proclaimed that this was a clear case of indifference between two choices, and that the rational solution was to flip a coin. I whipped a quarter out of my pocket and said, "Heads it's the West Coast, tails it's the East Coast." The coin landed tails up. "Well, that's that," I said. "Let's go for best two out of three," said he. I could understand that. But what I did not immediately understand was her dissatisfaction. She was not prepared to accept the result, either.

Later, after puzzling it over for a while and chatting about it with people who have better insight into human nature than I do, I decided that my coin toss solution had three fatal flaws. First, both of them really wanted to reach an agreement. They did not want a winner and a loser. A coin toss simply meant that one of them would win and one of them would lose. That could later become a source of resentment. I suspect, too, that they both considered this a test of their relationship. They were, after all, newlyweds. It usually takes newlyweds some time to reassure themselves that they haven't made a terrible mistake by getting married. If they could reach agreement under such difficult circumstances, it would mean that they could overcome adversity and discord together. It would be a positive sign of their long-term compatibility. Failure would be a red flag.

The second thing wrong with my coin toss solution was that deciding on the basis of a coin toss is not deciding on the basis of *reasons*. When we make important decisions in life, we naturally want to be able to say that we had good reasons for making our choices. We want to be able to convince ourselves that our choices duly reflect our goals, that we have done a good job of matching means to ends, and that we had a sober sense of the relative pros and cons of our alternatives. It seems somehow irresponsible merely to flip a coin. How do you explain *that* to your relatives?

But sometimes reasons do not point toward a clear choice. Sometimes two (or more) alternatives are equally reasonable. Where reasoning does not work, random choice is as good a basis for decision as anything else. Better, even, insofar as it actually *leads* to a choice. This, I think, was one of those cases. My friends had not yet convinced themselves of this, however. They needed time to see that reasoning would lead to an impasse. I do not know whether they ever would have admitted this to themselves, and to each other, but if so, it would still have been inappropriate for me merely to whip a coin out of my pocket on the spot. This would simply not have had the gravity or solemnity that such an important decision requires. It was a mistake, in short, to flip flippantly. What I should have done is suggest that they make a pact with each other to prepare an extravagant five-course candlelight dinner for two at the next full moon, drink a $100 bottle of wine, and, at the stroke of midnight, flip a silver dollar, binding themselves to the result. My guess is that embedding the random-choice decision rule in an appropriately solemn ritual might just have done the trick. Sometimes a high-quality decision-making process must gives atmospherics their due. My third mistake was to overlook this.

The example, I think, reminds us of the limitations and dangers of a coldly clinical approach to decision making. But care and attentiveness to the process of decision can still pay off. Our house-hunting example provides a good illustration. As long as you are self-reflective in your application of it, it is worth emulating when you confront an important decision of this kind—and the on-line tool at www.decisionhelper.com makes it easy to do exactly that.

A more careful and more systematic approach to buying a house certainly would have helped a friend of mine, anyway. Many years ago she dashed into town, hopped into a car with a realtor, and bought the very first house she saw. Later that night, at dinner, she was in the middle of crowing about the wonderful house she had bought in such a great neighborhood for so little money and with such little effort, when one of the other guests interrupted her. "Oh," he said, "you weren't deterred by the rail-road track in the backyard, then?"—to which my friend replied, as the color drained from her face, "*What* railroad track?"

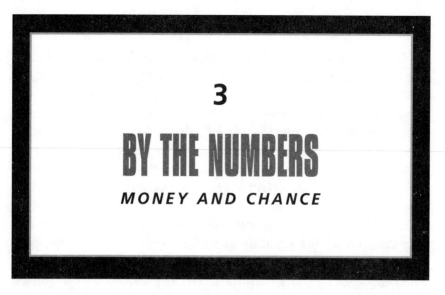

3

BY THE NUMBERS

MONEY AND CHANCE

There's a sucker born every minute.
—David Hannum (usually misattributed to P. T. Barnum)[1]

To this point we have used numbers liberally to help us work through examples of common decisions. In some of those examples, we used numbers to quantify things that are not really all that quantifiable—for instance, how well different houses or neighborhoods fare on the various criteria we care about when we go looking for a place to live. The scores we used were not ridiculous, but it is important to bear in mind that they did not convey precise information about the intrinsic worth of the things we were judging. Instead, they conveyed information about *our judgments* of those things. Robert Parker's famous scores in *The Wine Advocate* fall into this category. If you have a taste for wine, you can be quite confident that you will prefer a wine Parker rates 92 to a wine he rates 86, because he has an outstanding nose and palate. But if you are a connoisseur yourself, you might find on occasion that, for various reasons, you actually prefer a wine Parker rates 90 to a wine he rates 92. His scores give us accurate information about his well-informed judgments of things, but less than perfectly accurate information about the things themselves, because quality, unlike quantity, is rarely something to which you can assign a precise, objective number.

In other examples, we have noted that good-quality hard-and-fast numbers that actually give us objective information about the options we are considering may, in principle, be available, but that limits on our time, energy, and skills may make it impossible to find or to use that information effectively. My subway dilemma and the fork-in-the-path example fall into this category. In both cases, decisions had to be made quickly without the benefit of the detailed statistics that would have permitted a more accurate evaluation of the alternatives.

In still other examples, real numbers about genuinely quantifiable things have been readily available to us. Either the numbers were given right there in our decision problem, as in our Kafkaesque game show example from the previous chapter, or we could get them in the time available to us, as in our World Series example from chapter 1. It is this last type of decision that I would like to examine more closely now, because this is the kind of decision where it is generally easiest to choose and apply the various strategies we surveyed in chapter 2. These are the decisions, in short, that are often easiest to handle rigorously. Most such decisions involve money, so for much of this chapter I will concentrate on how to think about decisions involving money. Ironically, these are often exactly the kinds of decisions that we bungle most severely. (Sometimes the quality of our decisions depends heavily on how well we understand probability, too, so I will spend some time looking at that as well. The gamblers in the audience will especially like this part.)

Those of us who make costly mistakes about money, or who dig deep financial holes for ourselves from which we can see no easy way out, often do so in creative, unique ways. This is as true of countries and corporations as it is of individuals. If you are struggling to make ends meet, and if your debt load is getting you down, cheer up—at least you're not the United States, whose total public debt as I write exceeds $5 trillion, or Iridium, who only discovered how little demand there was for global satellite phones after spending more than $5 billion putting sixty-six satellites into orbit.[2]

Often, remedies for serious financial woes need to be custom-tailored to circumstances. If you find yourself in a serious financial bind, you should know that there are plenty of talented folks out there who make a good living helping people like you.[3] This chapter is no substitute for personalized professional advice from a qualified financial counselor. But it can help you spot weaknesses in your financial decision making that may have contributed to your present predicament, whatever it may be.

THINKING ABOUT MONEY

Money is a strange thing. Most of us have a love-hate relationship with it. Many of us can't live with it; most of us can't live without it. We like to think that we "manage" money, but the reality is often quite different. Either we find that we have no control over it at all, or that *it* controls *us*.

In finance as in war, it pays to know your enemy. What is this thing money? How does it behave?

Your dictionary and your economics textbook will tell you that money is a "measure of value" and a "medium of exchange." It certainly is a medium of exchange: you can trade money for almost anything. Whether it is truly a measure of value is more debatable. The dizzying heights the stock markets reached in the last few years clearly show that there can be a gaping rift between something's book value and its real value. Moreover, the expansion and contraction of the money supply do not seem to reflect real changes in the value of things in the world. As a measure of value, money is not very precise.

But in any case the textbook definition tells us nothing about how money behaves. It is important to know that money has a life and a mind of its own. It is capricious. It is cruel. It likes to lull you into a false sense of security, and then bite you on the heel. It is a bit like an ill-tempered cat.

To help us better understand money, it is useful to bear the following principles in mind:

- *Money evaporates quickly.* You can put $100 in your wallet, and without your even being aware of it, it will shrink almost to nothing within a matter of days. There is nothing you can do to prevent this. At best you can merely slow the rate of evaporation.
- *Making money is expensive.* You may have heard the old saw that to make money, you need money. This is a corollary of the TANSTAAFL Principle ("There Ain't No Such Thing as a Free Lunch"). The point is obvious when you think about making money through interest and dividends: if you don't have any money to put into a savings account or to invest, you can't earn any interest or dividends on it. But it is also true of other ways of making money. To sell a good or a service, for example, you have to buy tools or raw materials. This is as true for General Motors, which spends millions of dollars a year on plant and equipment, as it is for a squeegee kid, who can't ply his trade without a squeegee and a bucket.
- Generally, to make lots of money, you need lots of money. You can make millions if you have millions. You can't make millions if you are penniless. (There are rare exceptions to this rule, of course; you might win a lottery with a ticket that you found, or you might win a huge product liability lawsuit filed on your behalf by a pro bono lawyer. But these exceptions are extremely rare, and you would be foolish to rely upon them in your financial planning.) Thus you should always beware of get-rich-quick schemes. If they are legal, most likely they will not work. If they will work, most likely they are illegal.
- *Keeping money is expensive.* If you have a savings or an investment account, you are probably paying someone to hold it for you, through account fees and the like. In the good old days, money in the bank used to earn a rate of interest high enough to offset whatever account fees you used to pay. This is no longer necessarily true. Even after collecting interest, many of us pay the bank eight or ten dollars

a month for the privilege of keeping (and making more money on) our money. This may tempt you simply to stuff your money into your mattress. But . . .

- *There are costs to pay no matter what you do with your money.* There are two kinds of costs we do not always think about: (1) Opportunity costs; and (2) Transaction costs.

  "Opportunity cost" is a technical piece of economics jargon referring to the best alternative use of your money. You "pay" this cost by passing up that best alternative use when you decide to do one thing with your money rather than another. The opportunity cost you pay for a new car, for example, might be a luxurious vacation. The opportunity cost of stuffing your money in your mattress may be a good rate of interest on an investment.

  "Transaction costs" are the costs you pay just to spend your money. Some of these are transparent: taxes, fees, and commissions are all good examples. But sometimes they are less obvious. When you drive to the store to buy something, for instance, you probably don't think of the cost of the gasoline you burn, or a proportion of your other annual vehicle operating expenses, as part of the cost of your purchase— but they are. If you want to spend money at the store, and if you have to drive to get there, you can't avoid paying them. I will come back to this example in a minute.

- *Some of the most important costs associated with handling money are not monetary.* Money is a great source of anxiety. People fret about it all the time. When they spend it, they worry whether they have spent it unwisely. When they find themselves in a debt trap, they lose sleep worrying about how to get out of it. Even when things are going well, people fret about things going badly in the future.

  If you are the kind of person who experiences no anxieties about money, then you are truly blessed. For the rest of us, it is important to try to find a way of relating to money that is relatively comfortable psychologically—even if this means making decisions that are not likely to maximize our net wealth over the long run. This is precisely the same point I made in the previous chapter when I argued that your comfort level with risk should influence your choice of decision-making strategies. Risk-averse strategies, while not always expected-value maximizing in strictly monetary terms, can still be "rational" if you find risk psychologically painful.

Money all by itself is benign, but when we start mixing it with math, it can be deadly. Most of the decisions we make involving money require nothing more than relatively simple arithmetic such as addition and subtraction. These operations will not get us into deep trouble unless the amounts we subtract are chronically larger than the amounts we add. Usually the serious troubles arise when we start dabbling in multiplication and division—that is, interest rates and monthly payments. The numbers often look small and innocuous. This lulls us into thinking that they *are* small and innocuous. Generally, they aren't.

I was in an electronics superstore the other day and just happened to walk past the display of big-screen television sets. "YOU CAN AFFORD THIS!!!" the sign next to one screamed at me, "ONLY $139!" Gosh, I said to myself, $139 seems like a very reasonable price for a television set larger than most refrigerators. Then I noticed the small print informing me that this was the *monthly* payment for two years O.A.C. (which is supposed to mean "On Approved Credit," though it could just as easily mean "Our Avenue to your Cash") with a $500 down payment. I would have had to shell out $3,200 to buy the thing outright—before taxes, delivery, and setup (i.e., before transaction costs). To buy the set on the store's terms, taking into account the interest they were charging (at 12 percent), I would have wound up paying more than $3,800 all told (again, not including taxes, delivery, and setup). What made them think I could afford that? But their sales pitch was very clever. If you divide a large sum up into pieces, it doesn't seem so large. They would not sell nearly as many television sets if the sign read, "SPEND TWO MONTHS' SALARY ON THIS TELEVISION NOW, OR KICK IN ANOTHER $600 ON TOP

OF THAT AND WE'LL LET YOU PAY IT OFF OVER TWO YEARS!"

The same phenomenon largely explains credit card debt traps. The first time you get your credit card statement, you realize that you have a choice between paying the "new balance" or the "minimum payment due." That $3,500 charge for the television set ($3,200, plus tax, delivery, and setup) may seem quite daunting when you have only $1,000 in your bank account. But those nice folks at the credit card company only require $103.50! You can handle that. You gaily write a check for the lesser amount. But next month you start getting authorization denials as you bump up against your $5,000 credit limit, and your finance charges—at a whopping 18.5 percent—start piling up, too. Before you know it, you are in way over your head. By the time your credit counselor finishes helping you straighten out your mess—in part by holding a gun to your head while you chop your credit cards into tiny pieces—you have failed to make several monthly minimum payments, your credit rating is in the tank, and your big-screen TV wound up costing you way over $4,000.

A simple principle of mathematics is that whenever you multiply things a lot, they get big fast. The point is illustrated well by an ancient Persian legend my sixth-grade math teacher used to tell. The story goes like this:

A poor farmer rendered his king some great service, and the king wished to reward him with gold and jewels. The farmer asked instead if he could propose his own reward. The king, somewhat miffed at the farmer's haughtiness, nevertheless agreed to hear him out, threatening to punish him severely if the request seemed greedy on its face. Undaunted, the farmer placed one grain of wheat on a corner square of a chessboard, and said to the king, "This is what I ask. Place double the number of grains on the next square, and double that number again on the third, doubling the previous number for each square on the chessboard, and I will be satisfied with the total amount of grain as my reward." The king—no mathematical genius—thought he was getting off easy, and immediately agreed. But when he gave the order to deliver the grain, his officers returned to say that this was impossible, as there was not enough grain in the entire kingdom to make good on the pledge. "How can that be?" he demanded to know. "Did we not have an excellent harvest?" They explained that the problem lay not with the harvest, but with the chessboard.

A chessboard has sixty-four squares. It is true that the first square had only one grain on it, and the second only two. But since the number of grains on each successive square doubled, the number of grains on any given square was equal to the number 2 multiplied by itself once for each previous square. The number of grains on square number n, in other words, would be $2^{(n-1)}$. When n is small, this is not a particularly big number. But when n is 64, it is huge. The last square alone—square 64—would have 2^{63}, or 9,223,372,036,854,780,000 grains on it. The total number of grains on the chessboard would be 2^{64}, or 18,446,744,073,709,600,000. If one cubic foot of grain weighed ten pounds and contained 50,000 grains, the total would weigh more than 900 trillion tons and occupy more than 350 trillion cubic feet—enough to fill Lake Superior, Lake Huron, and Lake Erie with some to spare. That's a lot of grain.

I don't remember whether the story was supposed to be true. If so, I imagine the king, out of embarrassment and anger, had the farmer flogged. But it does nicely illustrate how numbers can snowball, and this applies equally well to money as to grain—though, admittedly, 100 percent compound interest rates are rare outside of gangland (compounded interest applies not only to the principal, or original amount, but also to accumulated interest).

Even realistic interest rates, however, can turn small amounts of money into big ones when compounding over a long enough period of time. This can work to your advantage if you are managing to save and are patient. Suppose, for example, that you opened a savings account in your child's name on the day of her birth with $100 and never deposited anything in it ever again. If the account bears 8 percent interest compounded annually, then by the time your child reaches the age of sixty-five, the value of that account will grow to $14,877.98. That's the good news.* The bad

---

*This assumes no account fees—probably an unrealistic assumption. Also, the future value of the account is likely to be diminished by inflation. The figure given is in current-year dollars.

news is that if you carry a $4,000 credit card balance (the average credit card debt in the United States) at 18.5 percent and pay $100 every month, it will take you five years to pay off the balance, even if you make no further charges, and at the end of the day you will have paid more than $2,000 in interest. That's enough to buy a decent-sized color television set.

There are three other things that it pays to be aware of when thinking about money. The first is that a good use of money is always something you can only judge relative to other possible uses. No use of money is ever good in and of itself. This is where the concept of opportunity cost comes in handy. Some people, for example, cannot resist bankruptcy liquidations. It doesn't matter what is being liquidated: 80 percent discounts are simply too good to pass up. They come home loaded down with things like crystal decanters and designer boots that were "unbelievable deals." But unless you *need* a crystal decanter or a pair of designer boots, this is a complete waste of money. A much better use of the money would have been to buy a carton of laundry soap at full price, if you happen to need laundry soap.

Second, accurately evaluating alternative uses of money can be complicated, even if it is not particularly tricky. Suppose you definitely need a carton of laundry soap, which the corner convenience store sells for $7.95, but which the supermarket two miles away is selling for the "unbelievable deal!" of 20 percent off ($6.35). Ever frugal, you may be tempted to hop in the car and drive two miles to the supermarket and two miles back. But you are forgetting about transaction costs. Your car gets twenty miles to the gallon in city driving, so at $1.45 a gallon, the trip will cost you twenty-nine cents in gasoline. You also lease your car for business purposes, and you have already exceeded your annual mileage limit. You are now paying a premium of fifteen cents per mile. That's another sixty cents. Driving to the supermarket will also reduce the business-use portion of your lease, which has tax implications—let's say to the tune of another sixty cents.* The real monetary cost of

---

*Assuming a four-mile round trip, a marginal tax rate of 36 percent on a $450 per month vehicle lease, 20,000 miles driven in the tax year, and operating expenses (insurance, license fees, fuel, maintenance) of $3,000.

the laundry soap at the grocery store is now $7.84. You saved eleven cents (before tax). You also spent an extra half hour getting the soap, and the traffic aggravated your blood pressure. Was this an unbelievable deal?

Third—and this is the most important point—the way you make decisions about money should reflect the reality that money is not something you can really afford to run out of completely. You always need it in some minimum quantity. Exactly what this minimum quantity is varies from person to person and from place to place. It depends, among other things, upon the cost of living where you reside, your number of dependants, your lifestyle, and your existing obligations. But you should be able to work out what that quantity is in your particular case. It is the amount you need to pay for food, shelter, clothing, medical care, other necessities of life, existing obligations such as payments on college loans, alimony, or child support, and so on.

Because you need a minimum amount of money all the time, you need to pay attention to your *cash flow*. This is the relative amount of money you have coming in and going out. You need to try to make sure that your income from all sources in any given month can cover your basic expenses. If you have some savings, a good friend or relative who will float you on a short-term basis, or a line of credit at a reasonable interest rate, you may be able to get by once in a while with a negative monthly cash flow. But if your cash flow is chronically negative, then you need to find a way to reduce your expenses, increase your income, or both.

It is prudent financial management to try to build in some additional cushion in your cash flow, so that you can cover unforeseen extraordinary expenses and save a regular amount each month for retirement, your children's college tuition, and that kind of thing. While not absolutely necessary every month, it is nice to include in this cushion some funds for such things as hobbies, vacations, and charitable contributions.

Any resources you may have above this cushion is a surplus which you can use in a variety of ways, but which you do not, strictly speaking, *need*.

It is helpful, then, to think of your financial resources in terms of a cake. ("Let them eat cake!") If you have no cake, you starve. All cakes have at least one layer. But yours could potentially have three, and this is what you would like to have. Still, as you work toward getting a nice, delicious three-layer cake, you have to keep an eye on the cake you have at the moment.

- If your cake has only one layer, you must protect it carefully. Take no risks with it. You can't afford to lose, or be swindled out of, your cake.
- If your cake has two layers, you can take *some* risks with it. You can give some away, or trade some for something else. If things go well, you will soon be able to afford a three-layer cake. If they go badly, all is not lost—you will still have enough cake to live on. Don't take too many risks with your two-layer cake, though, because this is the difference between simply being fed enough to stay alive and being fed comfortably.
- If you have a three-layer cake, you can afford to be generous and risky. After all, you don't need such a big cake.

The strategies you invoke when making financial decisions, in short, will depend upon how many layers your cake has.

Typically, if your cash flow is tight and you are not managing to maintain a cushion, your financial choices should be guided by a highly risk-averse strategy such as minimax, risk-minimization, disaster avoidance, or loss avoidance. Which one you pick to guide your decisions will depend on the circumstances and your own comfort with risk. But the general point holds: try to avoid gambling with your first-tier resources. If you have an adequate cushion, you can afford to accept risks that involve larger potential gains, but also larger potential losses—provided that you do not accept risks that could compromise the security of your first tier. If you are lucky enough to have surplus resources, you are more likely to choose on the basis of SEU maximization, which promises the highest long-run payoff—again, providing that the downside risks of the SEU-maximizing strategy would not be so severe as to compromise your cushion or your first-tier resources. If you are *really* risky—and, I might add, if you have no dependents—you might want to follow a maximax strategy every once in a while and take a shot at a really big payoff. The general point is this: don't take chances where you can't afford them; take more chances where you can.

The same principle applies to businesses as well as to individuals and households. Businesses need a minimum cash flow to survive. They must be able to meet payroll, pay suppliers, cover rent and other overhead, cover tax obligations, and so on. It is desirable for businesses to have some cushion to protect them from price fluctuations, the whims of the market, and unforeseen expenses. It is wonderful when businesses are flush with cash, so that they can expand, pay out handsome dividends and bonuses, make hostile takeover bids, and generally act like economic bullies. Smart businesspeople will follow risk-averse strategies when their finances are precarious, and riskier strategies when they are not.

Consider, for example, the question of whether you should buy an extended warranty. Manufacturers and retailers offer extended warranties on a wide variety of mechanical and electronic goods these days—everything from toaster ovens to stereos to automobiles. Normally, for an extra lump sum up front, you can extend for several months or years the period of time in which someone will repair manufacturer's defects free of charge.

Now, the first thing to recognize about extended warranties is that manufacturers and retailers would not knowingly offer them if they stood to lose money on them. This means that over the extended warranty period, the average cost of repairing whatever you bought is likely to be lower than the cost of the extended warranty itself. The average person will therefore be better off declining the offer to buy an extended warranty, and this is what the SEU principle would normally tell you to do. (Of course, sometimes manufacturers or retailers screw up and lose money on extended warranties. This can happen when a particular item they sell is so badly designed or manufactured that an unexpectedly large number of them come back for repairs. Consumers' organizations sometimes keep track of repair records, average costs of repairs, and extended warranty prices for various items, and if you consult this information, you may find from time to time that purchasing an extended warranty is actually SEU-maximizing. But most of the time it is not. And in any case, you probably don't want something for which it pays to buy an extended warranty, because it's most likely junk.)

So it is almost never SEU-maximizing to buy an extended warranty. Are there nevertheless circumstances when you should? Yes. If you can afford the extended warranty, but could not afford to do without the item in question and could not afford a major repair, you should consider buying one. It may be unlikely that you would ever need to pay for a major repair, but if your financial resources are limited, both the disaster avoidance principle and the minimax principle would tell you to accept the certain small loss of the cost of the extended warranty in order to avoid the uncertain (maybe even highly improbable) large cost of a major repair. Generally, you should *always* decline extended warranties when you are rich, and you should decline them for items that are relatively inexpensive to repair, or that you could live without, if you are poor.

The same reasoning leads people to buy life and homeowner's insurance. Insurance companies make a great deal of money, because a lot of people buy insurance and relatively few die prematurely, get burgled, or have their houses burn down. Put another way, the average person loses money buying insurance. Nevertheless, someone who is risk-averse will gladly pay a small monthly premium to guard against a possible catastrophe. Buying insurance is almost never expected-value maximizing, but it is often smart risk-management. It may seem counterintuitive to think that spending some of your precious cake on insurance is wise if it has only one layer, and foolish if it has three—but there you are.

To sum up, it is always important, when making decisions about money, to think strategically, to tailor your strategies to your financial circumstances, and to be sensitive to the full range of costs associated with your decisions—in particular, to the opportunity costs and transaction costs that never show up in sticker prices. Also beware that marketers and hucksters are very good at knowing how to pitch things to you in a way that makes it harder, not easier, to make sensible decisions. They know what will make you more likely to loosen your purse strings. Very often, you will have to go to the trouble to reformulate a sales pitch in order to see how it works to the merchant's benefit and not to yours. In the next chapter I will return to this theme and let you in on some handy psychological insights that will not only enable you to smoke out these tricks more easily, but also use them to your advantage.

THINKING ABOUT PROBABILITY

While not all of the decisions you make about money will involve an element of probability, some will—especially if you are a gambler—and it is prudent to spend a little time and effort exploring it. The average person on the street frankly doesn't have a clue about probability. This is why lotteries make so much money.

Probability tells you how likely something is to happen. You can assign a number to probability. As you will no doubt recall from chapter 1, probabilities can range from zero (no chance whatsoever) to one (certainty). For convenience, we use a lowercase p to denote the probability of something. For further convenience, we use a subscript just next to the "p" to denote the event whose probability we are talking about. So another way of saying "the probability of my winning the lottery is zero" would be like this:

$$p_{\text{(my winning the lottery)}} = 0.$$

This is true, by the way, because I don't buy lottery tickets.

We have to be careful about how we use the language of probability. Sometimes we say things are "probable" or "improbable" when all we really mean is that we think them likely or unlikely. Our reasons for thinking something likely or unlikely may be perfectly good. For instance, I think a nuclear war between China and the United States next weekend is unlikely. These two countries have never fought a nuclear war in the past. Clearly they would prefer to avoid one in the future if they can. As far as I know, nobody sits around flipping coins or rolling dice in Washington or Beijing on Friday nights to decide whether to have a nuclear war on Saturday morning. But still there is no way for me to attach a number to

$$P_{\text{(nuclear war between China and the United States next weekend)}}.$$

If you can attach a meaningful number to a likelihood, *that's* when it makes sense to talk about probability.

When can you attach a meaningful number to a likelihood? When you know the possible outcomes and can tell how often to expect them.

Consider the roll of a die. A die has six sides. A fair die has a consistent density, which means that if you throw it, any side has an equal chance of showing on top. (You can weight one side of a die, which changes its center of gravity and makes it a little bit more likely that one side in particular will come up. Here and elsewhere in the book I am going to presume that you, and everybody else you play dice with, is scrupulously honest.) When you roll a die, there are six possible results:

1 2 3 4 5 6

FIG. 1. THE POSSIBLE RESULTS
OF ROLLING ONE DIE

Each possible result is equally likely, so you can know with confidence that the odds of rolling a "1" are the same as the odds of rolling a 2, 3, 4, 5, or 6—namely, 1-in-6. You can express this also as 1/6, 17 percent or 0.16666 . . . (take your pick).

Notice what happens if you add up the odds of every possible result:

$$p_{(1)} = 1/6$$
$$p_{(2)} = 1/6$$
$$p_{(3)} = 1/6$$
$$p_{(4)} = 1/6$$
$$p_{(5)} = 1/6$$
$$+ \quad p_{(6)} = 1/6$$
$$\overline{p_{(1,2,3,4,5 \text{ or } 6)} = 6/6 = 1.0}$$

The sum of the probabilities of all possible results is 1. This is always true.

Now, you may think that if you rolled a die six hundred times, you would get 100 ones, 100 twos, 100 threes, 100 fours, 100 fives, and 100 sixes. Not necessarily. This is what you should *expect* to get before you start rolling, because this is what the odds would predict. It is, in other words, the best guess you can make. But there is actually an excellent chance that some numbers will come up more often than others. This is just in the nature of random variation. In other words, what you can *expect* in a mathematical sense is not *guaranteed*. The following results of six hundred throws would not be at all unusual:

- 105 ones
- 83 twos
- 102 threes
- 102 fours
- 113 fives
- 95 sixes

These results, in contrast, would be *highly* unusual (though not impossible):

- 4 ones
- 8 twos
- 523 threes
- 18 fours
- 20 fives
- 27 sixes

In fact—although this is counterintuitive—the odds of your rolling exactly 100 of each are very, very small. What you should expect mathematically, and what you should *actually* expect, are two quite different things. If you don't believe me, see for yourself: go to www.decisionhelper.com and click on "Dice Roller."

When you roll two dice together, a result of "one" is no longer possible, since no die has a "zero" on one of its faces. The smallest result you could get is 2 (a pair of ones, known in the gambling world as "snake eyes"). The largest possible result is 12 (a pair of sixes, or "box cars"). There are, then, eleven possible results, not six, when you roll two dice; namely, 2, 3, 4, 5, 6, 7, 8, 9, 10, 11, and 12.

Are these equally likely? No. Why not? Because while there is only one way of rolling a 2, and only one way of rolling a 12, there are many ways of rolling some of the other numbers. There are more ways of rolling a 7 than anything else (hence the phrase "lucky number 7"). Here are all the possible combinations of rolling two dice:

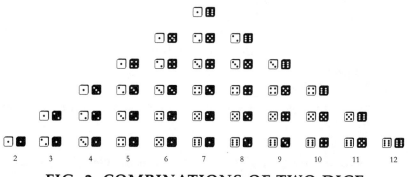

FIG. 2. COMBINATIONS OF TWO DICE

This, by the way, is a good example of a "frequency distribution." It shows you what proportion of the time you can expect a particular outcome. Notice that there are six ways of rolling a 7, five ways of rolling a 6 or an 8, four ways of rolling a 5 or a 9, three ways of rolling a 4 or a 10, two ways of rolling a 3 or an 11, and only one way of rolling a 2 or a 12. If you count up all of the possible combinations, you will find that they total thirty-six.

There are two important things to note about this. First, it is no accident that there are thirty-six possible combinations when you roll two dice. Each die has six sides, and $6 \times 6 = 36$ (i.e., 6^2). The total number of possible combinations if you roll *three* dice is $6 \times 6 \times 6 = 216$ (6^3); of four dice it is $6 \times 6 \times 6 \times 6 = 1,296$ (6^4), and so on. Second, notice that when it comes to adding up the total you roll with two dice, it doesn't matter which die comes up which number. A three and a four yields the same total as a four and a three. Thus the probability of rolling a seven *some way* is 6/36 (or 1-in-6); the probability of rolling a seven *by rolling a three and a four* is 2/36 (or 1-in-18); and the probability of rolling a seven *by rolling a three with the white die and a four with the black die* is only 1/36 (1-in-36).

To recap up to this point:

1. Probability always ranges from 0 (no chance) to 1 (certainty).
2. The sum of the probabilities of all possible outcomes is always 1.
3. The probability of something happening is the sum of the individual probabilities of all the possible ways it could happen.
4. To find the probability of two or more independent things all happening jointly, multiply their individual probabilities together.

Time for a little quiz. If you get all of the answers right, you can pat yourself on the back, because your understanding of probability is excellent—certainly more than adequate for most of the decisions you will have to make. If you get half right and half wrong, you shouldn't feel bad, but you can improve your decision making by thinking about probability a little bit more. If you get all of the questions wrong, you should sue your high-school math teacher.

Get your pencil ready; here we go.

1. Suppose you just rolled a die five times and it came up 6 every time. Does this make it (a) more likely that you will roll a 6 next time? (b) less likely that you will roll a 6 next time? or (c) just as likely as before that you will roll a 6 next time?

2. Suppose you flip three coins. Which of the following is the likeliest outcome? (a) They will all come up heads. (b) They will all come up tails. (c) One will be different from the other two. (d) It makes no difference; these are all equally likely outcomes.

3. Suppose you have to choose six numbers out of forty-nine for a chance to win a lottery. Which of the following combinations of numbers is least likely to come up? (a) 3-15-16-39-41-42; (b) 5-6-25-26-45-46 (c) 1-2-3-4-5-6; (d) They are all equally likely to come up.

4. You appear on a game show, and the host points toward three doors. He tells you that behind one door is a new car, and behind the other two there is nothing. He asks you to choose a door. You choose door number 1. He walks over to door number 2 and opens it, showing you that there is nothing behind it. He then asks whether you want to stick with door number 1 or switch your choice to door number 3. Should you switch?

5. Which of the following series of coin tosses is random, and which one did I make up (H=heads, T=tails)? No guessing, now.

   (a) H, H, T, H, H, T, T, T, H, H, T, H, T, H, T, T, H, H, H, H, T, H, T, T, T, H, T, T, T, H, H, T, T, T, T, T, H, H, H, H, T, H, T, T, H, T, T, T, T, H, T, H, H, T, T, H, H, T, T, T, H, T, T, T, H, H, H, T, T, H, H, H, H, T, H, H, T, H, T, H, T, T, T, T, H, T, H, T, H, T, H, T, H, T, H, T, H, T, T, H, T, H.

   (b) H, H, H, H, H, H, T, H, H, H, H, T, T, H, T, H, T, T, H, H, T, T, T, H, H, T, H, H, T, H, H, H, T, T, H, H, T, H, T, T, H, T, T, T, H, T, T, H, H, H, T, H, H, T, T, H, H, H, T, H, H, H, H, H, T, H, T, T, T, T, H, T, T, T, T, H, T, T, T, T, H, T, T, T, T, T, H, T, T, T, T, H, H, H, T, T, T, T, T, H.

6. You are back on the game-show circuit, still looking for a new car. The host invites you to play ball. He points you toward two identical large drums and tells you that you must distribute one hundred colored balls between them. Fifty of the balls are red, and fifty are black. He will then blindfold you and spin both you and the drums around. You must choose one ball from one drum (still blindfolded). If you choose a red ball, you win a new car. If you choose a black ball, you win nothing. How do you distribute the balls between the two drums to maximize the probability that you will choose a red ball?

7. You live in a country where 20 percent of the population gets pneumonia, 10 percent of the population gets tuberculosis, and 2 percent of the population develops diabetes. Which is more likely: that you will get pneumonia *and* tuberculosis, or that you will develop diabetes? Or are these equally likely?

8. You play the stock market. You notice that it has dropped for ten consecutive sessions. This is extremely rare. Is this a good time to buy?

Okay, let's go over the answers.

1. Suppose you just rolled a die five times and it came up 6 every time. Does this make it (a) more likely that you will roll a 6 next time? (b) less likely that you will roll a 6 next time? or (c) just as likely as before that you will roll a 6 next time?

If we assume that this is a fair die, the odds that it will come up 6 on any given roll are 1-in-6, no matter what you have rolled previously. The correct answer, then, is (c).

Many people mistakenly choose (b), for an understandable but incorrect reason: namely, it is very unlikely that you will roll the same number six times in a row (the odds of that are $1/6 \times 1/6 \times 1/6 \times 1/6 \times 1/6 \times 1/6$, or 1-in-46,656). But in this question, the first five rolls are history. There is no chance of them being anything other than six. The only thing that is uncertain here is what the next roll will be. Since a die has only six faces, not 46,656, the odds that you will roll a 6 are 1-in-6.

The mistake is to think of a series of fixed, determined events as still containing an element of chance. This is a common gambler's error, often called "The Monte Carlo fallacy." Remember: once you have rolled a die, it's rolled. It has no chance of being anything other than what came up. And the past has no effect on the likelihood of future independent events.

2. Suppose you flip three coins. Which of the following is the likeliest outcome? (a) They will all come up heads. (b) They will all come up tails. (c) One will be different from the other two. (d) It makes no difference; these are all equally likely outcomes.

Since a coin has only two sides, the odds of getting three heads in a row are $1/2 \times 1/2 \times 1/2$, or 1-in-8. You have the same chance of flipping three tails in a row. Thus one quarter of the time you will flip *either* three heads *or* three tails in a row ($1/8 + 1/8 = 1/4$). The rest of the time you will get two heads and one tails, or two tails and one heads, because these exhaust all the possible combinations of flipping three coins. Thus the correct answer is (c). If you don't believe me, go to www.decisionhelper.com and click on "Coin Flipper."

3. Suppose you have to choose six numbers out of forty-nine for a chance to win a lottery. Which of the following combinations of numbers is least likely to come up? (a) 3-15-16-39-41-42; (b) 5-6-25-26-45-46; (c) 1-2-3-4-5-6; (d) They are all equally likely to come up.

Many people would choose (c). They would be wrong. The correct answer is (d). The odds of winning a fair lottery with any combination of six numbers are the same as the odds of winning with any other combination of six numbers.

The reason many people choose (c) is because the numbers 1-2-3-4-5-6 make a nice sequence, and are all clumped at the beginning of the range of possible numbers 1 through 49. None of us has ever seen a set of winning numbers with these two characteristics. It just doesn't *look* random. The first sequence does. But it is neither more nor less likely to come up.

The second sequence doesn't look entirely random, either—but it is not as obvious a sequence as the third one. It has precisely the same chance of coming up as the other two.

There is a practical lesson here: if you insist on playing lotteries like this—which, as I will explain in a minute, is a dumb thing to do—you should always choose some sequence of numbers that doesn't look random. This is because many people deliberately avoid choosing such sequences, thinking them less likely to come up. If your sequence does come up, then, you are less likely to have to share the winnings with someone else—provided, that is, that others aren't following the same logic! (Thus you should pick a sequence, but not a very obvious one.) Don't fret too much about this, though. The odds of your six numbers coming up are negligible no matter which ones you choose. More on this shortly.

4. You appear on a game show, and the host points toward three doors. He tells you that behind one door is a new car, and behind the other two there is nothing. He asks you to choose a door. You choose door number 1. He walks over to door number 2 and opens it, showing you that there is nothing behind it. He then asks whether you want to stick with door number 1 or switch your choice to door number 3. Should you switch?

This is known in the math biz as "The Monty Hall Problem," named in honor of the famous host of *Let's Make a Deal*. Most people find the answer to this question the hardest of all to understand, so I am going to explain it a few different ways. I don't mean to insult your intelligence by doing this. The first time I heard this problem, I got it wrong, too.

The correct answer is that you should switch. Most people consider this counterintuitive, mistakenly thinking it makes no difference whether you switch or not.

The key thing to realize is that, since you picked a door at random, your odds of picking the door with the car behind it in the first place were 1-in-3. Let's suppose you picked the winning door. The game-show host will open one of the other two doors (it doesn't matter which; they are both losers) and invite you to switch to the door he didn't open. If you do, you will lose, because there's no car behind that door, either.

Your odds of picking a *losing* door were better: 2-in-3. In that case, the game-show host has no choice as to which door he opens. One of the other doors has a car behind it, and he can't show you that one. So he opens the *other* losing door (the one you didn't pick in the first place), and invites you to switch to what would prove to be the *winning* door. If you switch, you will win.

So: your odds of winning the car if you *don't* switch are 1-in-3, and your odds of winning the car if you *do* switch are 2-in-3. You should switch.

Now, if you're like most people, you are scratching your head at this point and don't quite get it yet. "How can that be?" you will protest. "The car has an equal chance of being behind any of the three doors." This is true. "The game-show host shows you one it isn't behind. Therefore it must be behind one of the remaining two." Also true. So far so good. "The odds of it being behind the door you picked are just as good as the odds of it being behind the one you might switch to. So it doesn't make any difference whether you switch or not."

Wrong. Let's look at all of the possibilities:

TABLE 11. "THE MONTY HALL PROBLEM"

You choose door number . . .	The car is behind door number . . .	The host opens door number . . .	If you switch, you . . .
1	1	2 or 3 (it doesn't matter which; they are both losers)	Lose
1	2	3	Win
1	3	2	Win
2	1	3	Win
2	2	1 or 3	Lose
2	3	1	Win
3	1	2	Win
3	2	1	Win
3	3	1 or 2	Lose

Notice that there are six possible ways of winning if you switch, but only three possible ways of losing if you switch.

If you're *still* not happy, why not try it out yourself? Go to www.decisionhelper.com and click on "The Monty Hall Problem."

5. Which of the following series of coin tosses is random, and which one did I make up (H=heads, T=tails)?

(a) H, H, T, H, H, T, T, T, H, H, T, H, T, H, T, T, H, H, H, H, T,
   H, T, T, T, H, T, T, T, H, H, T, T, T, T, T, H, H, H, H, T, H, T,
   T, H, T, T, T, T, H, T, H, H, T, T, H, H, T, T, T, H, T, T, T, H,
   H, H, T, T, H, H, H, H, T, H, H, T, H, T, H, T, T, T, T, H, T,
   H, T, H, T, H, T, H, T, H, T, T, H, T, H.
(b) H, H, H, H, H, H, T, H, H, H, H, T, T, H, T, H, T, T, H, H,
   T, T, T, H, H, T, H, H, T, H, H, T, T, H, H, T, H, T, T, H, T,
   T, T, H, T, T, H, H, H, T, H, H, H, T, T, H, T, T, H, H, H, H, H,
   H, H, T, H, T, T, T, T, H, T, T, T, T, H, T, T, T, T, H, T, T, T, T,
   T, T, H, T, T, T, T, H, H, H, T, T, T, T, T, H.

If you have a type A personality, you probably counted the number of heads and tails in each series to see which one had the closer number of each, reasoning that since heads and tails are equally likely, over a large number of flips they should each come up 50 percent of the time. Nice try. That would have been one possible basis for choosing which one was likely to be random. However, after I determined that my random series had 47 heads and 53 tails, I made sure that my nonrandom series did, too. So you had to look for some other feature to distinguish the two.

The random series is (b). Now, you may have looked at it and decided that it was *not* the random series, because it has several features that seem intuitively unlikely. For example, it starts with six straight heads. It also has a long string of seven heads in a row, and an additional string of six straight tails toward the end. These may have seemed unlikely to you. But in fact, they are *highly* likely. If you flip a coin a hundred times, the odds are very good that you will get at least one string of seven in a row, and excellent that you will get at least one string of six in a row. The first series has no string longer than five in a row, and it has only one of those. The probability of that happening over the course of one hundred flips is very, very small.

The mathematical proof of this is more complicated than is

worth bothering with here, but the point is important: there is often a considerable difference between what seems unlikely psychologically and what is in fact unlikely numerically (a point that applies equally to question 3). The same phenomenon explains the general amazement when two people in a room discover that they have the same birthday. In fact, if you picked any twenty-three people at random, the odds are better than even that at least two of them will share a birthday.[4] You can exploit this phenomenon to your advantage, by the way: stay tuned for question 8.

6. You are back on the game-show circuit, still looking for a new car. The host invites you to play ball. He points you toward two identical large drums and tells you that you must distribute one hundred colored balls between them. Fifty of the balls are red, and fifty are black. He will then blindfold you and spin both you and the drums around. You must choose one ball from one drum (still blindfolded). If you choose a red ball, you win a new car. If you choose a black ball, you win nothing. How do you distribute the balls between the two drums to maximize the probability that you will choose a red ball?

People either tend to get the answer to this one very quickly, or they agonize for a while and decide that it doesn't matter how you distribute the balls. If you fall in the latter category, you may have assumed that you must split the balls evenly between the two drums. The question doesn't specify that.

You maximize your chances of choosing a red ball by putting one red ball in one drum, and the other 99 balls in the other drum. The probability of your choosing a red ball is the sum of the probabilities of choosing each drum (1/2 or .5) times the probability of choosing a red ball from among all the balls in it. If you put just one red ball in one drum, and if you choose that drum, you are guaranteed to choose a red ball. If you choose the other drum, your chances are still close to 50 percent (49-in-99) of choosing a red ball. The overall probability of your choosing a red ball with this distribution is therefore $(0.5 \times 1) + (0.5 \times [49/99])$, or just under .75 (.74747. . .). There is no distribution better than this. If you distributed the balls equally between the two drums, the probability of choosing a red ball would only be .5.

7. You live in a country where 20 percent of the population gets pneu-monia, 10 percent of the population gets tuberculosis, and 2 percent of the population develops diabetes. Which is more likely: that you will get pneumonia and tuberculosis, or that you will develop diabetes? Or are these equally likely?

This was a trick question. You have to know a little bit about medicine or public health to get the right answer: namely, that you are more likely to get pneumonia and tuberculosis together. This is because these various probabilities are not entirely independent. If they were—that is to say, if these three diseases were randomly distributed in the population—then the correct answer would be that the likelihoods are equal. Your probability of developing dia-betes (.02) would equal your probability of getting pneumonia (.2) times your probability of getting tuberculosis (.1). But if you have tuberculosis you are more likely to get pneumonia than someone who does not (and vice versa), because these diseases both com-promise your lungs and your immune system. In other words, their incidence is correlated. The correlation is not perfect—if it were, everyone who had tuberculosis would also have pneu-monia—nevertheless, the fact that they are somewhat correlated means that your probability of getting both is at least a little bit higher than .02.

This question highlights the importance of being sensitive to which probabilities are independent and which are not. There are many situations like this one. For example, if you live in a cold cli-mate, the probability of having your electricity go out *and* having your pipes burst is not simply the product of the probability of each event happening independently—because if your electricity goes out, your furnace will not work, and *that's* when your pipes are likely to burst.[5]

8. You play the stock market. You notice that it has dropped for ten con-secutive sessions. This is extremely rare. Is this a good time to buy?

This is another trick question, because it does not belong in a quiz about probability. The stock market does not rise or fall by chance. It rises or falls as the result of the deliberate choices of individual investors, none of whom is flipping coins or rolling dice to decide what to do with his or her money.

Ten consecutive losses for the stock market may be highly unusual, but whether you should expect the market to turn around or to continue to drop depends entirely upon context. If the market fundamentals look good and if the buzz on Wall Street has it that the correction is over, it's a good bet that investors will start buying again. But if the fundamentals look terrible and the Bears are rampaging, you have no grounds for optimism and no reason to expect prices to rise.

Whether you win or lose in the stock market, then, depends upon your ability to read market indicators and to gauge the mass psychology of investors. It does not depend upon your understanding of probability. Interestingly, though—and perhaps a little perversely—you can sometimes make money in the stock market exploiting other people's misunderstandings of this point. If enough investors think that an eleventh straight losing session is highly improbable just because it's rare, then they will bet with their money on a turnaround, driving the market up. The belief that eleven straight losing sessions is unlikely, therefore, can become a self-fulfilling prophecy. This is the difference between markets and dice: no matter how many people think that rolling five straight sixes makes another less likely, the real odds never change.

COMMON PERILS AND PITFALLS

People who make mistakes thinking about money and probability often do so for perfectly understandable reasons. Sometimes you can chalk up mistakes to a simple lack of knowledge. I am always shocked, for example, at how many high-school kids simply do not know how bank accounts, loans, credit cards, and investments work, because no one took the trouble to sit them down and teach them. It is true that that these can be terribly complicated subjects, especially if you get into things like options and derivatives. But parents and teachers do children a great disservice by not promoting basic financial literacy. It is somewhat more forgivable that people misunderstand probability. Much of it is simply counterintuitive, as our quiz clearly indicated.

Some of the mistakes we make about numbers are the result not of a lack of knowledge, but of normal psychological tendencies. Even very smart people fall into these traps every once in a while. A couple of winters ago, for example, we had an especially cold February where I live. Pipes burst all over the place. In March, the local newspaper ran a front-page story on this, quoting a meteorologist to the effect that while the normal average daily high temperature in February is –1° C, that particular February the average daily high reached only –4° C. "In other words," he said, "it was four times as cold as normal." Gosh, I thought; it's a good thing the normal average daily high was not 0° C, or February would have been *infinitely* colder than normal! The funny thing was that neither the reporter, nor his editor, nor any of the normally pedantic letter-writers picked up on this. We simply see the number 4 and the number 1 and automatically think that whatever we are measuring with those numbers relate meaningfully in a ratio of 4-to-1. We don't bother to ask whether the number scale is arbitrary.*

Another common source of error is the difficulty we all have of comprehending very large and very small numbers. By *comprehend* I do not mean *use correctly*; I mean *appreciate the magnitude of*. We can all agree that Bill Gates is a very rich man. As I write, his net worth is almost $85 billion. This means that as an economic unit, he is bigger than Chile or Egypt (as measured by Gross Domestic Product) and IBM (as measured by annual revenue).[6] But how many of us can really grasp just how much money $85 billion is? One strategy is to try to visualize it in terms of the things we might

---

*If Canadians measured temperature in degrees Fahrenheit, instead of degrees Celsius, the normal average high would have been 30°, and the actual average high 25°. Our mathematically challenged meteorologist might then have calculated that this was only slightly less than 17 percent colder than normal. This would have been an equally meaningless calculation.

The only valid metric for purposes of this comparison is degrees Kelvin, where at 0°—absolute zero—all motion theoretically stops. Comparing two numbers on the Kelvin scale provides a meaningful ratio of energy levels. On this scale, the ratio of actual to normal average daily high temperature would have been 268°/272°. Our cold February, then, would have been slightly less than 1.5 percent colder than normal.

buy with it. But it still boggles the mind. How do you visualize 1.7 million top-of-the-line Lexus sedans?

The difficulty we have of grasping the magnitude of large and small numbers makes it difficult for us to appreciate (for example) extremely small and extremely high probabilities. As we try and fail to grasp just how unlikely things with small probabilities truly are, we naturally let our minds fill in the blanks with lousy proxy indicators. Take, for example, fear of flying. At one level, this is a natural fear. Many people are afraid of heights to begin with, and even if you passed high-school physics, your gut may refuse to believe that there is anything reliably holding up an airplane. But the clincher is the fact that we can all recall in vivid detail a slew of graphic, horrendous air disasters. They always make the front page, where they tend to linger for days. The fact that we can so easily recall horrible accidents inclines us to believe that the likelihood that any given plane will crash is much higher than it really is (psychologists call this the *availability heuristic*: we estimate likelihood not with reference to actual statistics, but with reference to how readily we can recall prior examples). You cannot soothe a nervous passenger by telling him that his odds of being killed each time he boards a commercial airliner in the United States are 1-in-3.67 million.[7] This fraction is simply too small for him to grasp. It is not appreciably different psychologically from (say) 1-in-5,000.

Since I teach international politics, I often have students come tell me that their parents don't want them to travel to Israel because of the terrorist threat. "Is it really very dangerous there?" they will ask. "Oh, yes," I always reply. "You are taking your life in your hands if you go to Israel. But as long as you stay off the roads, you'll be perfectly safe." A thousand or more people may die on Israeli roads in any given year. In a bad year, a few dozen may die at the hands of terrorists. But the terrorists make the international headlines, and so nobody worries about the drivers.

The triumph of psychology over mathematics largely explains why the gambling industry does so well. There is an iron law of gambling: over the long run, you cannot win. You can't even break even. You are guaranteed to lose.[8] You can only win in the short run—and even then, you are more likely to lose than to win. Why, then, do people gamble?

First and foremost, people tend to overestimate their chances of winning (or, put another way, they underestimate their chances of losing). Sometimes this is because they do not understand how games of random chance are stacked against them by design. Often it is simply because they have difficulty truly grasping the sheer magnitude of the odds they face. The ease with which they can recall *other people* winning leads them to overestimate the likelihood that *they* will win, too. Let's go over a few examples to see how this works.

Question 3 from our quiz describes a very common and very popular lottery: you pick six numbers at random from 1 through 49. If all six numbers come up, you win the jackpot. Typically, each combination you pick costs you a dollar. The following rather daunting equation gives us the total number of different possible combinations of six numbers 1 through 49:

$$\left(\frac{1}{6!}\right)\left(\frac{49!}{(49-6)!}\right) = 13{,}983{,}816$$

If you aren't sure what the exclamation marks mean, they are factorials. The factorial of any whole number is that number multiplied once by each smaller whole number. In other words, I could have written the equation this way:

$$\left(\frac{1}{6\times5\times4\times3\times2\times1}\right)\left(\frac{49\times48\times47\times46\times45...}{(49-6)\times42\times41\times40\times39...}\right) = 13{,}983{,}816$$

But never mind the left-hand side of the equation. The term on the right-hand side is what interests us here: *there are almost fourteen million different combinations!* Your odds of buying a winning lottery ticket, in other words, are worse than your odds of being the only person picked at random from the entire population of greater Los Angeles. You are *much* more likely to be struck by lightning, or to be killed in a car or a commercial airliner.

I use this example to explain to my students why buying a lottery ticket is never the SEU-maximizing thing to do. I start by asking how many of them buy a lottery ticket at least occasionally. Usually, 80 to 90 percent of the class will raise their hands. I then go through the math, supposing a jackpot of $2 million. If they decide not to buy a ticket, the cost they pay is nothing and their probable gain or loss is nothing—for a total expected utility of zero. If they decide to buy a ticket, however, they face a sure loss of a dollar and have one chance in almost fourteen million of winning $2 million. Adding up the expected utilities, we get

$$(-1 \times \$1) + ([1/13{,}983{,}816] \times \$2{,}000{,}000) = \$-0.86.$$

The expected value of the lottery ticket, in other words, is a loss of eighty-six cents. They are much better off keeping their dollar.

My students usually then start raising objections. The first one usually says, "But you can't win if you don't play!" This is true, but irrelevant. The odds of winning are so small that, for all practical purposes, they approximate zero. "Just imagine the freedom!" another will say, echoing the local Lotto 6/49 ad campaign. "It costs nothing to daydream," I reply, "so why not keep the dollar?" A mathematically talented student will sometimes then suggest that you *should* buy a ticket once the jackpot exceeds $14 million, because at that point, buying a ticket has a positive expected utility. It doesn't, though. As the jackpot grows, more and more people buy tickets, making it increasingly likely that even if you picked the right combination, you would have to share your winnings with someone else. Finally, someone will usually pipe up that people win the lottery all the time, so why not them as well as anyone else? Here the availability heuristic rears its ugly head. No matter how many touching stories you read about impoverished retirees hitting the jackpot with the last dollar in their pocket, their extremely good fortune will not change yours for the better. You aren't the slightest bit more likely to win just because they won. In fact, every time someone else wins, they clear out the jackpot and drive down the expected utility of your next ticket.

Once in a while, a student will say, "I have a friend whose friend's neighbor's cousin's dad won four million bucks." This provides a particularly potent availability heuristic, because you feel some kind of connection to this lucky individual. You may not know him personally, but the fact that such a short chain of acquaintances links you together makes your own chance of winning the lottery seem all the less remote to you. Actually, though, this kind of connection is not unusual. Right now you probably know someone who knows someone who knows someone who knows someone who knows someone who won a big jackpot. This is what the "Principle of Six Degrees of Separation" would lead us to expect: if you pick any two people at random in the whole world, the odds are pretty good that you can trace a chain of no more than five intermediate acquaintances between them.[9]

When all the objections stop, I stand in triumph before my class and ask for yet another show of hands. "How many of you are going to *continue* buying lottery tickets *now?*" Typically, 80 to 90 percent raise their hands again, and I continue my lecture, dejected.

Lottery officials are clever enough to know that some people will stop buying tickets week after week if they never win anything, so they typically give out smaller prizes for matching fewer than six numbers. You may win $10 if you match three numbers, for example, $100 if you match four, or $1,000 if you match five. This ensures that people will win small amounts often enough for almost everyone to know at least one small-scale lottery winner. This encourages them to think that they can win, too. But of course, the math still works in the lottery's favor. The intake from ticket sales is always greater than the payout in winnings. This means that the average amount of money each lottery player spends on tickets will always be greater than the average amount of money each lottery player wins. Put another way, no matter what the schedule of winnings may be, the expected utility of buying a ticket will always be less than zero.

Other games involve better odds of winning, but if you truly understand probability, you will still avoid them. A typical slot machine, for instance, may pay back eighty-six cents of every dollar it takes in. This gives the house a guaranteed 14 percent long-run advantage. The house advantage in roulette varies from 1.35 to 7.89 percent, depending upon the bet, and depending upon whether the wheel has one green slot, as in Europe, or two, as in the United States. The fact that the dealer wins ties in blackjack gives the house an insurmountable long-run advantage in that game. Players have the best odds in Las Vegas craps. But even here the house has a minimum advantage of .006 percent on the player's best bet. No matter what you do, how hard you try, or what game you play, you cannot make money over the long run by gambling.

This doesn't mean that clever people haven't tried. Many of the schemes they have come up with over the years are based upon the Monte Carlo fallacy, or some similar error. You can buy software programs, for example, that will pore over past winning lottery numbers in search of numbers more likely to win in the future. These are a complete waste of money, even at the "unbelievable deal" of 80 percent off.

Other schemes are indeed guaranteed to make you money, but only under unrealistic conditions. One of the most interesting of these is a roulette strategy called the "Martingale" or "Doubling-up" system. A roulette wheel has eighteen red numbered spaces, eighteen black numbered spaces, and either one or two green spaces ("0" and "00"). Among the bets you can place is a bet that on the next spin of the wheel, the ball will land on a red space. If it does, the payoff is even money (meaning you get your wager back, plus winnings of an equal amount). According to one version of the Martingale system, you start by placing a $10 bet on red. If you lose, you double the bet. If you lose again, you double it again. You keep doubling the bet until you win, whereupon you pocket all but ten dollars and start over. Eventually you will win, because eventually the ball will land on a red number. No matter how many spins it takes to win, according to this system, you always stand to gain the amount of your first bet. Table 12 shows why.

TABLE 12. THE MARTINGALE SYSTEM

Spin	Bet	Payoff if you win	Cumulative loss if you lose	Net gain or loss if you win
1	$10	$10	$10	$10
2	$20	$20	$30	$10
3	$40	$40	$70	$10
4	$80	$80	$150	$10
5	$160	$160	$310	$10
6	$320	$320	$630	$10
7	$640	$640	$1,270	$10
8	$1,280	$1,280	$2,550	$10
9	$2,560	$2,560	$5,110	$10
10	$5,120	$5,120	$10,230	$10
11	$10,240	$10,240	$20,470	$10
12	$20,480	$20,480	$40,950	$10

Quiz question number 5 holds the key to the explanation for why this strategy will not work. When you spin a roulette wheel repeatedly, the odds are excellent that you will get quite long sequences of red or black results. After your seventh loss, you will seek to place your bet for $1,280, but the croupier will refuse to allow it, because the house limit is $1,000. Even if you won with a $1,000 bet on your eighth try, you would be $270 in the hole, because your cumulative loss through seven spins was $1,270.

The best reply to my argument that gambling is never utility maximizing is this: "Gambling is fun." Many people take a great deal of pleasure from it. Perversely, misunderstanding probability increases the pleasure, because the excitement is greater the more likely you believe you are to win. It turns out that ignorance is bliss after all! Some people get more pleasure out of spending a dollar on a hopeless lottery ticket than from any alternative use. While in strictly monetary terms this is still a bad gamble, nevertheless pleasure must factor into our utility calculations somehow. Put another way, as long as you are an irrational person, gambling *can* be rational.

Some people don't enjoy gambling. I'm one of them. I don't enjoy it in part because I consider it a violation of the practice-what-you-preach principle. But once upon a time I went to Las Vegas to deliver a lecture. (Honestly, I'm not making this up.) My mother, who understands the odds but enjoys small-scale gambling, had never been to Vegas. She asked me if I would lose $20 on the slot machines for her, as a personal favor. Being a good son (more or less), I said I would. But I wanted to do it as quickly as possible. So I asked my host where I was likely to lose $20 in slot machines most quickly. He suggested the Luxor, a spanking-new pseudo-Egyptian monstrosity that at the time set new records for tastelessness (records since shattered by other Las Vegas hotels, I understand). The Luxor had $2 slot machines, so we figured I could be in and out of there in no time. But no matter what I did, I simply couldn't lose. Several times I got down to my last $2 token, but each time the machine paid off on my last spin. After two hours of sheer frustration at my failure to lose, I gave up and pocketed the $40 I had won. I believe I may be the only person to have gone to Las Vegas expressly not to gamble and who came home unhappy about having doubled my money. Who says God has no sense of humor?

Unfortunately, gambling can be very addictive for those who enjoy it. If you have a tendency to gamble compulsively, you must be very careful not to allow the thrill of gambling to trump your strategic decision making. Many people find professional help indispensable. But it is generally a good idea to budget your gambling money whether you are an addict or not, and never to permit yourself to exceed your budget. The size of that budget should reflect careful consideration of your financial resources. Whether you gamble at all should be a strategic calculation. If your cash flow is tight and you have no cushion, you are wise never to gamble. If you are rich, you can probably afford it. But you will rarely go wrong if you persuade yourself that your gambling budget is just like an entertainment budget: something you should not expect to recoup once you have had your fun. If you do win, pocket your winnings and count yourself lucky. Don't expect to win the next time. Similarly, if you play a lottery, you would be wise to think of the price of your lottery ticket as a charitable contribution for which you will not receive a tax receipt. You can then have fun in good conscience.

The final peril I would like to touch upon is the danger of mis-interpreting frequency distributions. You will recall from our dis-cussion of dice that there are more ways to roll a seven with two dice than any other number, which means that a seven is the single most likely outcome. Sometimes you can deduce the probability of something just by looking at all possible outcomes, as we did with dice. But sometimes you have to go digging for information to find out how frequently things happen in the real world, and this can make certain kinds of mistakes especially hard to avoid.

You may be familiar with a "bell curve." This is a common shape of a frequency distribution. Suppose you lived in a midsized town and you measured the height of all fifteen hundred resident adults. Most likely, you would get a result like this:

FIG. 3. ADULT HEIGHTS

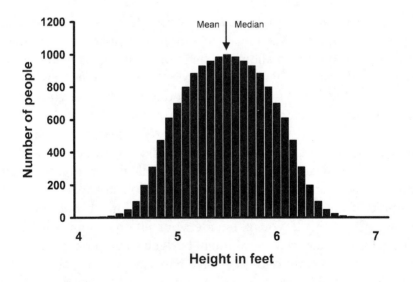

We call a shape like this a "normal distribution." It has a few inter-esting features. First, the "mean" of the distribution—i.e., the average height—is right smack in the middle (in my contrived example, 5'-6"). The distribution is also symmetrical about the mean, and there are exactly as many adults who are taller than average as there are adults who are shorter than average (hence the "mean" height is the same as the "median" height, since the median divides the population in two equal groups). Notice also that there are some very short people and some very tall people in your town, but the total number of people in the two "tails" of the distribution is really quite small. The vast majority of people are between five and six feet tall. Knowing this distribution, you could predict the probability of choosing at random someone of any particular height. You are more likely to pick someone of average height than of any other height, but the probability of this still isn't very great. Only 1,000 adults in your town are exactly 5'-6" tall, so p(picking someone 5'-6" tall) is only .07 (1-in-15). Still, the probability of picking someone of any other particular height is lower.

What would happen if you measured up the youngsters, too, and included them in your distribution? You might get something like this:

FIG. 4. EVERYBODY'S HEIGHTS

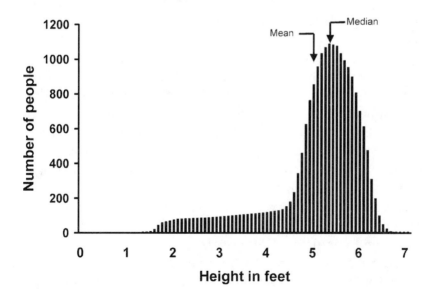

Notice that the distribution is no longer bell-shaped. This is because the overwhelming majority of children are shorter than adults. Very few kids are under a foot and a half (hardly any come much smaller than that to begin with), and very few are over six feet tall (though a few gangly teenagers are). Because the distribution is no longer symmetrical, the mean height is no longer the same as the median height. However, you could still predict the odds of picking at random someone of any particular height if you knew the actual distribution.

Lots of things have normal bell-shaped frequency distributions, and lots of things don't. Sometimes you can get a pretty good sense of an overall frequency distribution just by "sampling" it. You wouldn't need to measure all 20,000-odd people in your town, for instance, to have a pretty good idea of the general shape of the overall distribution. You could get a decent sense of that just by measuring several hundred. But that's another story we needn't bother with here. The point I want to make now is that people sometimes make mistakes in judgment because they don't understand what frequency distributions say about *specific individual people*—which is, generally speaking, not a whole lot.

Suppose you are a man approaching your seventy-third birthday. You have recently read that the average life expectancy for men in your country is seventy-three years. You may think that your time is almost up. Not likely. The fact that the average male lives for seventy-three years does not all by itself suggest that you will shortly check out. In fact, the frequency distribution for male life span is a funny shape. If you have survived past the age of two, you are in fact quite likely to live longer than seventy-three years, because males do a fair amount of dying as infants (somewhat more than females do). If you have survived past the age of twenty-five, you are very likely to live *well* past seventy-three, because the ages of sixteen to twenty-five are also prime male dying years (mostly because of traffic accidents, handguns, overdoses, and mindless adolescent risk taking). If you are relatively fit, do not smoke, drink alcohol in moderation, maintain a good body weight, have a cheerful disposition, are happily married, and have a dog, you will probably be around for a long time yet. You are guaranteed to die some time, of course, but the average male life expectancy does not predict any particular man's date with the Grim Reaper.

My favorite story about misunderstanding frequency distributions involved a young woman who showed up with her mother at a hospital emergency room and announced that she was there to have her baby. The nurse behind the desk asked her how far apart her contractions were coming. "Oh, I'm not having any contractions," the young woman replied. "Then why are you here?" asked the nurse. "Because today is my due date," she said. I can forgive the young woman, but *what* was her *mother* thinking? In fact, only 5 percent of children are born on their due date. Ninety-five percent are born before or after. Of those born after, almost all are born within three weeks of the due date, because obstetricians will induce labor if nature is being too slow. This means that you are less likely to come into the world three weeks late than three weeks early. The frequency distribution is not a smooth bell-shaped curve around the due date. It has a shape more like figure 4, above.

It is not always obvious why some things are more likely at certain times rather than at others. But if you have enough information about frequency distributions, you can often make choices that increase or decrease the likelihood of certain outcomes. Your doctor, for instance, can give you a wealth of information about mortality and morbidity rates that will help you make informed lifestyle choices that can really pay off.

THE BOTTOM LINE: KNOWING WHEN TO CHOOSE HOW

It is a good idea to practice distinguishing choices that involve genuine elements of random chance from those that do not, but which we often describe misleadingly in the language of probability anyway. If you are flipping coins, rolling dice, or choosing numbers, you can meaningfully talk about the probabilities of all of the various possible outcomes you face, and you can do true SEU calculations. If you are investing in the stock market, you cannot. No matter how many people tell you that the market will "probably" rise, or that the price of a given stock is "likely" to increase dramatically, as I mentioned earlier there is no meaningful way to attach numerical probabilities to these outcomes. You may discover that the long-term historical return on the stock market is 10 percent per year, but in no way does that guarantee that you will do better with your money by putting it in the stock market than (say) by buying a CD bearing 6 percent interest—even over the long run. There is nothing preventing the stock market from going into a deep, long slide, as it would if the world economy collapsed.[10] If you are a risk-averse person—as you should be, if your finances are tight—you will prefer the CD every time, simply because you can be confident that its downside risk is much smaller. If you are rich, you may prefer the stock market if your judgment of trends and fundamentals inclines you to be bullish, because you can better afford to lose what you invest if it turns out that you are wrong. You make your decision by looking at your financial position and choosing the appropriate strategy. You do not—because you cannot—simply calculate and compare the expected utilities of your two options.

Being smart about numbers, then, means not only understanding a little bit about how numbers work, but also knowing when to approach them one way and when to approach them another. A savvy decision maker goes beyond even this: he or she understands not only how numbers work, but how people actually work with numbers. This is the province of psychology, and this is where we turn next.

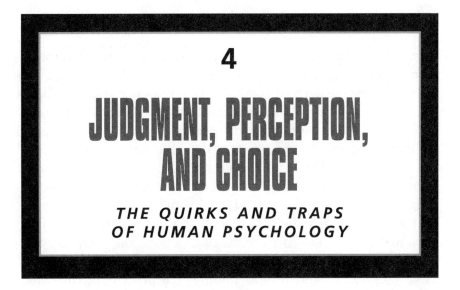

4

JUDGMENT, PERCEPTION, AND CHOICE

THE QUIRKS AND TRAPS OF HUMAN PSYCHOLOGY

I hate to lose more than I like to win.

—Jimmy Connors

I mentioned in the last chapter that the average person does not make money buying insurance or extended warranties. Yet people readily buy both. A classical economist might be tempted to call this behavior "irrational." It would be, if all we should care about is maximizing our long-term wealth. But money isn't everything. Peace of mind is important, too. Real people often make decisions that may look "suboptimal" from a classical economist's perspective but which make perfectly good sense to you and me.

But real people also do a number of odd things that are neither rational nor sensible. For example, people who would use a credit card to pay $1.50 for a gallon of gas, even if they could get a five-cent-per-gallon "discount" for paying cash, will often pay $1.45 cash to avoid a five-cent credit card "surcharge." But in fact it doesn't matter what you call it. It's the same gas at the same cash or credit price either way. Most people would also go much farther out of their way to save $5 on something that normally sells for $15 than they would to save $5 on something that usually costs $125. But five bucks is five bucks. Suppose you go to a play and discover when you get to the box office that you have somehow lost $10 from your wallet. You are more likely to buy a $10 ticket anyway than if you had bought a ticket in advance and discovered on arriving at the theater that you had lost it. For some reason, people treat the loss of a ten-dollar bill differently than the loss of a ten-dollar ticket. What sense does that make?[1]

Psychologists who study how real people make decisions have discovered a number of very interesting deviations such as these from the coldly calculating "rational" ideal. They have catalogued a number of common biases and other sources of error in our perception, judgment, and evaluation of alternatives. They have also documented the powerful influence emotions can have on our decision making. In this chapter I introduce and explore some of these fascinating (and useful) findings.[2] Bear in mind that not everything I will discuss applies equally to everyone. The extent to which people exhibit decision-making "pathologies" (translation: systematic goof-ups) varies widely from person to person. But I'll bet you will recognize some of them in your own decision making, as I do in mine. If so, you can take comfort in the knowledge that you are a normal human being.

Some of the odd patterns we exhibit and some of the common errors we make are impossible to eliminate from our decision making entirely. They are, as it were, consequences of the ways in which we are wired. But others we can train ourselves to catch on self-reflection. We can get better and better at avoiding them. Over the long run, then, an awareness of these patterns and tendencies can help us improve the effectiveness of our decision making.

In some cases, knowledge of these patterns makes it possible to figure out ways of influencing other people's behavior. Clever marketers, for example, know how to pitch things to you in ways that make you much more likely to open your wallet and dump it on their laps. If *you* are aware of these patterns, you can resist their nefarious manipulations. You can also use this knowledge to influence others' decisions, too.

REFERENCE POINTS AND RISK TAKING

If we were all the perfectly rational expected-utility maximizers that classical economists seem to think we are, the main question we would ask ourselves whenever we faced a choice is: "How can I get the most of what I want?" Commonly, though, we ask a very different question: "Do I stand to gain or lose?"

Now, at first glance, it may not seem that there is a large or an interesting difference between these two questions. But there is. One of the crucial insights of behavioral decision theory—that branch of psychology that studies how people actually make decisions involving an element of chance—is that people tend to have very different attitudes toward risk depending upon whether they face prospects of loss or prospects of gain. We tend to accept bad gambles to try to avoid losses, but we pass up good gambles to secure gains.

Much of the pioneering work in this field has been done by Daniel Kahneman and Amos Tversky using clever questionnaires. For example, Kahneman and Tversky asked their subjects whether they would prefer a sure gain of $3,000 or an 80 percent chance of winning $4,000 and a 20 percent chance of winning nothing. By a four-to-one margin, their subjects preferred the sure gain of $3,000. (So would I, by the way.) But when they offered them a choice between a sure *loss* of $3,000 and an 80 percent chance of losing $4,000 (and a 20 percent chance of losing nothing), their subjects preferred the gamble by a margin of more than eleven-to-one.[3] (I would too.) In both cases, Kahneman and Tversky's subjects passed up the expected-utility-maximizing choice. It is easy enough to calculate this. In the first question, the expected utility of the preferred alternative (the sure gain of $3,000) was $3,000 × 1.0 = $3,000, whereas the expected utility of the gamble was higher: $4,000 × .8 = $3,200. In the second question, the expected utility of the preferred alternative (the gamble) was −$4,000 × .8 = −$3,200. Again, the expected utility of the less popular alternative (the sure loss of $3,000) was higher: −$3,000 × 1.0 = −$3,000. Kahneman and Tversky's subjects, in short, are lousy gamblers.

And so are most of the rest of us. This is what the social scientists call a "robust" finding: many studies have demonstrated that people accept risks when facing prospects of loss, but avoid risks when facing prospects of gain. This is related to the tendency we have to find more pain in loss than pleasure in gain (as Jimmy Connors put it, "I hate to lose more than I like to win"). The odds are pretty good that you exhibit this tendency yourself: all other things being equal, you will take more chances to try to avoid a loss than you would to try to secure an equivalent gain.

While this tendency may not be expected-utility maximizing in strictly monetary terms, many of us would insist that it makes perfect sense. After all, few of us are so rich that we could shrug off a loss of $3,000. This would be a major disaster. We would be in real trouble. Trouble is trouble. $4,000 worth of trouble isn't that much more serious that $3,000 worth of trouble. If you can't swim, it doesn't much matter whether you are drowning in 30 feet of water or 40. So taking a 1-in-5 chance of avoiding any loss at all is perfectly reasonable, even if it carries with it an 80 percent chance of an even bigger loss. This is certainly what the disaster avoidance principle ("Choose the option with the smallest chance of disaster") would tell us to do. The gamble has an 80 percent chance of disaster, while the sure loss of $3,000 has a 100 percent chance of disaster.

On the other hand, we could all use an extra $3,000. An extra $4,000 would be even better—but why jeopardize the windfall? Take the money and run. This is what minimax would dictate. The sure $3,000 has a better worst outcome than the gamble, which carries a 1-in-5 chance of no gain at all.

This line of reasoning obviously makes most sense if your financial resources are tight. If you are fabulously rich, there is no reason here to base your decision on the disaster avoidance or minimax principle. You might as well play the odds properly. Accept the gamble for gains, but decline it for losses. Most of Kahneman and Tversky's subjects were college students, so their preferences don't surprise me.

Accepting risks to avoid losses but shunning it to secure gains, then, is a perfectly sensible thing to do in certain financial contexts. But it is not always sensible, and yet this tendency is very strong.

Consider the following question Kahneman and Tversky put to their subjects (the proportion who preferred each option appears in square brackets):

> Imagine that the U.S. is preparing for the outbreak of an unusual Asian disease, which is expected to kill 600 people. Two alternative programs to combat the disease have been proposed. Assume that the exact scientific estimate[s] of the consequences of the programs are as follows:
>
> - If Program A is adopted, 200 people will be saved. [72 percent.]
> - If Program B is adopted, there is a 1/3 probability that 600 people will be saved, and 2/3 probability that no people will be saved. [28 percent.]
>
> Which of the two programs would you favor?[4]

Notice that the two programs have the same expected value: saving two hundred lives. Kahneman and Tversky's subjects preferred the risk-averse choice.

But the same options framed in terms of *lives lost* rather than *lives saved* elicited a completely different preference:

> - If Program C is adopted, 400 people will die. [22 percent.]
>
> - If Program D is adopted, there is a 1/3 probability that nobody will die, and 2/3 probability that 600 people will die. [78 percent.][5]

In this case, subjects preferred the risky choice. Simply by reframing the problem in the language of losses, Kahneman and Tversky induced a preference for risk.

A friend of mine used these studies to good advantage when he went house hunting. He found the perfect house in an ideal neighborhood, and entered into a negotiation with the vendor. The list price of the house, however, was higher than his budget would allow. After a few rounds, my friend made a final offer right at the maximum of his price range. But the vendor was unwilling to entertain any bid lower than what he had paid for the house a few years earlier—even though the market had soured in the meantime. They found themselves at an impasse, $15,000 apart. My friend's realtor came back to deliver the bad news that the vendor had rejected his final offer and did not wish to hear from him again unless he sweetened his bid by $15,000. "How many offers has he had on this house, and how long has it been on the market?" my friend asked. "Yours is the first bid in three months," the realtor replied. "Is he motivated to sell?" my friend asked. "He is beside himself," said the realtor, "a total wreck." "Then try this," my friend said. "Point out to him that he may not get another bid for another three months. He may not get another bid at all. Even if he does get another bid, he may not get his price. The carrying costs between now and then are huge, and he will have no choice but to pay them. If he accepts my bid, he saves a ton of money." The realtor made the pitch in these terms, and the vendor immediately accepted my friend's final bid.

This was clever negotiating. My friend reframed the vendor's problem and induced a different risk preference. Throughout the bidding, the vendor was fixated on getting back the money he had paid for the house in the first place. This was his *reference point*, and anything less than that he interpreted as a loss. In three months, the house attracted only my friend's bid. The problem was that the vendor saw it as a $15,000 loss. Rather than suffer a sure $15,000 loss, he preferred to gamble on the possibility that he would get an offer later that would entail no loss at all. What my friend did (via his realtor) was to shift the vendor's reference point from the price he paid in the past to the price he would have paid in the indefinite future, if and when he attracted another bid. *This* price included not only the original purchase price of the house, but all of the carrying costs in the meantime as well. My friend's bid, when seen against this future reference point, now looked like a sure gain, not a sure loss. The vendor accepted the new reference point. Being risk-averse for gains, he now preferred the sure small gain my friend's final bid represented to an uncertain but possibly larger gain somewhere down the road.

Notice, by the way, that if my friend had instructed his realtor to point out to the vendor that he had already paid significant carrying costs since he first listed the house, and that by accepting his bid he could prevent further such losses, he was far less likely to be persuasive. He would not have changed the vendor's reference point. He would have been asking the vendor to accept a sure loss in preference to taking a gamble on the possibility of a better future bid. The vendor, like most of Kahneman and Tversky's subjects, was clearly willing to accept risks to avoid sure losses.

The selection of the reference point was very important here. This raises the question, How should you establish a reference point from which to measure gains or losses? This is a different question from the question, How *do* people establish a reference point? Let's look at each in turn.

An economist would tell you that you *shouldn't* establish a reference point. You should not think in terms of gains or losses. You should think in terms of net assets. Any reference point you pick will be arbitrary from a rational-choice point of view.

My view is a little different. I would agree with the economist that many reference points you might pick would be arbitrary. For example, suppose you went to Las Vegas for a week in 1995 with $2,000 in your pocket and came home with $3,000. A few years later you went back for another week with another $2,000 and came home flat busted. If on your return your friends asked you, "Hey, how did you do in Vegas?" what would you say? Would you say you lost $1,000 (your net loss for both trips), or that you lost $2,000 (the loss from the second trip only)? Most of us would say that we lost $2,000, because we would have "normalized" (adjusted our reference point) for the earlier winnings. Psychologically, we would have treated the two trips as discrete events. Yet if you won $1,000 on the first day and lost $2,000 the next, when someone asked you how much you had won or lost you would probably say that you had lost $1,000. You would not have normalized for the first day's winnings. You would have treated the two days of gambling as one event. But why should you normalize your reference point in one case and not the other? There is no logical reason—only a *psychological* one. This is an example where the selection of a reference point is arbitrary, and the economist is on firm ground.

There are, however, some reference points that make a great deal of sense, logically or practically. These are *not* arbitrary. For example, the price you paid for a stock when you bought it makes eminent sense as the reference point for determining whether you gain or lose money when you sell it. I know of no government that insists that you calculate capital gains with reference to the *lowest* price the stock hit while you held it, nor of any government that permits you to calculate capital gains with reference to the *highest* price a stock hit while you held it (a reference point that would get you off ever having to pay capital gains tax at all!). You would consider the first reference point unreasonable, and the government would consider the second one unreasonable. You would both be right.

As I suggested in the previous chapter, the amount of money you need to cover your basic expenses makes a great deal of sense as a financial reference point. It is a sensible beacon to use for determining how much risk to tolerate in your financial decision making. I would not insist that you should *always* accept or shun risks when facing prospects of loss as defined by this particular reference point—as I suggested a minute ago, when choosing between two options that carry a chance of disaster, the magnitudes of the two disasters may be less important than the probabilities that you will suffer them. But I would suggest that the simple fact that you need adequate cash flow over the long run makes it entirely appropriate to invoke different strategies in different fiscal contexts. Hence it is possible to make a more compelling case for some reference points than for others, and the economist would be wrong to think that all reference points are equally arbitrary.

How do people choose their reference points in real life? Nobody knows for sure. There seem to be many possibilities. People often just treat the status quo as a reference point, and there are some normal psychological tendencies that reinforce this. One is the *endowment effect:* people sometimes demand more to give up an object than they would be willing to pay to acquire it in the first place. If someone wanted to buy your fountain pen, for example, you might not be willing to part with it for less than thirty bucks— but if you were in the marketplace for a fountain pen yourself, the most you would be willing to pay for the very same pen might be $20. It's not entirely clear why people behave this way. One possibility is that we simply become attached to things we own. But it reinforces our tendency to think of what we already have as the benchmark against which we define gain and loss. (The status quo is all the more likely to serve as our reference point if it hasn't changed for a very long time, or if we have recently gained something. Other things being equal, people tend to normalize quickly for gains. If my friend had bid on a house in a hot real-estate market, the odds are that the vendor's reference point would not have been the price he had paid for the house a few years earlier, but the considerably higher "market value" of his house at the time of sale. The status quo is *less* likely to serve as a reference point if we have recently suffered losses. People quite understandably normalize slowly for losses. Who likes loss?)

When the status quo does not define our reference point, many other things might. People's *conceptions of entitlement*, for example, can be very powerful. I study international politics, so some of my favorite examples of how conceptions of entitlement can shape reference points involve territorial claims. States will often take great risks to avoid losing (or to try to get back) territory they rightfully believe to be theirs, even though the territory itself may be barren, useless wasteland. Yet states rarely take risks to get territory to which they do not feel entitled, even when it is rich and productive.*

---

*Among the most fateful transfers of territory in modern history was the German annexation of the French provinces of Alsace and Lorraine at the end of the Franco-Prussian War (1871). The wound this left in the French national soul poisoned Franco-German relations right up to the First World War. French and German reference points are quite interesting here. France never normalized for the loss of these provinces in 1871. But neither did Germany normalize for their gain. Most Germans thought of them as conquered French territory, not as part of Germany. At the end of World War I, France recovered Alsace and Lorraine. It is interesting to note that Germany objected to many of the terms the victorious allies dictated to her—but not to this one. It was as though the territorial reference points of 1870 had never changed. This only makes sense if we understand the power of the sense of territorial entitlement to shape people's understandings of what is and is not an acceptable state of affairs.

At still other times, people's *aspirations or ambitions* can define their reference points. Mussolini wanted a "New Roman Empire" and took outrageous risks to get it. Hitler wanted to control Eastern Europe and recklessly gambled for it.

Sometimes a conception of *what one needs to feel secure* frames people's choices. In 1941, for example, Japan's military leaders felt that their country's survival depended on secure access to food, energy, and raw materials. But Washington's oil embargo, imposed in response to Japan's misbehavior in China, painfully demonstrated their vulnerability. So they took what they knew at the time to be a desperate gamble unlikely to succeed: a surprise attack on Pearl Harbor. They didn't believe it would work—they simply thought there was a small chance that it *might* work. If everything went well, the attack would knock out the American Pacific fleet long enough for Japan to seize and fortify a defensive perimeter. From this position of strength, they hoped, they might be able to negotiate an acceptable modus vivendi. Inaction, they thought, would bring certain disaster. Thus they accepted a bad gamble to try to avoid what they believed to be a sure loss.

Sometimes a *dramatic change* provides an opportunity to establish a new reference point. If you have bottomed out in Las Vegas, both financially and emotionally, you may boldly move to a new city, take up a new career, and try to establish a clean slate. It would be natural psychologically for you to reset your counters in that case to zero. Your new life in your new home would establish new baselines for you. You would let go of all of your old reference points. Often this is a wise thing to do: when you have suffered a long string of debilitating losses, one of the best ways of restoring your mental and fiscal health is to write off your past and start afresh. But there is a sense in which this is nothing more than creative bookkeeping and healthy self-deception, because there is no way to unlive your past life.

In fact, writing off past losses is among the hardest things to do. Gamblers routinely make bigger and more desperate bets after a long string of losses in a desperate attempt to recoup them, simply because they are unwilling to forget about them. The technical term for this kind of behavior is "escalating commitment to a losing course of action," and it is easy to explain as a form of risk-acceptance in the domain of losses.[6] The phenomenon applies to countries and businesses as well as to individuals. The United States' long, hopeless, escalating commitment in Vietnam can be seen as a refusal to write off the sunk costs in blood and treasure of a failed policy. Disgraced British trader Nick Leeson brought Barings Bank to its knees by throwing vast sums of good money after bad in a vain attempt to recoup earlier huge losses. In these cases, the operative reference point was the beginning of a series of costly decisions, and the carnage did not end until the people making the decisions essentially bottomed out.

Various things, then, shape people's actual reference points, and you will usually need to do some detective work to figure out which reference point someone has in mind at any given time and on any given issue. Sometimes it is possible to manipulate people's reference points, and sometimes it is not. My friend succeeded brilliantly with the previous owner of his house. No one seriously thinks Hitler could have been talked into rethinking his. But as a rule of thumb, it is generally easier to influence the way in which someone else frames a choice if you can do so *before* they have settled on a reference point. In the business world, this is known as "shaping expectations," and it is terribly important: whether your company's stock rises or falls on its quarterly earnings report depends less on its actual performance than on what people expect you to report. Through optimistic and pessimistic statements, press releases, and the like, you can nudge people's expectations in one direction or another. Careers can depend on this. A CEO who guides her company to a $1 million profit when investors and stockholders anticipate a $2 million profit should probably dust off her résumé. But her future is secure—at least until the next earnings report—if Wall Street expects a $2 million loss and she reports one only half that big.

The effect of reference points on risk taking is not the only crucial insight of behavioral decision theory, but it is an important one because it has so many real-world applications. There are other important insights as well, however, and before moving on it is worth flagging a few.[7] Some have to do with how people edit or simplify problems before they make decisions; another concerns the weights we give extreme probabilities. Let me introduce these and illustrate them with the kinds of questions that elicited them in the laboratory, and then turn to some everyday examples of how they work.

In 1953, the French economist Maurice Allais discovered that people tend to give too much weight to outcomes they consider certain (compared to outcomes they merely see as probable). We call this the *certainty effect*. As we saw, most people would prefer a sure gain of $3,000 to an 80 percent chance of winning $4,000. But if we modify these two choices—in effect, offering people a 1-in-4 chance on each option—they will reverse their preferences. Most people prefer a 1-in-5 chance of winning $4,000 (1/4 of the original 80 percent chance) to a 1-in-4 chance of winning $3,000.[8]

The *isolation effect* is a term psychologists use to describe people's tendency to ignore the components of risk that their alternatives share, focusing exclusively on the differences. This can lead to inconsistent preferences, because you can often break down the components of risk in your alternatives in various ways. Consider, for example, the following simple two-stage game:

Stage 1:

- Game proceeds to Stage 2 ($p = .25$).
- Game stops and you win nothing ($p = .75$).

Stage 2:

Choose A or B:
- A: Win $3,000 for sure.
- B: Take an 80 percent chance on winning $4,000 (with a 20 percent chance of winning nothing).

You must decide which second-stage alternative you would choose before the game starts.

Most people choose the sure $3,000 if they get to the second stage (choice A). But if you do the math and combine the elements of risk in both stages of the game, you will discover that this is precisely the same choice I presented two paragraphs ago. If you choose A, you really have only a 1-in-4 chance of winning the $3,000 that you can get "for sure" if you reach the second stage of the game, because the odds are 3-in-4 that you will never get to stage 2. Likewise, you have only a 1-in-5 chance ($p = .2$) of winning $4,000 if you choose B, because the odds are only 1-in-4 that you will have the opportunity to take that "80 percent" shot at the bigger payoff ($.25 \times .8 = .2$). People ignore stage one entirely when making this choice, because it is common to both second-stage alternatives.

A third important phenomenon is our tendency to give too much weight to very low probabilities. This is *not* the same as *overestimating* low probabilities, which we discussed in the previous chapter. Many people buy lottery tickets because they think they are more likely to win than is actually the case. That is overestimating your chances of winning. If you *overweight* a low probability, that means you know the probability, and you understand that it is very small, but you let it influence your decision making disproportionately. Most people, for example, would prefer taking a 1-in-1,000 chance of winning $5,000 to a sure gain of $5. In effect, they prefer a lottery ticket over its expected value (these two alternatives have identical expected utilities). On the other hand, most people would rather give up $5 than take a 1-in-1,000 chance on losing $5,000. This is like paying a small premium to avoid an unlikely small loss.

These tendencies taken together help explain, for example, why people buy insurance. At first glance, you might think that people's willingness to buy insurance is somewhat puzzling, given their willingness to take risks to avoid losses. An insurance premium, after all, can be seen as a sure loss, and the choice *not* to buy insurance can be seen as a gamble to avoid that loss. In fact, generally speaking it is a *good* gamble, because the decision not to buy insurance will have a higher expected utility. But there are various ways in which clever marketers can prevent people from framing their decision in this way and take advantage of the certainty effect, the isolation effect, and the tendency to overweight small probabilities. No one trying to sell you homeowner's insurance, for example, would ever make the following pitch:

> (Sound of a telephone ringing)
> "Hello?"
> "Hello, Mr. Smith? I hope I'm not calling at a bad time. My name is Jones, and I'm calling on behalf of Suboptimal Mutual Life and Casualty. Do you have a minute?"
> "I'm having dinner."
> "Fine. How would you like to suffer a small sure loss to avoid an improbable disaster? For the very reasonable monthly loss of $49, we will offer you protection against various kinds of catastrophe that you are not even remotely likely to suffer in your lifetime."
> "Can you call back?"

No, Jones would be out of a job in no time. A successful insurance salesman will offer you "protection" against "loss and damage" (the very low probabilities of which he would *never* draw to your attention—though most people understand intuitively that they are not particularly high). He would stress that you were buying an iron-clad right to reimbursement, subject only to a deductible and certain limits and exclusions. Once you buy the policy, you get the schedule of coverage, normally printed in tiny type, that makes clear just how many possible causes of loss your policy will not cover. It is common for homeowner's policies, for example, to exclude or limit reimbursement for damage caused by earthquakes, flooding, vandalism, vermin, and a bunch of other things. In fact, then, when you buy homeowner's insurance, you are buying only a *chance* for reimbursement, because there is some probability that if you suffer a loss, the cause will be an uninsured peril. But no good salesman would ever pitch it to you this way.

The various ways in which people frame decisions, edit and simplify their alternatives, and weight probabilities give clever marketers all kinds of avenues for steering you toward one choice rather than another. They can try to reframe your decision for you, get you to shift your reference point, distract your attention from some of the risks associated with your choices, highlight others, and combine and separate your risks in ways that make you look at them quite differently. They can also combine these techniques with others that we saw in the previous chapter. For example, they can break large numbers down into small, innocuous-looking pieces by advertising monthly payments more prominently than total costs in interest and principal. Lotteries can encourage you to overestimate your chances of winning big by showing in their ads only pictures of winners celebrating their winnings (have you ever seen ads showing millions of disappointed losers tearing up their tickets?). Sales clerks trying to sell you extended warranties try to focus your attention on "peace of mind" and "free repairs," not on the fact that the average cost of an extended warranty is higher than the average cost of repairs during the period of coverage. Slogans such as "You may never see prices this low again!" or "The Sale of the Century!" are deliberately designed to mislead you into thinking that you are certain never to do better than to buy now, when in fact almost certainly you *will* see prices this low again—for example, at the *next* Sale of the Century. Advertising a "suggested retail price" higher than an item's regular full-sticker price hoodwinks you into thinking that you are actually saving money when you are not. Even the silly general practice of knocking a penny or a nickel off the list price of something can work dramatically, because it takes advantage of the natural human tendency to focus most heavily on the first number in a sequence. A store will sell far more widgets for $49.99 than it would for $50, even though most people would never even miss the penny they saved if they dropped it on the street.

It generally pays, therefore, to think about how choices are presented to you, and whether there are alternative representations—especially if you are thinking about spending a lot of money. When I bought my first car, for instance, a salesperson from the dealership called me up to make the pitch that I should buy the car on terms through the manufacturer's credit arm. She went through a ten-minute presentation designed to convince me that I would save money by accepting their offer of five-year financing at 8.5 percent interest. She went through various other possible ways I might pay for the car and tried to convince me that hers was the best option I had. Every time I suggested that some other alternative might be superior, she would draw my attention to a different feature of her offer: it had a lower up-front cost than paying cash; it had a lower monthly payment than a bank loan; it left me with more equity in the car than did a lease (this was back in the days before leasing became so popular with car dealerships). She went on and on about what I would gain or lose, shifting deftly from one reference point to another (my current wealth, my future wealth, my cash flow, and so on). Only by resisting her attempts to manipulate my frame, my reference point, and my evaluation of the alternatives was I able to make the decision strategically. At the end of the day, I turned her down. My own assessment revealed that while her option was good for the manufacturer and for the dealer, it was not especially good for me.

SHORTCUTS, BIASES, AND OTHER NORMAL ERRORS

The patterns and tendencies we have discussed to this point are especially evident in people's preferences between alternatives with known probabilities and payoffs. But frequently the decisions we make require us to discover or to estimate probabilities, payoffs, or both. They are not always given to us in the problem itself. Nobody is omniscient, and even when good-quality information about these things exists, often the constraints on our time and resources make it difficult for us to get it. This does not prevent us from making decisions. Instead, we try to estimate these things, often very impressionistically. This is unavoidable, but rarely very precise, and is often an important source of error. I would like to turn now to some of the ways in which normal information-processing can lead to errors in judgment, perception, and evaluation. In the next section I will look at how throwing emotion into the mix makes things especially interesting.

In chapter 3, I noted that people often estimate the probability of an event by reflecting on the ease with which they can recall earlier instances. Many people think aviation disasters are far more likely than statistics indicate, for instance, because they can recall lots of vivid, horrific examples. I noted that psychologists call this the *availability heuristic.*

"Heuristic" is a ten-dollar word for "shortcut." It comes from the Greek word meaning "to find." Heuristics are not always misleading. Sometimes they can be both efficient and accurate. You probably do not know the proportion of people in the world who are noseless, but you probably don't know any noseless people yourself, either, and this may incline you to think that the number must be very small. And so it is. The vast majority of people have a nose. Searching your memory for people you know who have no nose is much quicker and easier than trying to dig up accurate statistics, and will lead you to an estimate that is probably good enough for your purpose (say, to gauge the potential market for a new nose polish you have invented). But obviously there is enormous room for error here. We can all recall examples of extremely unusual things, and the availability heuristic often leads us to overestimate their prevalence or likelihood.

Psychologists have documented a number of other heuristics we also commonly use.[9] One of these is *representativeness*: we often make judgments about things by zeroing in on the characteristics they have that we believe are typical of some larger group or class. The representativeness heuristic provides one way of diagnosing illness, for example. Doctors frequently decide what disease you have by comparing your symptoms with those typical of various diseases. Whichever disease's symptom profile fits your illness best is one a doctor is likely to diagnose. Again, often this is a very efficient and very accurate procedure. When good doctors do this, they are aware that this is what they are doing, and they are also aware that it is a shortcut prone to occasional error. If your symptoms are serious, your symptom profile ambiguous, or if they are unable to rule out something nasty, they will typically go beyond this, ordering a battery of blood tests, X rays, and other fancy things. A good doctor will only stop with representativeness when there is little doubt about what ails you, and no indication that it could do you serious harm.

Representativeness is certainly a better heuristic for doctors to rely upon than is availability. You don't want your doctor diagnosing you with the disease of the month just because she sees so many cases of it (though if your symptom profile fits, the availability heuristic is likely to bolster her confidence in her diagnosis). But representativeness has its dangers, too. Among other things, it leaves you vulnerable to myths and stereotypes.

Representativeness is also a common source of mistaken judgments of likelihood. Recall question 3 from our probability quiz in the previous chapter: most people judge it far less likely that they could win a lottery with a combination of numbers such as 1-2-3-4-5-6 than with a combination such as 3-15-16-39-41-42. This is because the second series *looks* random, and the first series doesn't, and we tend to believe that only random-looking sequences win lotteries. The representativeness heuristic also seems to be responsible for some instances of "the conjunction fallacy." This is the error of thinking that two events or conditions occurring together is more likely than one of them occurring alone (a mathematical impossibility). If you took a group of people through a hospital ward and asked them at the end of the tour how many of the patients they thought might be gay men with AIDS, for instance, you might well elicit higher estimates than if you simply asked how many patients they thought might have AIDS. Men lying in hospital beds rigged up to IV bags look just like we would expect AIDS patients to look. Society (wrongly) tends to think of AIDS as a disease that specifically afflicts homosexuals. Many people (also wrongly) assume that a very high percentage of gay men have AIDS. Seeding the thought that any given patient might be gay therefore triggers an overestimate because the stereotypes overlap and reinforce each other. But, in fact, the probability that a man is gay *and* has AIDS cannot mathematically be greater than the probability that he simply has AIDS (whether or not he is gay).

A third common heuristic goes by the name of *anchoring and* *adjustment.* Quite simply, this refers to the tendency to make judgments of value, magnitude, likelihood, or degree relative to some "anchor," or initial available value. If you can manipulate that initial value, you can sometimes exert quite a strong influence on someone's judgments. This particular heuristic is an especially dangerous occupational hazard for teachers. Suppose a student writes quite a bad essay, making a grade of C–, because she was sick, her dog died, and her house burned down all at the same time. She is stoic, however, and refuses to make excuses by telling you her troubles. She is also brilliant. The next time, she hands in a much better essay. Now, the fact that you gave her a C– on her first essay may incline you to give her second essay a grade of B+. But the same essay, if it had been handed in first instead of second, you might have graded A, and the poorer essay, if it had been handed in second instead of first, you might have graded C+. This is *anchoring and adjustment.* The implication for students is clear: put your best effort into your first assignment! (Similarly, if you sit down to grade a stack of essays, there is a danger that your grades for the group as a whole may be too high across the board if the first essay is excellent, and too low if it is terrible. This is because the first essay "anchors" the rest.*)

Many of the decisions we make require that we gauge the motivations and intentions of others. Some of these decisions are real minefields, and perfectly normal information-processing tendencies can push you headlong into them. Let's look at a particularly delicate hypothetical example.

You are a talented and attractive young lawyer who recently had to change jobs because you were the victim of sexual harassment in your previous office. For months your boss flirted, insinuated, cajoled, and finally threatened your promotion if you did not sleep with him. You resigned instead, but had a hard time finding

---

*To circumvent this problem, some schools and universities have a policy that grade distributions must meet certain constraints: for example, that the average for a group as a whole must be B–; that no more than 15 percent can be A– or better; and that no more than 15 percent can be D+ or worse. This is called "grading to a curve," and it is a violation of a basic principle of statistics, which states that highly unusual distributions are likely every once in a while.

another job because your former boss used the grapevine to poison your reputation.

You finally land a position at another firm where one of the junior partners, who knows your former boss to be a snake and who sympathizes with your ordeal, decides to take you on. Things go fine for a few months, but when the junior partner under whom you are working leaves to take a job in another city, she is replaced by a Mr. Smith, who seems very attentive to you. He smiles a great deal and pays you lots of compliments. He frequently asks you to team up with him on cases. (Someone in the office tells you that he *always* teams up with young women.) Sometimes you have to work late, and he is very solicitous of your welfare. He brings in dinners for both of you after hours and insists on paying for them. Occasionally he suggests that you have dinner out together. You begin to notice that he is dying the gray out of his hair and cutting it more stylishly. He begins to wear a more potent aftershave. He starts wearing dapper suits.

One day, Mr. Smith makes what you consider an inappropriate comment on your appearance. You realize that you are uncomfortable in his presence. You start trying to avoid him. You make sure you leave at five o'clock every day, when everyone else goes home. He asks you to work late with him a few times, and each time you find some excuse. As your anxiety mounts, your workload increases, and you make a few minor mistakes. He calls you in to explain them. You say something vague about going through an unusually stressful period of time. He offers to help, and laments the erosion of your collaboration. He tells you that he can make things easier for you if you want him to. Flustered, you rush out of his office, and deliberately avoid him for a week.

You get your performance review. It is generally positive, but the praise is qualified and, in some places, noticeably faint. You get a mediocre raise. You learn at the water cooler that Mr. Smith has been telling the other partners that they may have to let some people go who have not been performing up to standard. You start to panic.

You need to see Mr. Smith on a matter of business, and make

an appointment to meet him in his office. At the last minute, his secretary calls to say that he is unavailable, but that he is willing to meet you that evening after hours. As you put down the phone, you feel that your situation is becoming unbearable. You must decide whether to pretend that nothing is wrong, confront him and clear the air, or simply quit.

Actually, our Mr. Smith is a thoroughly decent chap. He is by nature friendly and polite. He is gay, but not out. He has just found a new partner, who just so happens to be in the fashion business. His partner persuades him to get a new haircut, cover up his graying hair, change his aftershave, and dress with more style. Mr. Smith is a strong liberal who believes in promoting women's careers in law. He goes out of his way to offer the few women lawyers in his office extra help, and makes a point of teaming up with them on cases. He believes that compliments boost self-esteem, and makes what he believes to be pleasant and harmless remarks on appearance. Being solicitous and observant, he notices that you look as though you are under increasing stress. He sees you stumble a bit. He does not wish to pry, but he wants to find out subtly what is wrong so that he can figure out how to help. He lets you know that he is eager to do so. He wants you to know that he knows you are capable of excellent work, so he ventures to say that he laments the fact that you have not been working together quite so closely as before. The senior partners ask for his comments on your performance review, and he makes a very strongly positive statement and argues for giving you the highest possible raise. (Unfortunately, some of the other partners have caught flak from your clients for your little mistakes, and they insist on watering down his raves and giving you just an average pay increase as a signal to you that you need to be more careful. Mixed though your performance review is, it is much better than those of the three young Ivy League whippersnappers the firm just took on as interns, who have been a complete disaster. The partners are thinking about terminating all three because they spend most of their time playing Solitaire, surfing eBay, and arguing about Chinese food. A secretary overhears a conversation to this effect, but does not catch any names. She spreads the word at the water cooler that someone's job is in jeopardy.) Mr. Smith is pleased to discover that his secretary has booked you in to see him, assuming that you must have decided to seek his help on whatever is bothering you, but at the last minute he is called into court. He tells his secretary to let you know that he will be back at five o'clock and would be happy to stick around long enough to discuss whatever it was that you wanted to see him about.

What we have here is a serious case of misperception. You have Mr. Smith all wrong, and because of this, you are about to make a fateful decision on the basis of just terrible information. And yet I think we would all agree that your misreading of the situation is perfectly understandable. According to cognitive psychology, it may even have been virtually impossible to avoid.

Your judgments and perceptions in this case were shaped and reinforced by a series of perfectly normal psychological processes. First, your prior experience with sexual harassment *primed* you to interpret Mr. Smith's ambiguous behavior as nefarious. Everything he did was consistent with the hypothesis that he was a sexual predator—albeit a more subtle sexual predator than the last one you had to deal with. While his actions were also consistent with the hypothesis that he was merely trying to be pleasant and helpful, you do not have any recent experience of a pleasant and helpful male boss, so it is not surprising that you would naturally incline toward the former interpretation.

Priming effects can have a powerful influence on how we interpret things. Perhaps the best illustration I know of the potency of priming is a practical joke I pulled on a close friend of mine many years ago. We were both a few years out of graduate school, at that stage in our careers when junior faculty members start to get nervous about their upcoming tenure decisions. My friend had just published his first book, and felt, with some justification, that his prospects for tenure depended heavily on whether the reviews were positive. He asked me repeatedly when I thought the reviews might start appearing in the journals, obviously nervous with anticipation.

Having a modest wicked streak, I saw here an opportunity for a good prank. I wrote a bogus review of his book that began, as most academic book reviews do, with a brief statement of what the book was trying to do and where it fit in the existing literature. I found some things about the book to praise lightly. I wrote this first part in the driest academic style I could muster. A few paragraphs in, I started to get more critical. I pointed to important works my friend had overlooked or ignored. I questioned his methodology. I questioned his originality. As the review went on, the criticisms became more and more outrageous. I questioned his integrity. I questioned his competence. I was vicious. By the end, the review had degenerated into an ill-tempered ad hominem attack that was so far over the top (I believed) that my friend would have to realize that it was a joke. To make it increasingly obvious that it was a joke as it went on, I made up all the footnotes to books and articles my friend had supposedly overlooked, and I made their titles and their authors' names more and more ludicrous. I seeded the text and the notes with little snippets of personal information that only his closest friends could possibly have known. I even gave myself away in a footnote toward the end.

The review complete, I arranged with the editor of the leading journal in the field to send it to my friend with a cover letter on journal stationery announcing "double-barreled good news": first, that his journal had received the enclosed review and planned to publish it in the next issue; and second, that the review was quite negative. "There is nothing like a biting critique to make people sit up and take notice of your work!" he wrote. He said that the reviewer had "pulled his punches" in several places, however, and that he and his editorial staff planned to work with the author "to sharpen the criticisms."

When my friend received the package from the journal, he tore it open immediately and began to read. As he tells the story, his face fell and he turned white. He started to panic. Before he got halfway through, he ran to the library to try to track down the "important books and articles" he had supposedly overlooked and ignored. He couldn't find them, of course, since they didn't exist. He pressed his colleagues into action. Before long he had his whole department trying to identify the fictitious author of the review and the fictitious citations. Finally, one of his colleagues who read calmly through the entire review and noticed the little personal jabs and inside jokes said: "Um . . . did you read the whole thing?" I came home that evening to a message on my answering machine in my friend's trembling voice. All it said was: "Revenge is a dish best served cold."

What had happened here is that the editor's cover letter had established in my friend's mind the complete legitimacy of the review. He noticed that the review included highly personal information and references to things about him that an academic reviewer could not possibly have known. He was puzzled that he could find no information on the alleged author or the fictitious references. But he put these concerns aside. They didn't make him rethink his prior assumption that this was a real review. The editor's cover letter had primed him too well to doubt it.

I am not a cruel man by nature. If I had known that my friend would react so badly, I never would have done it. I simply could not imagine that he could get halfway through the piece without catching on and doubling over with laughter. I underestimated the power of priming effects.

My friend did have his revenge, in a way—though completely inadvertently. After my prank, *I* was primed to expect one from *him* in retaliation. One day a few months later I received a phone call from someone I had never heard of, informing me that *my* first book had won a prize I had also never heard of. The fellow on the other end of the line asked me to prepare a speech and make all kinds of travel arrangements to come collect it. "Ha!" thought I; "Nice try!" I knew that my friend had spent a couple of years at the place that supposedly awarded this alleged prize, and I imagined he had simply asked one of his friends to call me and try to get me to show up unannounced for a nonexistent award ceremony. So I did nothing. A few weeks later I got an irate phone call from someone else entirely asking me why I had not yet bothered to inform them of my travel plans. She stopped just short of calling me a stuck-up ingrate.

But I digress. Let's go back to your law-firm predicament.

Priming can certainly explain a lot of your misperceptions. But there are other perfectly normal psychological phenomena that can help explain them, too. Three of these I find particularly interesting. They are the *egocentric bias*; the *proportionality bias*; and the *fundamental attribution error.*

The *egocentric bias* is the common tendency we have to exaggerate our own role in shaping other people's behavior. In other words, we simply tend to overestimate the extent to which people act with us in mind. Mr. Smith did not change his appearance because of you, but because of someone else. He was not attentive and complimentary to you in particular—he is attentive and complimentary to his female colleagues in general. It was not you that the partners were thinking of terminating; it was those good-for-nothing interns.

The *proportionality bias* leads us to infer other people's intentions from the apparent costs and consequences of their actions. Mr. Smith clearly invested a lot of time and money in you—not quite as much as you thought, mind you, since the egocentric bias led you to attribute the costs of his clothes and his hair to you; but a significant amount nevertheless. Quite naturally, you inferred that he must have cared a lot about you. You did not know that he spent equal time and money on others. Nor did you know that he is very rich, which means that the money he spent on you was really of little consequence to him. He *does* care about you—but not as much as you think, and not in the *way* you think!

The *fundamental attribution error* leads us, in certain circumstances, to exaggerate the extent to which people's behavior reflects their personal dispositions, and to underestimate the extent to which their behavior reflects the circumstantial or situational constraints they face. It can also lead us to attribute much greater coherence and meaning to other people's behavior than the evidence really warrants.* You interpreted everything Mr. Smith said and did as evidence of a predatory disposition and a master plan of conquest. You assumed that everything was coherent and

---

*I provide a more elaborate statement of the fundamental attribution error in the glossary that I fear would be unnecessarily confusing here.

deliberate. For example, you assumed that Smith alone was behind your mediocre performance review, and that it was mediocre because of his failure to make headway trying to get you into bed. You did not imagine that others would have had a hand in shaping your review. You also assumed that he deliberately had his secretary cancel your meeting at the last minute so as to engineer an after-hours meeting. It did not even occur to you that he might have been called away on short notice by something completely unrelated and totally beyond his control.

It's possible that some of your misperceptions were also the product of your *image* of men. Images are collections of beliefs about people's motivations, intentions, attitudes, dispositions, and so on. You can have images of individual people, small groups, or large groups. We all work with images all of the time, and your images can exert a powerful influence on how you interpret people's actions. They provide a set of lenses and filters that make it more likely that you will interpret what people do in a way that is consistent with your image. We form images quickly, and often on the basis of little information. But once we have formed an image, it becomes highly resistant to change. We have, as it were, an unconscious double standard: we require much more information to *change* an image once we have formed it than we required to create it in the first place. Elizabeth Bennet's problem in *Pride and Prejudice* was precisely this: she formed her negative image of Mr. Darcy quickly, on the basis of just a few encounters, and only slowly and reluctantly revised it. It took an overwhelming amount of information that did not fit that image to make her change it. Hence the word "prejudice" in the title.

Your image of men may have included a belief that all they think about is sex, and that all men are, at heart, sexual predators. (I hear a few of you out there saying, "Yes? What's your point?" I'm not going there.) If so, this certainly would have reinforced your tendency to interpret Mr. Smith's behavior accordingly. Notice that while the result here is essentially the same as the priming effect of your earlier sexual harassment experience, these are different psychological mechanisms. The experience of your earlier job might have led you, through priming, to misinterpret Mr. Smith's behavior even if you did *not* have an image of men as obsessed sexual predators. By the same token, if you had had an image of men as sexual predators, but no prior experience of harassment, you might have misinterpreted Mr. Smith anyway— though not because of priming.

The upshot here is that there are many different ways of making mistakes. Not all of them are avoidable. We cannot always monitor and check judgments that we make almost instantaneously, and often subconsciously. Sometimes the information that would enable us to avoid mistakes is simply unavailable. Mr. Smith was certainly not helping you read him correctly, because he was actively hiding details about his personal life that would have inclined you to interpret his actions differently. You were not allowed into the senior partners' meetings, and so you could not know that you weren't the person they were thinking of firing. You were not there when Mr. Smith got his last-minute call to go into court, so you could not know that circumstances, not cunning, led him to ask his secretary to reschedule your meeting. But it is interesting nonetheless to speculate how you would have behaved if you had been aware that a variety of normal psychological processes made it more likely, not less, that you would interpret Mr. Smith's ambiguous behavior in the way that you did. Perhaps you would have looked more actively for clues supporting an alternative explanation. Perhaps you would have gently probed him, or others in the office, for relevant information. Perhaps you would have been more willing to give him the benefit of the doubt. If so, under our scenario, your relationship with him would have unfolded rather differently, and far more satisfactorily for both of you. It would only have been a matter of time before you discovered that he was not a threat to you.

It is true, as they say, that "an open mind is an empty mind," and it is impossible to be *fully* open-minded on anything. We can only make sense of the world on the basis of some prior understanding of it. But it is helpful to ask yourself periodically which particular perceptual lenses you have on at any given moment, and also to reflect on possible alternative explanations for other people's behavior. If you know what some of the more common shortcuts, biases, and errors are, you can keep a better lookout for them.

EMOTION AND DECISION MAKING

So far we have been exploring psychological patterns that can lead you astray even when you are calm. They are, one might say, "cold" cognitive traps to which everyone is subject any time they try to process nontrivial information. But when our emotions become engaged in our decision making, interesting things can happen, too.

Because we tend to think of reason and emotion as incompatible, you might be tempted to think that when your emotions are excited, your decision making can only get worse. Not necessarily. Studies have shown that most people perform better on information-processing tasks when they are under moderate stress. We have all experienced the heightened alertness that adrenaline brings. As Samuel Johnson once said, "[W]hen a man knows he is to be hanged in a fortnight, it concentrates his mind wonderfully."

You can also learn a lot about yourself from an intense emotional experience. Love, hatred, hope, joy, despair, fear, anger, lust, jealousy, envy, pride, infatuation, and resentment can all teach you something useful about what you value, what you want, who you are, and who you would like to be. When intense emotions subside is often the perfect time for reflection and introspection.

So emotion does not always hinder effective decision making. Nevertheless, as you might expect, there are ways in which one's emotions can make it harder, not easier, to make a good decision. Most simply, emotions can tire you out. Fatigue reduces our alertness, slows our synapses, and makes it harder for us to keep more than just a few bits of information in play at any one time. In effect, it temporarily reduces our IQ. Intense emotion is particularly draining, but no one can maintain a high level of performance for very long even under just moderate stress. Stress eventually degrades your performance. It becomes positively harmful to you, physically and psychologically, when it is too intense, lasts too long, or occurs too frequently.

Even when your energy level is high, emotions can trip you up. One thing they can do is give you tunnel vision. When you are desperately infatuated with someone, for example, you can usually forget about trying to get your mind to focus on something else. When you are together with the object of your desire, you are paralyzed with rapture. When you are apart, you daydream constantly about being together. When your brain is occupied with sweet thoughts of romance, there are no free clock cycles left for quality decision making.

Emotions can also short-circuit your decision making. If you discover the object of your infatuation in bed with someone else, for example, you may be surprised to find a moment later that you are holding a broken table lamp in your hands and that your lover's lover is unconscious on the floor beside you. You did not exactly *decide* to attack, but your rage demanded instant gratification and essentially made the decision for you. Crimes of passion are never the result of a quality deliberation.

These are fairly obvious ways in which emotion can frustrate effective decision making, but there are subtler ways as well. Among other things, emotions can cause many of the same kinds of misjudgments as "cold" cognitive processes.

To some extent, we can explain certain mistakes in terms of our striving to meet basic human needs. We all try to avoid fear, shame, and guilt. We all need self-esteem. We crave social approval. We need to have a sense of accomplishment, and we need recognition of that. We need to have a sense of control over our lives. If we make mistakes in judgment because we are subconsciously trying to satisfy these needs, we are making "motivated" errors (in contrast to the "unmotivated" errors I talked about in the previous section, which are simply occupational hazards of thinking).

Some of the motivated errors people make can be traced to their basic personality or to their life history. We can see this most clearly in a good psychobiography. One can make a pretty good argument, for example, that Adolf Hitler's manias and psychoses probably had something to do with a traumatic childhood, sexual repression, and deep self-loathing.[10] Among his most notable personality traits was a proneness to aggressive rage. This helps explain why his decisions were often reckless, ill-conceived, and ill-considered. Hitler was a man very much driven by his demons, and his decision making reflected it. In fact, he was such a lousy decision maker that Allied leaders actually worried during World War II that somebody might assassinate him. They didn't want a competent military strategist to succeed him.

My favorite psychobiography is Alexander and Juliette George's fascinating study of Woodrow Wilson.[11] (Wilson was the last president of the United States to hold a Ph.D., and his terrible performance in office has, I fear, ruined the chances for the rest of us.) Wilson was self-righteous and pigheaded. He was a control freak. He lapped up flattery, and he took all opposition personally. The Georges trace this powerful personality trait to childhood anxieties about being unable to satisfy the demands of an overbearing, perfectionist father. From a very early age, Wilson sought power and adulation to compensate for low self-esteem. His pathological inability to compromise wrecked his vision of a rule-governed international order after World War I. When he asked the Senate to ratify the Treaty of Versailles, which included his grand scheme for a League of Nations (the failed forerunner of the current United Nations), he absolutely refused to entertain any amendments, because this would compromise his design of the League and his control of the process. He allowed his disagreements with Sen. Henry Cabot Lodge to degenerate into an all-or-nothing power struggle and lost sight of the larger issues. The Senate never ratified the treaty. The United States never joined the League. Wilson suffered a fatal stroke.

When people's basic psychological needs go unmet for long periods of time, gratifying them becomes an irresistible priority. If the world does not oblige them, they will find ways of trying to make it do so. They will try to create the world that they need.

It is normal, for example, for people to divide the world into an in-group and an out-group. Membership in an in-group gratifies our self-esteem and our need to belong. It does so all the more effectively if we can persuade ourselves that our in-group is good, and the out-group is evil. This is why we have nationalism and football. It is also why we have neo-Nazis. If you are white, not very smart, sexually repressed, socially outcast, unemployed, and overly fond of playing *Mortal Kombat,* the odds are that your self-esteem is in the tank and you crave membership in, and affirmation from, some in-group. You may stumble upon some number of people with similar characteristics who have chosen to address their unmet needs by shaving their heads, wearing jackboots, tattooing swastikas on their chests, and generally comparing themselves favorably to out-groups such as blacks or Jews whom they can pretend are responsible for their own failures. If you join them, you will find yourself reading books, magazines, newsletters, and newsgroups with such a bizarre angle on the world that you may ultimately convince yourself that you can trigger a nationwide white supremacist uprising just by detonating a fertilizer-and-diesel-fuel truck bomb outside a federal building somewhere. This is what we would technically call a "bad decision." It is a decision based on faulty information. Nobody is going to rise up and overthrow the government because of your terrorist lunacy. Even if they did, they wouldn't necessarily embrace your crackpot politics. Why would you think they would? Because your striving to satisfy your deep psychological needs led you into a delusional world of your own.

Your psychological needs can also have a profound effect on how you interpret the actions of others. Every once in a while a member of our in-group does something that we consider bad. Motivational psychology tells us that we are likely to explain away the bad actions of our in-group members by appealing to situational constraints ("He had no choice; he had to do it"). But if a member of an out-group had done the same thing, most likely we would have explained it in terms of his character or disposition ("He is evil").

Sometimes people make errors in judgment not because of their personalities, but because of the situations in which they find themselves. Some situations, for instance, arouse fear, anxiety, and debilitating stress. Under great time pressure, and facing the prospect of loss, we often search inadequately for information, make biased estimates of probability, deliberate superficially, evaluate alternatives hastily, and commit to a course of action prematurely. This can have a snowball effect. Every bad decision we make can make our situation worse and worse, increasing our anxiety. In the face of looming catastrophe, we often try to convince ourselves that we have not erred. We clutch at straws. We find ways of ducking responsibility. In extreme cases, we may withdraw or break down.

The outbreak of the First World War provides a classic illustration of situation-induced decision-making pathologies. When Austria-Hungary decided in the summer of 1914 to smite Serbia, Germany gave Austria an imprudent degree of encouragement and support, because Austria was Germany's sole remaining Great Power ally. At the time, Kaiser Wilhelm, his chancellor, and his foreign secretary did not anticipate that Austria's actions would pull Russia and France into war as well, triggering a general European conflagration. In part, this was because their sycophantic and ambitious ambassadors abroad were mostly telling them what they wanted to hear, systematically downplaying the dangers of German policy. (Only the German ambassador to London, Prince Karl Lichnowsky, provided clear, accurate, and dire warnings of his host country's likely responses. His superiors dismissed his "alarmism," and wrote him off as having "gone native.") When at last the handwriting began to appear on the wall, German policy makers desperately searched for some way out of the hole they had dug for themselves, and German diplomacy lost any semblance of coherence. Panic set in. Things went from bad to worse. At the eleventh hour, the kaiser could stand the stress no longer. He left Berlin for Potsdam to have a nervous breakdown in peace while Europe descended into war.

This is a classic case of motivated errors and situational stress combining to produce lousy decisions across the board.[12] We see in the story evidence of a number of common pathologies:

- *Wishful thinking.* German leaders overestimated the likelihood of outcomes they considered desirable, and underestimated the likelihood of outcomes they found painful to contemplate.
- *Selective attention.* German diplomats and leaders filtered out information suggesting that Austria's move against Serbia would escalate to a general European war.
- *Denial.* When unable to filter out such information, German leaders refused to accept it, in part by trying to discredit its source.
- *Bolstering.* When unable to ignore or discredit such information, German leaders went out of their way to try to find contradictory evidence with which to overwhelm it.
- *Hypervigilance.* As the crisis peaked, German leaders began a frantic, chaotic last-minute search for new options and new information, none of which they were in a position to process properly owing to time pressure and stress.
- *Defensive avoidance.* Faced with the unavoidable realization that his policy had failed catastrophically, the kaiser sought to avoid the psychological pain of having to acknowledge his mistakes and his responsibilities by burying his head in the sand.

It did not help matters that Germany's leaders in 1914 ranged from mildly to severely incompetent. But while the kaiser, at least, was certainly a neurotic of the first degree, most of the errors that led to the First World War were the result not of the personalities and dispositions of individual leaders, but of the particularly stressful circumstances under which they were operating.

Emotion, then, can be the enemy of sound decision making, and can work against it in a variety of ways. How do we prevent this?

Many of us flatter ourselves that our reason is the master of our emotions. Even if we don't believe that, we tend to think of that as a weakness or a deficiency in us. In other words, we hold up as an ideal the capacity to suppress or transcend emotion to permit calm, objective deliberation. Actually, as we shall see in chapter 6, this is a gendered (masculine) ideal that no one can ever fully realize, and I, for one, am glad that no one can. What a bore such a person would be! But this is not to say that we should always indulge our emotional impulses. We should try to find some way for emotion and reason to coexist in peace.

To the extent that emotions proceed from beliefs, we can control our emotions if we can persuade ourselves, or permit others to persuade us, that our beliefs are wrong. But there are limits even to this. No matter how many accident-statistics you trot out, and no matter how carefully you explain Bernoulli's principle, some intelligent people will still be afraid to fly. No matter how many times we open the closets to show our children that there are no monsters inside, some will still fear them. Therapy helps some people who are chronically unable to make sensible decisions because of their personalities or life experiences, but for others it has no effect whatsoever. Our emotional lives are notoriously resistant to tinkering.

Often the best way to try to prevent our emotions from getting in the way is to move our decision making *out* of the way. If you can avoid the kinds of situations that trigger powerful and debilitating emotional responses, you will prevent those responses from complicating your decisions. Sometimes you cannot avoid the situations themselves, but can afford to allow your emotions to run their course before you decide on a response. My wise old grandmother always used to say that you should never make an important decision when you are tired or angry. She had a policy of waiting at least twenty-four hours before responding to someone who had irritated her. This was easier for her in her day than it is for us in ours, of course, because she did not have e-mail. But practicing restraint can really pay off.

An emotional response is a bit like a roller coaster. The peak is usually right near the beginning. After a short time, there is a dramatic drop. After a few ups and downs, with perhaps some twists and turns, things eventually level off and the ride comes to an end. Jane Austen's Mr. Bennet knew this very well. "No, Lizzy," he said, deflecting his daughter's attempt to comfort him for a monumentally stupid decision, "let me once in my life feel how much I have been to blame. I am not afraid of being overpowered by the impression. It will pass away soon enough."

If you simply practice trying to wait out the roller coaster, you do not give your emotions a chance to wreak havoc on your decisions. The single wisest thing President Kennedy did in his handling of the Cuban missile crisis was to wait until his anger had subsided before choosing his response to the discovery of the Soviet deployment. If he had chosen his response immediately, or even the following day, he would probably have chosen to bomb and invade. This might have been the opening salvo of World War III. But within forty-eight hours, his anger had cooled to the point where he could more carefully assess the possible costs and benefits of the various military and nonmilitary options before him. He was wise, in short, not to decide too quickly.

Sometimes we can neither avoid emotional situations nor postpone our responses to them. So it goes. There are limits to our ability to escape or to manage our human nature. We will occasionally stumble into cognitive and emotional traps no matter how well we understand them in the abstract, and no matter how studiously we practice avoiding them. There are two attitudes we can take to this: we can berate ourselves for our failings and bemoan our humanity, or we can shrug it off as the unavoidable consequence of being human. I see no reason to prefer the former attitude to the latter. How dull it would be never to make a mistake. How sad it would be to lament our humanity, too—especially given the lack of alternatives.

5

DOING THE RIGHT THING

MAKING MORAL CHOICES

Two things fill the mind with ever new and increasing wonder and awe, the more often and the more seriously reflection concentrates upon them: the starry heaven above me and the moral law within me.
— Immanuel Kant, *Critique of Practical Reason*

So far we have been looking at decision making from a purely instrumental perspective. We have started with the question, "What do I want?" and have explored how best to get it. To this point we haven't bothered to ask whether our goals are praiseworthy ones, and we haven't explicitly factored into our discussion considerations of right and wrong.

In some of the examples we have discussed, it would have been ludicrous to do this. In the ordinary course of events, it is a matter of complete moral indifference which Chinese restaurant you decide to patronize, or which fork in the path you decide to take. But even seemingly innocent decisions such as whether to buy lottery tickets may, in fact, raise profoundly moral questions. Should you buy lottery tickets if the opportunity cost is nutritious food and decent shelter for your children?

Our discussion thus far can certainly help you answer this question. You may be in the habit of buying lottery tickets because, as a destitute single parent, you are trying to win enough money to provide your children with opportunities in life that they are unlikely to have otherwise. This is certainly a noble motive. But the previous two chapters should have enabled you to see why this is a vain hope. You are much more likely to serve your children's interests by spending what little money you have on the necessities of life. While this offers no possibility of a windfall, it is much the better gamble. A clearer understanding of money, probability, and some of the psychological traps that lead people to gamble can therefore help you make sound moral decisions.

But we still need to have a hard look at moral deliberation as such. How does it differ from purely instrumental decision making? In what respects is it the same? What twists and complications does it involve?

I want to suggest that moral reasoning is not quite so radically different from instrumental deliberation as many people seem to believe. One can approach moral choices in much the same way as nonmoral ones. The nine steps to effective decision making still apply. But there is a crucial difference, and it lies primarily in the weight you give to certain implicated values when moral considerations are at stake.

It is a sad commentary on modern society that a discussion of moral reasoning in a book about decision making requires a certain amount of justification at the outset. An alarmingly large number of people today hold morality in contempt. They fall into two categories. The first are people whose primary guiding question in life is, "What's in it for me?" They think of moral principles not as useful and important aspects of their daily lives, but as quaint, unnecessary relics of a bygone era, much like antiques and Charles Dickens novels. In their struggle to climb the socioeconomic ladder as quickly and as painlessly as possible, they do not much care whether their actions harm others or contribute to some common good. When caught and convicted of massive tax fraud, the only thing they regret is not fudging their books more cleverly. Such people are not fully to blame for their moral degeneracy. Modern material society constantly bombards us with messages that we are failures if we do not somehow manage to live the lifestyle of the rich and famous. It is hardly surprising that the weak-minded cannot resist the subliminal pressure to cut corners.

The second group of moral skeptics cannot plead weakness. Their problem is intellectual smugness. These are the people who deride morality as a religious vestige, a mechanism for social control, or a weakness that stems from our inability or unwillingness to stare the cosmos in the face and admit that our existence has no meaning. On this view, morality is for wimps. I do not propose to take on the nihilists here. This is not a book about metaphysics. I would merely ask them: "How do *you* know?" And I would encourage them to go see Alfred Hitchcock's *Rope*.

What both groups fail to understand is that moral deliberation is not something that people invented. It is an integral part of who we are. Human beings are moral beings by nature. By this I do not mean that we always do the right thing. Clearly we do not. I mean instead that we have a natural capacity to think in moral terms, and a natural inclination to take moral considerations seriously. We might want to call this a natural "moral faculty."* Only very young children, the severely mentally disabled, and the criminally insane cannot make moral judgments. Normal adults can. And normal adults do. Stifling one's moral sensibility is a bit like stifling one's appreciation of beauty, one's need for human contact, one's need for challenge and stimulation, or one's need to sneeze. You may be able to do it, but the inevitable result is that, at some level, you will be miserable. It is one of the characteristics of our species to suffer whenever an element of our basic humanity is stifled or neglected. There is no such thing as a happy nihilist.

Morality therefore plays a central role in a normal, healthy human life. We neglect it at our peril. But how do we give morality its due? How do we make moral choices? How *should* we?

---

*Professional philosophers might shun this particular phrase, since it connotes the now-discredited Moral Intuitionist position. I am using the term here in a purely psychological sense.

RULES AND CONSEQUENCES

You are the lone doctor in a small Florida town. One of your patients has ALS, or Lou Gehrig's disease—a fatal degenerative nerve disease that leaves its victims paralyzed and speechless, though alert. Your patient's condition has deteriorated so badly that you doubt whether he will live more than a few months. He is bedridden, breathing only with the help of a ventilator, and is being fed intravenously. He is in torment. He begs you to end his suffering. He wants you to administer a lethal dose of barbiturates. He has no family or friends to live for, and no hope of recovery. He also has no way of ending his own life, since he no longer has control over his limbs. Someone would have to help him. He trusts you, and no one else, to do it humanely. What do you do?

One way of deciding what to do is to ask whether the *kind* of act requested of you is consistent with some set of moral rules or principles. You identify the relevant body of rules or principles, and you simply check to see whether the act is permitted (or, at least, not forbidden). This is *deontological* moral reasoning—a word that comes from the Greek root for "that which is binding." If you are a devout Catholic or Muslim, you are likely to say no. Both religions condemn euthanasia and doctor-assisted suicide.[1] Florida state law prohibits it, too. So does your Hippocratic Oath (at least as most in your profession interpret it). There are several bodies of rules, then, that you might consider binding, and that would prohibit you from doing what your patient has asked you to do.

Another way of deciding what to do, however, is to ask which alternative would have the most desirable outcome. Which option would result in the greatest balance of pleasure over pain? This is *consequentialist* reasoning. If you were to decide *this* way, you might well agree with your patient's request. He is in anguish. You can end his suffering. You would not be hurting anyone else by doing so. There is no one to object. He is likely to die soon anyway, so it is unlikely that anyone would even know if you hurried his end along.

Broadly speaking, these are the two most common modes of

moral reasoning. The example is a useful one because most people have strong opinions on euthanasia and doctor-assisted suicide, and yet virtually all of us acknowledge that both ways of approaching the problem have some merit. Most of us would agree that, all other things being equal, people ought not to kill other people—and especially that doctors ought not to kill their patients. But we would also agree that, all other things being equal, we should relieve people's suffering, try to make people happy, and respect people's strong, well-considered self-regarding wishes. This is simply a case where we can't have it both ways.

Most religious ethical traditions have a deontological core. They include some basic list of injunctions that people are supposed to apply in their daily lives. The Ten Commandments, for instance, lie at the heart of the Judeo-Christian ethical tradition. They are simple do's and don'ts. They say things such as "Honor thy father and thy mother" and "Thou shalt not kill." They do *not* say: "Honor thy father and thy mother when, on balance, this makes people happier than not honoring thy father and thy mother," or "Thou shalt not kill, except when killing someone results in saving more lives than would be saved by not killing."

The purest example of a deontological ethical system is one developed by Immanuel Kant. Kant was an eighteenth-century Prussian philosopher whose great works represented a bold attempt to reconcile faith and reason. His ethical system is notable for its abstraction and its hard-core universalism. He argued that all people in all times and places were subject to precisely the same moral law, and that the commandments of this moral law were something we could deduce through an exercise of reason alone. He developed the argument primarily in two almost impenetrable works, *Grounding for the Metaphysics of Morals* and *Critique of Practical Reason* (known in the philosophy biz as "the Second Critique," since the longer and even more impenetrable *Critique of Pure Reason* came first). At the end of the day, what Kant offers us bears a strong family resemblance to the familiar Golden Rule: "Do unto others as you would have others do unto you." But beneath the superficial similarity lies quite a subtle and sophisticated argument.

Kant was keenly aware of the tension in human nature between our desires and instincts on the one hand, and our reason on the other. As a species we are stuck, as it were, somewhere between animals, who do not have reason and who therefore act only in accordance with desire, and God and the angels, who, being perfect, are above desire, and who therefore must act in accordance with reason alone. Obviously, it is better to be godlike than animal-like, Kant thought, so we should strive to give reason dominion over our desires.

Kant held that our capacity for reason is the source of our dignity and makes us worthy of respect. All humans, having reason, have the same dignity, and are therefore worthy of the same respect. If you treat people merely as instruments, cogs, or means to some end—as you do, for example, if you use them merely to gratify your own base desires—you do not show them the respect to which they are entitled as human beings. The imperative to treat people as ends in themselves rather than merely as means to some other end is the essence, for Kant, of the moral law. It is our primary duty.

Kant felt the distinction between duty and inclination so acutely that he thought if you did the right thing because it gave you pleasure to do so, you weren't really acting morally. A moral person acts for the sake of duty alone. I have always had a hard time with this part of his argument. It seems to me that he comes very close to saying that, to be a moral person, you have to have immoral desires. And if you enjoy doing nice things for people, according to Kant, you're not acting morally. You're simply indulging your desires. By definition, morality can't be fun. This is a hard doctrine. But Kant was nothing if not uptight. He had unbelievably rigid habits. He was famous, for example, for taking a walk at precisely the same time every day, and for following exactly the same route. He was so precise and so dependable in this that his neighbors literally used to set their watches by him. One day he failed to show, and the townsfolk rushed to his house fearing he had died. They found him engrossed in reading Rousseau's *Emile*. For the first and only time in his life, he had lost track of time.

How, exactly, do we know the right thing to do in any given case, according to Kant? This is reason's job. What is right for one person must be right for all people in the same situation. To decide whether something is morally permissible, then, you simply ask yourself whether you could will that the maxim of your action become a universal law. (The "maxim of your action" is the general principle of which your action is an example.[2]) That may not be terribly clear, so let's look at some examples.

Suppose you are an adolescent male. Your mother leaves the house for a few hours and you promise that you will practice the piano while she is gone. Your friend calls and asks if he can come over to play *Mortal Kombat*. You say, "No, I promised Mom I would practice the piano." "Aw, c'mon," says your friend. "She'll never know whether you did or not." What, according to Kant, should you do?

What you *really* want to do is break your promise to your mother. To decide whether this is all right, you first formulate a universal version of what it is that you would like to do. In this case it would be the maxim: "Anyone may break a promise whenever they wish." Next, you ask yourself what would happen if this were, in fact, general practice. Would this generate some kind of logical paradox? Would it thwart your particular purpose in this particular instance (Kant would call this a "contradiction in intention")? If so, you should not do it. In either case you could not "will that the maxim of your action be a universal law."

As you think things over, you realize that if people could break promises whenever they liked, no one would have confidence in other people's undertakings. The very idea of a "promise" would be meaningless. The statement, "I promise to practice piano for half an hour while you are out" would not mean, "I undertake to practice the piano," or, "You can be confident that I will practice the piano." At best, it would mean something like: "Get off my back." That may be what you *really* meant in the first place; but since universalizing the maxim transforms your promise into a nonpromise, which is paradoxical, you cannot break your promise, according to Kant.

The phone rings. You are deeply engrossed in a game of *Mortal*

Kombat with your juvenile delinquent friend. It is your mother. "I'll be home in five minutes; did you practice the piano, as you promised?" she asks. You want to lie. You don't want the earful of abuse you will get if you tell the truth. You imagine the universal law, "Anyone may tell a lie when convenient." Now, you cannot will that this be a universal law without frustrating your object in telling a lie, because for the lie to work, the person to whom you tell it must believe it to be true. If everyone lied at will, nobody would believe what other people said. Your mother certainly would not believe you. You would get the abuse anyway. Since universalizing the maxim would generate a contradiction in intention, you cannot lie.

It is a little ironic that Kant was the prophet of universal moral reason. The man never left his hometown of Königsberg. He started to travel to Berlin once, but a few miles out of town he got cold feet and turned back. He may therefore have seen less of the world than any other moral philosopher in history. Nevertheless, he was definitely on to something. Moral reasoning clearly does require a certain disinterestedness. It is not a cover for personal desire. Moreover, what is right for one person must be right for any other person in exactly the same circumstance. Otherwise, morality is arbitrary and ethical deliberation impossible.

There are problems, however. Some of these problems involve trying to put Kant's system into practice. What do we do, for example, if we are forced to choose between two evils? Suppose your best friend confesses to you that he has been cheating on his wife, but before he tells you this, he makes you promise never to tell another soul. His wife then calls you up and asks you whether he has admitted to having an affair. You must either break a promise or tell a lie. There is no avoiding one or the other. Kant does not help us here.

Second, Kant does not tell us how we are supposed to formulate the maxim of our action. It may be that "Anyone may tell a lie when convenient" fails a universalization test, but what if we were to formulate it more precisely—for example, "Anyone may tell a lie to save another's life"? Or, "Anyone may tell a lie to save another's life on Saturdays in May when there is a full moon"? As far as I can tell, neither of these would generate a contradiction in logic or intention.

Most of us, I suspect, would have no difficulty telling a lie to save another person's life. Indeed, in 1797, Benjamin Constant took Kant to task on precisely this point. He wrote the following rebuttal:

> The moral principle stating that it is a duty to tell the truth would make any society impossible if that principle were taken singly and unconditionally. We have proof of this in the very direct consequences which a German philosopher [this would be Kant] has drawn from this principle. This philosopher goes as far as to assert that it would be a crime to tell a lie to a murderer who asked whether our friend who is being pursued by the murderer had taken refuge in our house.[3]

But Kant permitted no exceptions. He replied in a famous essay called, "On a Supposed Right to Lie because of Philanthropic Concerns."[4] "To be truthful (honest) in all declarations," Kant wrote, "is ... a sacred and unconditionally commanding law of reason that admits of no expediency whatsoever." You cannot lie to the murderer. You can, however, hope that your friend escapes out the back while you answer the front door.

This example points to what must surely be the most serious difficulty with Kant's single-minded indifference to the consequences of our actions: it simply does not ring true. Who among us is willing to agree that consequences are completely unimportant? Who among us really agrees with the ancient maxim, *Fiat justitia et ruant coeli*—"Let justice be done and let the heavens fall"? If it takes a little injustice to prop up the heavens, that strikes me as a price well worth paying. In fact, I would go so far as to say that some lies are not only harmless, but positively required by the duties of kindness, politeness, or self-preservation. There are times and places when one definitely ought not to answer a question truthfully ("Do I look fat?" "Did you have a good time at my party?" "I see you didn't finish your haggis; are you not hungry?").

Deontological ethical systems can deal with these problems in various ways. Religious systems, for example, often acknowledge an authoritative interpreter—some individual or some council—whose job it is to sort out ambiguities, contradictions, and tensions with common sense. Others supplement, modify, or water down core moral principles to accommodate people's intuitions about justifiable exceptions. While some Christians are pacifists, for example, most Christian churches do not take "Thou shalt not kill" as an absolute prohibition. They accept that killing can sometimes be justified. There was no way to stop the Nazis without killing a lot of people—even large numbers of innocent people—and most Christian churches simply accepted this as the lesser of two evils. Relatively few people, in short, think that the consequences of our actions are always irrelevant to the morality of our decisions, and even people who take rules very seriously indeed generally acknowledge this.

Are the consequences of our actions the *only* things that are relevant to the morality of our decisions? A hard-core utilitarian would say yes.* Utilitarianism is the best example of a purely Consequentialist ethical system. It is the view that the right action in any given case is the one that maximizes utility.

Utility is a concept that should be quite familiar to you by now, but there is one important difference in the meaning of this term when we use it in a moral (as opposed to purely instrumental) context. When utilitarians talk about utility, they don't mean *yours* in particular, but that of humanity as a whole, of society, or, at the very least, of those affected by your decision. Someone who seeks to do the right thing, on this view, will act in accordance with the Greatest Happiness Principle: "Choose the action that will result in the greatest happiness for the greatest number."

Jeremy Bentham (1748–1832) was the founder of modern utilitarianism. He was just as rigid in his own way as Kant was in his, and he was just as ingenious. Bentham's view was that the only thing truly good in itself is pleasure. More pleasure is better than

---

*Strictly speaking, I should say *act-utilitarian* here, but that would quickly become tiresome. I will introduce the nuance later, when I need it.

less. Moreover, pleasure is pleasure—it doesn't matter how you get it. In a now famous phrase, Bentham said that "the game of push-pin is of equal value with the arts and sciences of music and poetry."[5] Push-pin was an old English child's game that involved trying to cross other players' pins with one's own. Judging from context, Bentham must personally have thought it a mindless waste of time.

If pleasure is the only good, and if more pleasure is better than less, then making moral decisions is a fairly straightforward task of maximizing pleasure. Bentham proposed that we make such choices in accordance with what he called a "hedonic calculus": we should estimate how much pleasure and pain the available alternatives would cause all of the affected parties, and choose the alternative with the greatest balance of pleasure over pain.

Suppose, for example, that you had to choose between playing poker with your friends or watching a movie with your wife. You might make your decision in roughly the following way:

TABLE 13. HEDONIC CALCULUS FOR PLAYING POKER

Units of pleasure (+)/pain (–): Playing poker with your friends

You	Pleasure from playing cards with your friends	9
	Guilt from disappointing your wife	–2
Your wife	Disappointment at not watching movie with you	–10
	Pleasure in knowledge that you are enjoying yourself	1
Friend 1	Pleasure from playing cards	5
Friend 2	Pleasure from playing cards	5
Friend 3	Pleasure from playing cards	3
Total happiness score		**11**

TABLE 14. HEDONIC CALCULUS
FOR WATCHING A MOVIE

Units of pleasure (+)/pain (–): Watching a movie with your wife

You	Pleasure from watching movie with your wife	5
	Guilt from disappointing your friends	–8
Your wife	Pleasure from watching movie with you	10
	Guilt about your not playing poker with your friends	–8
Friend 1	Disappointment at not playing cards	–3
Friend 2	Disappointment at not playing cards	–3
Friend 3	Disappointment at not playing cards	–1
Total happiness score		**–8**

According to this calculation, you should clearly play poker with your friends. You would be maximizing overall utility. In fact, one might go so far as to say that, from a utilitarian perspective, watching a movie with your wife would be an immoral act.

I am sure most people would agree that, all other things being equal, it is better to promote the greatest happiness of the greatest number. But all other things are rarely equal, and finding problems with the hard-core utilitarian view is a bit like shooting fish in a barrel. We all know that some people have a greater capacity to experience pleasure and pain than do others, for instance; how do we factor that into the equation when we try to maximize pleasure? What is a meaningful metric to use to compare how much pleasure people get from very different kinds of activities? What if someone gets pleasure from torturing others; should their pleasure count equally with everyone else's? If your pathological liar child who is addicted to *Mortal Kombat* is drowning and you have to choose between saving him and saving a stranger's child who just so happens to be a virtuoso pianist, should you let your own child drown? If your own child is the virtuoso, how many strangers' children would you have to be able to save before the utility-maximizing thing to do would be to let your kid go under? And does your wife not have a better claim to your attentions than your friends do?

The essence of the difficulty with the utilitarian view comes out clearly in the following rather amusing story:

Peter Singer is a professor of ethics at Princeton, and he's the quintessential moral utilitarian. Singer believes that an action's morality cannot be judged by any transcendent standard. Instead, he suggests we ask whether a particular action will increase the sum total of happiness in the world.

For example, as George Will commented about Singer, "Should one spend a sum to ease the suffering of a family member or send the same sum to ease the sufferings of 10 Sudanese?" Singer's answer would be to send the money to Sudan, because doing so would increase the world's total amount of happiness. He also argues for allowing parents to kill their handicapped newborns, and favors euthanasia for the sick and the elderly—people who can no longer enjoy their lives and who create a burden on others.

But Singer's beliefs were put to the test when his own mother became sick with Alzheimer's. You will be relieved to know that, instead of starving his mother to death and thus increasing the world's supply of happiness, Singer is behaving hypocritically. He spends thousands of dollars providing his mother with nursing home care.

Singer sheepishly acknowledges the hypocrisy of his actions. "It's not the best use you could make of my money, that's true," he admits. But he then rationalizes his inconsistency: "It does provide employment for a number of people who find something worthwhile in what they're doing," he says.

Hogwash. A better explanation is that Peter Singer the son trumps Peter Singer the philosopher.[6]

Just as we are unwilling to agree with Kant that consequences are *never* important, we are unwilling to agree with utilitarians that consequences are all that matter.

The chinks in the utilitarian armor appeared early—most notably, with John Stuart Mill, whose father, James Mill, played Robin to Bentham's Batman. In *Utilitarianism* and *On Liberty*, Mill committed two utilitarian heresies in an attempt to rescue utilitarianism from powerful intuitive objections. First, Mill denied that push-pin was as good as poetry. He distinguished between "higher" and "lower" pleasures, and argued that if people had the opportunity to experience both, they would prefer a small quantity of a higher pleasure such as poetry to an infinite quantity of a lower one such as push-pin. (To me this seems just plain wrong. Having tasted both higher and lower pleasures, I prefer a moderate helping of each to a large helping of one and none of the other.) Second, Mill strongly defended the notion of individual rights. (This seems better.) But it is hard to know how you could justify individual rights if the most important thing is always to maximize the greatest happiness of the greatest number. After all, the painful sufferings of one Christian don't even come close to outweighing the gratification of a whole amphitheater of delighted Romans and one hungry lion. How do you justify the Christian's right to life on utilitarian grounds?

Philosophers have long suspected John Stuart Mill of being a closet deontological thinker, unwilling or unable to break with a domineering father who started young John Stuart on Greek lessons at the age of three. But later utilitarians attempted to field objections in a more sophisticated way. Probably the best adjustment is "rule utilitarianism," which differs from "act utilitarianism" in prescribing action in accordance with a set of rules which themselves tend to maximize utility. Thus if people would be happier on balance if other people kept their promises, you should always keep your promises, even if in any given case more people would be happier if you broke one.

This ingenious attempt to reconcile rules and consequences fails on at least two counts, however. First, the more seriously you take the rules, the more rule utilitarianism itself looks vulnerable to the very same objections that plagued Kant's view. Presumably, since we are happier on balance if people tell the truth and keep their promises than we would be if people lied and broke promises at will, a strict rule-utilitarian would agree with Kant that you ought not to lie to the murderer at your door. Second, the more seriously you take the rules, the less seriously you can take the underlying reason for embracing them—for if the whole point of the rules is to maximize utility, why would you pass up a utility-maximizing alternative just because it happens to be inconsistent with a generally good rule?

These are the kinds of problems that keep philosophers awake nights. I flag them only to make two simple points: (1) our moral intuitions tell us that rules and consequences are *both* important; and (2) it is hard to know how to reconcile them, manage the trade-offs between them, or weave them together in real day-to-day decisions.

Recently I had an interesting experience that illustrates this. I got off the subway and started walking toward my office. On the way I passed an outdoor bank machine. For some reason, I glanced at it as I passed—and there, sticking out of the cash slot, were three $20 bills. I stopped and looked around. No one was in sight. For a fleeting second, I felt a twinge of glee at having found $60. But almost immediately I realized that somebody had withdrawn the money and simply forgot to collect it when they took their bank card and their receipt from the machine. Not only did this money rightfully belong to whoever did this, he or she may have really felt the loss of $60. (Wealthy people, I suspect, withdraw larger sums than that.)

When I got to the office, I called the bank and explained what happened. At first, the woman who answered the phone couldn't believe that I had bothered to call. This I took as a sad commentary either on her or on society, I'm not sure which. But when she collected herself, she checked and discovered that the rightful owner of the money had already called and begged for mercy. She told me that they would credit his account right away. "What do I do with the money, then?" I asked. "Oh, just drop it off at the nearest branch," she said. "Do I need a file or a reference number or something like that?" I asked. "Nope; just drop it off."

It was then that I experienced that classic tension between rules and consequences. On the one hand, the money clearly didn't belong to me. "Finders keepers" may work in the schoolyard (though I doubt it), but it definitely didn't apply here. It was clear that this was now by right the bank's $60. If I kept it, I would, in effect, be stealing. So the deontological thing to do was clearly to return the money.

But what about consequences? The person who forgot to take the money from the bank machine was off the hook. The bank had credited his account. The marginal utility of $60 to the bank was completely negligible. This was a corporation that made $2 billion in profits the previous year. To them, $60 was dust. Lint. Nothing. To me, $60 was something. And returning it to the bank would take time and effort. As they say: "No good deed goes unpunished." Clearly, according to the Greatest Happiness Principle, I should keep the money.

Of course I returned it. I am more of a Kantian than a utilitarian. But I *don't* think that consequences are completely unimportant. I have to admit that if I had been destitute—if that $60 meant food or medicine for my sick, hungry child—I would have kept it. The bank didn't know who I was. They had no way of checking to make sure I returned the money. There was no way I would have suffered from anything other than a sense of guilt—and that would have passed soon enough. Exactly how desperate would I have had to have been before I decided to keep the money, rather than return it? I'm not sure. Moral reasoning is hard. Stay tuned.

WHOSE MORALITY?

Moral reasoning is not only hard; it is also controversial.

There is an interesting difference between what people consider *desirable* and what they consider *right*. Things can be more or less desirable. Exactly how much you want something can be a matter of degree. But if you think something is right, you think it is right, period. Generally speaking, you don't consider some things "a little bit right" and others "very right." This gives moral judgment a kind of absolute character. It also means that when people disagree about what is right and wrong, it is often hard to reach a compromise. Some people, for example, think that if you take another person's life, you should pay with your own; others think that capital punishment is unconscionable. Some people think a woman has an absolute right to decide whether to carry her fetus to term; others think she has no right to make that choice whatsoever. Some people think it is always wrong to steal; others think that there are times and situations not only when stealing is morally permissible but positively required (we have this last disagreement to thank for *Les Misérables*). There is no splitting-of-differences in any of these cases. There is no half-death penalty. Either you abort a pregnancy or you don't. You can't partially steal something.

Smart, well-intentioned people disagree on what is right and wrong. Moreover, their disagreements often have a strident tone. Moral debates are especially heated and disruptive. And yet we must all make moral choices. How do we know which choices to make, given the likelihood that well-meaning people will often urge us to make different and incompatible decisions? Should the fact that people disagree on moral judgments influence our moral decision making? If so, how?

Sometimes moral disagreements arise because people make choices impressionistically. This is a prime source of inconsistency, too, and the inconsistencies can make our choices appear hypocritical to others. Few of us have a systematic approach to moral reasoning. We tend to follow our gut, and our gut is especially bad at catching logical errors. This is because it has far fewer gray cells than our brain does. Our gut has redeeming virtues that make it worth listening to, of course: it is especially good, for instance, at communicating to our brains the content and intensity of our moral convictions. But when more than one value is at stake, we need the discipline of logic and systematic thought to make effective use of what our gut is trying to communicate to us. To the extent that sloppy moral reasoning causes moral disagreement, it should be possible to reduce it simply by thinking more systematically.

But there is still a larger problem. Even when you sort out the ambiguities and iron out any logical flaws, people sometimes still reach different judgments about what is right and wrong. Philosophers call this *descriptive ethical relativism*. Some people confuse this with *normative ethical relativism*—the view that what might be right for one person might actually be wrong for another person. You may hold this view if you think that "values" are a matter of personal taste, or that "one person has no right to judge another." Most people don't buy this. They tend to think that their own moral judgments are the right ones, and that people who disagree with them are either mistaken or evil.

How do we *really* know what is right or wrong? Science cannot help us here. Moral commitments, like religious beliefs, are not susceptible to proof. They are at least to some extent a matter of faith.

Does that mean there is no such thing as right and wrong? No. The fact that moral claims cannot be proven scientifically does not mean that they are false, just as the fact that the existence of God cannot be proven scientifically is not itself a proof that God does not exist.

So what do we do?

A good way to begin grappling with this problem is by being careful not to overstate the disagreements. For example, people don't actually disagree about the meaning of right and wrong in the abstract. They can't. If people meant entirely different things by moral concepts such as "good," "bad," "just," "unjust," "right," "wrong," "fair," or "unfair," they could not sensibly argue about how to apply them. It is an interesting ethnological fact that people of all cultures tend to use the same basic set of moral concepts in the same general way. Furthermore, once you take into account the situational contexts of the judgments people make, you find that there is actually much less disagreement about how to apply these terms than you might think.[7] Descriptive ethical relativism is not radical moral disagreement. It is merely disagreement on how to apply abstract concepts in concrete cases. Think of it as "moral disagreement on the margins."

From this perspective, acute moral debates actually take place within a fairly narrow range. Consider the intense disagreement between advocates and opponents of the death penalty. Both groups actually agree on a number of crucial things. They agree, for example, that innocent people have a right to life, and that if you are guilty of killing an innocent person other than by accident or in self-defense, you ought to be punished and punished severely. They also agree that innocent people ought not to be punished for crimes they did not commit, even if their punishment might have a positive social effect (that is, they would agree that people wrongly convicted of murder ought to be set free, even if a grisly televised electrocution might deter future murders or gratify the public's desire for revenge). Moreover, not all of their disagreements are moral disagreements. They might disagree, for example, on an empirical question, such as whether capital punishment actually does deter future murders (it doesn't). Essentially, their moral disagreement revolves around two quite focused issues: (1) whether retribution *in kind* is the appropriate punishment for murder; and (2) whether in killing an innocent person you relinquish your own right to life.

Their debate may be hot-blooded, but it is a debate over a fairly narrow range of issues. This is why we call it a *moral* debate. We would hardly call it a moral debate if the protagonists argued (for example) that there is nothing wrong with murder; that murderers should be rewarded for their marksmanship; or that murder is all right as long as it is done creatively and with a sense of humor. These positions are simply beyond the pale.

Moral debate, then, is a little bit like an argument over whether the thermostat is set too high or too low. The range of respectable disagreement is somewhere between 65° F and 75° F. People who lobby for 50° or 94° are weird; people who lobby for 20° or 110° are just plain nuts.

This insight makes it a little easier for us to bracket the metaphysical questions (which neither this book nor any other can answer satisfactorily) from the practical ones. The fact that people disagree on details but not on moral fundamentals suggests one of two things. One possibility is that there is a moral order to the universe—a true "right" and "wrong," as it were—that we as human beings with limited cognitive capacities are simply unable to grasp fully. Our vision is imperfect. Most of us can see its general shape, but few (if any) of us can see its subtle contours precisely. In fact, we cannot even know who among us sees the details better, and who sees them worse, because no one has an objective vantage point from which to judge. But since almost all of us see it roughly, our moral disagreements reflect nothing more than minor variations in perception.

Another possibility, however, is that there is no intrinsic moral order to the universe, but that for one reason or another—having to do with evolutionary pressures, perhaps—we as a species have simply developed a moral sensibility with a widely but imperfectly shared set of core moral commitments. On this hypothesis, the nihilists would be right on a crucial metaphysical point: the universe *is* meaningless. But they would be right only as the result of a lucky hunch. They would have no way of knowing for certain that they are right. And they would *still* be unhappy.

Now, I am sure that anyone with a glimmer of intellectual curiosity would like to know which is the case. We would all like to know whether there is a Truth with a capital "T," and if so, what it is. This is a natural human longing. But the important point here is that *it can make no practical difference for everyday decision making* whether there is an intrinsic moral order to the universe or merely a general human moral sensibility best understood as an evolutionary by-product or the result of some contingent historical and sociological processes. If there is an intrinsic moral order to the universe, you certainly want to be in synch with it. There is no reason to think that general moral sensibility would be radically *out* of synch with it, and so you can defensibly stake out ground anywhere within its rather narrow range. On the other hand, if there is no intrinsic moral order to the universe, you *still* want to stake out ground within the parameters of general moral sensibility—for society will make your life miserable if you don't.*

From whose morality, then, should you seek guidance? From your own—if it falls within the normal range of human moral sensibility. All well-established moral traditions, and most people's moral intuitions, include a fairly long list of guidelines with ceteris paribus ("all other things being equal") provisos. There is general agreement that killing, lying, stealing, and cheating are bad; that promoting the health and happiness of others is good; that people have duties to relieve the suffering of others; that people have espe-

---

*This line of thought bears some resemblance to Pascal's Wager. Pascal knew he could not prove the existence of God, but that professing faith was a no-lose proposition: if God existed, he would reap the rewards of faith in the afterlife; if He did not, he would be no worse off.

cially strong duties to care for family members, and for fellow members of the village, clan, tribe, nation, or country; and that the young and the aged deserve special care and attention. What unites these powerful intuitions is a sense of other-regarding concern. Morality, at bottom, is about caring for others. It is not primarily about caring for ourselves. We can be fairly confident that if someone's moral intuitions prescribe gratuitous violence, deception, or selfish exploitation, either they have lost touch with the cosmos, or some defective gene has screwed up their moral development.

Moral disagreements arise chiefly when morally normal people must choose between various ceteris paribus obligations. Some would refuse to kill anyone in order to defend their kin; others would do so at the drop of a hat. Some people would never steal food; others would do so to feed their starving children; still others would do so to feed any starving person. These differences are difference within the normal range of human moral sensibility.

By the time we reach adulthood, most of us have developed fairly detailed moral sensibilities. We do so in large part through training. We are taught what is right and wrong at our parents' knees, in school, in our communities, or in churches, mosques, and temples. We learn right and wrong also by observing the actions of people around us whom we love, trust, and respect. In short, our moral commitments are the result of social training and reinforcement.

For the vast majority of us, the precepts we learn fall well within the normal range, even if, from another social, cultural, political, or religious perspective, some of them appear wrong-headed and objectionable. But they are the best you have. As long as your moral commitments are essentially other-regarding and humane, they are really unimpeachable. You can—and should—freely participate in dialogue about your moral commitments with those who disagree with you (as they should participate in dialogue with you about *theirs*), because this will give you the opportunity to rethink and update your own moral commitments in the light of the experiences and arguments of others. But at the end of the day the single best lodestar you have is the set of principles and convictions that you have internalized over the years, and that have helped shape who you are.

Moral decision making therefore requires that you begin with your own moral commitments. This in turn requires that you spend some time and energy exploring them, thinking about them, and, if necessary, changing them in the light of your considered judgment. In this respect, as in all others, effective decision making depends critically upon self-knowledge. You should always be open to the possibility that others will persuade you to change your mind about some moral issue—but to change your mind, you first need to know it.

THE MORAL DECISION-MAKING PROCESS: A CLOSE LOOK AT A HARD CASE

Let us return, then, to the question of how you can handle rules and consequences in your moral decision making.

Moral considerations can bear on a decision in various ways. Some decisions are moral ones from the ground up: your task is simply to decide which of your available options is the best one from a moral point of view. This would be the case, for example, if someone offered to make a cash donation in your name to a charity of your choice. All you need to do here is decide which charity would put the money to the best use, morally speaking. At other times your decision may be an essentially instrumental one, but one or more of your options may raise moral concerns. Your decision in chapter 1 whether to cheat on your exam, so as to get the A you need to get into law school, falls into this category. Some of your other options, such as studying hard, raise no moral problems whatsoever.

Sometimes your moral commitments will be so strong and so clear that your decisions will be easy. If you are a confirmed pacifist, and if you receive a draft notice in the mail, you will have no difficulty choosing between reporting for duty and claiming a conscientious objector exemption. However, you may not be so lucky as to live in a country that allows such an exemption. Or, you may not qualify for an exemption because you are not a practicing member of a recognized pacifist religious community. In either of these cases, you may have to choose between serving and dodging the draft. If serving involves you even peripherally in killing people, you will understandably be unwilling to do it. But would it be worth doing if the alternative were ten years in jail? Being shot? Having your family rounded up and shot?

Whenever you face a moral choice without an obvious answer, it is possible to approach it with the same method and care as you would approach any other decision. The nine steps to effective decision making can still apply. Typically, the chief complication is the fact that you will have to choose between two or more absolute principles, or find some way to factor both rules and consequences into your decision. This is hard to do rigorously. And yet, since we do exactly this impressionistically on a daily basis anyway, we might as well try to do it systematically. Let's have a look at a way of doing this with respect to a difficult moral dilemma more and more people are having to face all the time: deciding how to care for an aging parent.

Advanced industrial countries are in a period of profound demographic change. Because of advances in medicine and improvements in lifestyle, people are living longer and longer. At the same time, birth rates have declined dramatically. The result is that the population as a whole is aging. Whereas the median American was only 34.6 years old in July 1996 (meaning that half of the population was older, and half younger), the median age is expected to rise to 37.2 in 2010 and 38.7 in 2035. Between 2000 and 2050, the proportion of the U.S. population in their prime years of economic productivity (twenty to sixty-five years of age) will shrink from 59 percent to 53 percent, while the proportion of people over sixty-five will increase from 13 percent to 20 percent. Hence the concern for "fixing Social Security" and saving Medicare. Figure 5 shows the absolute projected numbers and their relative proportions.[8]

With the passage of time, more and more families will be faced

FIG. 5. THE AGING OF THE U.S. POPULATION

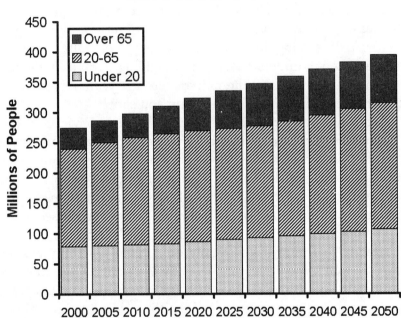

with having to decide whether to care for their aging Baby Boomer parents at home, or find alternative arrangements, such as senior communities, assisted-living facilities, and chronic-care institutions. These are profoundly moral decisions, because children clearly have a duty, where possible, to provide for their parents' care and comfort in their twilight years. Organized religions are quite explicit about this (remember "Honor thy father and thy mother"?), but it is plain that even secular humanists and hardcore Princeton utilitarians tend to agree.

At the same time, it is easy to imagine that discharging your duty toward your aging parents might get in the way of other moral duties you might have, or might have important consequences that you should factor into your decision somehow. Let's see how one well-meaning daughter used a systematic approach to help make a difficult moral decision.

Fred and Ginger are successful professionals with no children of their own who live in an upscale suburb of Los Angeles. Fred has no particular religious commitments and doesn't fight for any causes other than repealing the capital gains tax. He rebelled against his parents' doctrinaire socialism shortly before entering business school, where he took to reading Nietzsche and Ayn Rand. He believes that the main things that matter in life are fine wines, music, and fast cars (he has three of them). Ginger is a devout Presbyterian. She was always very close to her parents, and developed a strong sense of family loyalty. She was their only child. Her mother sacrificed a promising career as a dancer to raise her, and Ginger would gladly have done the same for her own child, if she and her husband had ever managed to conceive. (Fred never told her that he had long ago calculated that a vasectomy was cheaper than rearing a child, and had had his tubes snipped one day on his lunch break.)

Ginger's mother is recently widowed, and cannot bear to live by herself. She is lonely, frightened, and suffers from terrible arthritis, which makes it difficult for her to climb stairs, open jars, or even take a bath by herself. She is also beginning to suffer serious hearing loss, and has frequent attacks of dizziness and vertigo that her doctors say are caused by Ménière's disease. During a recent bout of vertigo, she fell over and broke her hip. She is now recovering in the hospital, where doctors say she will have to remain for at least six weeks.

Ginger's mother is independent-minded and professes that she does not wish to be a burden on others, but she can no longer live on her own. One of her doctors tells Ginger that her mother has confessed to him that she has had regular nightmares about being put in an institution and abandoned. The doctor asks Ginger whether she and her husband might be able to take her into their home when she is ready to leave the hospital.

Ginger broaches the subject with Fred. He goes ballistic. The last thing he wants in his house is an invalid, he says, especially a Bible-thumping one. Ginger points out that she feels an obligation to care for her mother. Fred magnanimously concedes that he can understand that, and insists that he would happily contribute to the cost of the best old-folks' home money can buy. A fight ensues.

It ends with Fred shouting that Ginger can choose between him and her mother as he slams the door on his way out for a soothing drive in his Porsche.

Fred's proposition sounds like an easy choice. But for no apparently good reason, Ginger loves Fred. She feels that it is her duty as his wife to take his preferences into account. Somewhat at a loss, she picks up her well-thumbed copy of *Decisions, Decisions*, spending particular time browsing chapters 1, 2, and 5. She pulls out a sheet of paper, on which she writes the following:

1. Objectives
    • Provide care and comfort for Mom.
    • Prevent rift with Fred.

2. Obvious options
    • Mom moves in.
    • Seniors' home.
    • Full-time live-in care for Mom?
    • Something else?

3. Implicated values
    • Duty to Mom
    • Duty to Fred
    • My sanity
    • My marriage
    • Self-respect
    • ~~Money?~~ (Probably not an issue here)*

---

*As an aside, it is worth noting how different this deliberation would be if Fred and Ginger were poor. Money certainly would be an issue. Some of the options Fred and Ginger consider here simply would not be affordable. We generally recognize many of the difficulties the poor face in our society, but we often overlook the fact that poverty can make it significantly harder for people to solve certain moral problems simply because it can constrain the set of available options. This does not mean that it is harder for the poor to act morally, since the right thing to do in any particular case is the best of the *feasible* options. But from the perspective of the poor, the fact that the rich have an easier time solving their moral dilemmas simply by virtue of being able to entertain a wider array of alternatives must surely be galling.

4. Importance of decision
   → VERY HIGH!

5. Time/energy budget for decision
   → Two weeks; Mom needs decision by then. Will take time off work if necessary.
   • One week to identify full slate of options
   • One week for evaluation and choice

6. Strategy
   → Optimize; want to find best possible solution.

She puts down her pencil and starts thinking about options.

After a couple of hours on the phone brainstorming with her friends, Ginger hears Fred return. He is having a brief guilt trip for being so hard and unfeeling, and he and Ginger kiss and make up. He announces that he has got the names and addresses of the best seniors' homes in the county, and he volunteers to find out about their facilities, cost, and availability. Ginger agrees to let him do this, and he spends the next few days gathering the information.

Meanwhile, Ginger's friends come up with an intriguing idea. Why not build an addition to the house with a separate entrance, and let Ginger's mother move in there? She would literally be right next door, and if she needed help, she could get it in a flash. She would be able to spend a great deal of time with her daughter, and Fred could see as much or as little of her as he cared to do. It would preserve a sense of privacy and independence, and would enable Ginger's mother to feel that she was not imposing herself on her daughter and that good-for-nothing son-in-law whom she can barely stand anyway. If the addition were all on one floor, built for full accessibility, and wired with the proper emergency alarms, her mother could function in it quite well. Help would be just a few moments away whenever she needed it.

The "Granny suite" option seems to have quite a lot of intuitive appeal, but Fred insists on checking out the seniors' homes before reaching any final decision. Ginger is not averse to this, since she has decided to optimize anyway: she wants to make her choice on the basis of good-quality information about *all* of her options. So she makes a few appointments for tours. She tells her mother that she is doing this, but she notices her mother's face blanch even as she nods her agreement that this is a sensible suggestion. Together, Fred and Ginger tour three facilities, two of which look wonderful to Ginger—and downright marvelous to Fred—but it is plain from Ginger's mother's demeanor when they report on their tour that she would just as soon spend the rest of her life behind bars.

Ginger asks her mother how she would feel with a full-time, live-in attendant. She replies that that would be fine, but from her tone of voice it is obvious that she does not like that idea very much, either. She has always lived with family and has never been very comfortable with strangers.

A roadblock arises. A contractor Ginger has called to consult about building a Granny suite informs her that city bylaws do not permit this. Two neighboring towns do, however. The Granny suite option now requires buying or building a new home in another community. It would take more than a year to build a new home; that is simply too long, given Ginger's mother's situation.

Ginger enlists the help of a realtor to scour nice neighborhoods in nearby towns for properties with on-site Granny suites. There are two on the market that sound nice. Both are probably affordable, given the likely selling price of Fred and Ginger's current home.

Ginger is beginning to sense that moving is going to be the best option. She has not yet sat down to evaluate all of the alternatives in careful detail, but she can tell that the seniors' homes are simply going to be too painful for her mother psychologically, and that Fred is not going to tolerate having her mother move in with them. But he is comfortable in their home and attached to it. He is also lazy. It will take something of a sales job to make him warm up to the idea of selling and moving on fairly short notice.

Ginger sits Fred down and says she wants to talk with him. She begins by affirming just how much she values him and their marriage. He says he feels the same way. She then starts talking about how important it is to her to make sure her mother is comfortable and safe in her old age. Fred interrupts and asks her to cut to the chase. She tells him that she has discovered that they cannot get a permit to add a Granny suite onto their existing house, and that if they want to pursue this kind of solution, they will have to move. Fred starts listing objections to moving—how much they like their home, how happy they are in their neighborhood, how expensive and disruptive moving can be, how they will have to leave some of their best friends, and so forth and so on. Ginger admits that these are reasons against moving, but she asks him simply to keep an open mind about all of their options, and to come with her the next day to check out the two listings the realtor has found. Reluctantly, he agrees.

Ginger is not above a little subterfuge and manipulation. She has told the realtor that she expects her husband will resist the option of moving, and she has explained why. She has also told the realtor about her husband's passion for wine, music, and cars, and has indicated that she would be especially interested in looking at houses that were suitably equipped. The two houses with Granny suites both have enormous wine cellars, fabulously expensive in-home audio systems, and four-car garages. Ginger asks the realtor to make a big deal out of these features in Fred's presence. He does, and Fred takes the bait. He is in a noticeably better mood at the end of the day than he was at the beginning.

Back home and with some time to herself, Ginger pulls out the sheet of paper and continues working on it.

7. Options.
- Mom moves in.
- ~~Seniors' home.~~ (Too hard on Mom.)
- Full-time live-in care for Mom. (Would have to be new place; old place has too many stairs.)
- Move to new house with Granny suite.

Ginger eliminates the second option by aspect. She is simply unwilling to bring her mother's worst nightmare to life.

It is time to evaluate the options. Ginger wants to have a first go at this herself, because she will have to think about some hard issues that would make Fred uncomfortable. Later she will work through them together with Fred, perhaps slightly differently. But she wants to see exactly how the options stack up in her own mind, and why.

Acknowledging that she is dealing with things that are not really quantifiable, Ginger decides that she wants to go through a numerical exercise anyway, just to see whether it leads her to conclusions that feel right to her. She begins by listing all of the considerations that are important to her, and how much weight she thinks they ought to have in her decision (she decides to score them each out of 100). She looks back at her list of implicated values and reflects upon them as follows:

- "Duty to Mom" she interprets as a concern for her mother's comfort and care. These are two quite different considerations, since her mother might be more comfortable in one situation, but might receive a higher standard of care in another.
- "Duty to Fred" she interprets as a concern for her husband's happiness.
- "My sanity" is a concern for her own mood and stress level—itself a moral consideration to some extent, since (all other things being equal) she feels that she has a duty to care for herself. But she wishes to distinguish this from her physical or material comfort, which she will factor into the decision under a separate category.
- Her husband has indicated explicitly that their marriage may be at stake in the decision, so "My marriage" also appears on her list. This is the main thing she does not want Fred to see just now.
- "Self-respect" is a function of how well she thinks she is living up to her duties as she understands them. She decides that this is covered by her concern for her mother and her concern for Fred, and as she does not want to double count those, she scratches this from her list (the importance of her own self-respect will be reflected in the weights she gives these other considerations).

- She originally scratched money from her list of implicated values, since she did not think that financial constraints were likely to play a significant role. She is, at any rate, keen on doing the right thing in the light of more important considerations, and does not much care about the cost. However, Fred has already objected to at least one option (moving) because it is expensive, and as she will want to work through the decision together with Fred, she feels she should include "Cost" on her list of implicated values, even though she plans to give it a weight of zero.

Fred has also raised concerns about their own comfort and convenience, and as she thinks about this, Ginger realizes that, while these are not moral considerations as such, nevertheless these are things implicated in the decision and about which she is not completely indifferent (although she suspects that Fred cares about them more than she does). So she decides she should consider these as well. "Comfort," she decides, has three components: how much they like the house they live in; how much they like their neighborhood; and how close they are to their friends. "Convenience" simply refers to the amount of hassle involved in pursuing any given option.

After much thought, she decides to give each of these considerations the following weights:

TABLE 15. GINGER'S WEIGHTS

Consideration	Weight
Mom's comfort	100
Mom's care	100
Fred's happiness	40
My sanity	30
My marriage	60
Cost	0
Comfort of house	10
Quality of neighborhood	5
Proximity to friends	5
Convenience	2

Ginger admits to herself that she cares more about her mother's comfort and care than she does about her marriage. In other words, she feels her duty to her mother more acutely than her duty to her husband. This is another thing she does not want Fred to know just now; but she recognizes the importance of ranking these considerations in her own mind, in case she must choose between them later.

She now scores each option on each dimension (out of 10, since she feels she cannot make finer distinctions), multiplies it by the relevant weight, and adds up the total. Table 16 shows the result. From Ginger's perspective, moving to a new house with a Granny suite is clearly the best option.

TABLE 16. GINGER'S SCORES

Consideration	Weight	Mom moves in	Full-time live-in care for Mom in new place	Move to new house with Granny suite
Mom's comfort	100	8	2	10
Mom's care	100	9	9	9
Fred's happiness	40	0	10	6
My sanity	30	1	2	7
My marriage	60	1	10	8
Cost	0	10	2	4
Comfort of house	10	8	8	8
Quality of neighborhood	5	10	10	8
Proximity to friends	5	10	10	3
Convenience	2	10	8	8
Total score	352	1990	2356	2981

There are two things worth noting about this exercise. First, Ginger takes her duties very seriously. They carry a great deal of weight with her. She is truly an other-regarding person. This is characteristic of people with a strong moral sense. Of course, she is no martyr. She shows evident concern for her own sanity, and while she does not weigh purely material factors very heavily in the decision, she is not completely indifferent to them, either. Second, she acknowledges that she is not the best person to estimate Fred's happiness with any of these options. Fred is. She is merely guesstimating here. She would really like Fred's input. But she doesn't want to show him her figures, since he would surely be upset to learn that she cares less about him than about her mother, and indeed would do the right thing by her mother even at the cost of her marriage if necessary.

Ginger asks Fred to go through the same exercise (diplomatically replacing "Ginger's happiness" for "My sanity," since the latter term connotes a certain amount of exasperation at being caught between mother and husband that Fred might resent). She invites him to add any additional considerations to the list that she might have overlooked. He asks what she means by his "happiness" as distinct from his marriage, the quality of the house they will live in, and so on. He also wants to know how he factors in the wine cellars and stereo systems. She explains that by his "happiness" she means his mood and stress level in general, not his physical comfort, though it may be that an option that scores well on one dimension will also score well on the other, since they may well be related. But they are somewhat different considerations. She suggests that he factor in the wine cellars and stereo systems under "Quality of house." As he looks over her list of implicated values, he decides that it covers everything worth factoring into the equation.

Fred raises one important objection, however. He wants to evaluate the seniors' home option. Ginger explains that, in her view, this would simply be too cruel to consider. She wants to eliminate it by aspect. Fred responds that if they are going to go through the exercise, they might as well go through it more thoroughly than less thoroughly, and that if the seniors' home option is that bad, it will drop out anyway. Ginger agrees. Table 17 gives Fred's evaluation of the options.

TABLE 17. FRED'S SCORES

Consideration	Weight	Ginger's mother moves in	Full-time live-in care for Ginger's mother in new place	Move to new house with Granny suite	Ginger's mother moves into seniors' home
Ginger's mother's comfort	10	5	8	9	8
Ginger's mother's care	10	5	10	7	10
My [Fred's] happiness	80	0	10	8	8
Ginger's happiness	60	1	6	7	0
Our marriage	60	1	8	9	1
Cost	20	9	3	5	7
Comfort of house	70	8	8	7	8
Quality of neighborhood	20	10	10	8	10
Proximity to friends	10	10	10	4	10
Convenience	10	8	10	6	10
Total Score	**350**	**1340**	**2840**	**2610**	**1980**

Fred's evaluation has several interesting features. First, he is not particularly other-regarding. He is somewhat selfish and hedonistic. He cares more about the comfort of the house he lives in than he does about his own wife's happiness. He cares very little about his mother-in-law's comfort and care. What he cares about most of all (surprise!) is his own happiness. A tear wells up in Ginger's eye as she looks over his weights, since they so clearly reveal a nature about which she had long been striving to delude herself. But at some level she admires his honesty, and she takes some comfort in the fairly high weights he has given both her happiness and their marriage. She notes with satisfaction, too, that even by his own reckoning, Fred does not think much of the seniors' home option. Even Fred confesses to being surprised by this, but on further reflection he acknowledges that this is true. He sees clearly enough that this would make Ginger miserable and do serious damage to their marriage, which would also slightly affect his mood and stress level. While he disagrees with Ginger that her mother would be uncomfortable in a seniors' home, this disagreement does not dramatically affect his evaluation of the options, because he has assigned such a low weight to her comfort anyway.

At this point it has become clear that the choice is between two alternatives: finding a new place for Ginger's mother with full-time live-in care, or moving to a new house with a Granny suite. Fred has ranked these first and second respectively, and Ginger's rankings are the reverse. The time has come to try to integrate the two evaluations somehow. Emboldened by Fred's brutal honesty in admitting both to himself and to his wife that he cares more about his own happiness and comfort than about either his marriage or his wife's happiness, Ginger drops her reluctance to letting Fred see that she cares more about her mother's comfort and care than she does about him or their marriage.

There remains the question of how to meld the two evaluations. From Ginger's perspective, there are two problems. First of all, she does not believe that Fred is giving his moral obligations due concern. Part of her rebels at the thought that his relatively weak sense of duty might defeat her relatively strong sense. This is, at bottom, a moral decision, she feels, and she believes the views of people who take moral considerations seriously ought to carry more weight than the views of moral cretins. She is certainly inclined to think that Fred's failure to cultivate his moral sensibility, and his tendency to indulge his selfish impulses, have made him a fundamentally unhappy man. His pleasures are transient; he obviously has little self-respect; and he spends most of his life under a cloud. What he really needs to do is exercise his other-regarding muscles. But is there any possibility of convincing him of this? Is there any chance that he would agree to allow her evaluation of the alternatives to count for more in their collective decision making than his? Not likely. In any case, while he is not an especially other-regarding person, he is not a sociopath who cares nothing at all for others, either. His moral impulses may be weak, but they are not nonexistent. She may disapprove of his weights, but she does not feel that she has a right to dismiss them out of hand.

The second problem Ginger perceives is that she and her husband have disagreed on some of their assessments—most importantly, those having to do with her mother's care and comfort. Ginger, for example, scored her mother's comfort with live-in care a mere "2," whereas Fred scored it "8." Ginger certainly believes that she is in a better position to judge her own mother's comfort than is Fred. But does she want to risk a fight on this point?

Ginger decides to see what happens if she simply takes the two evaluations at face value and puts them together. She notices that there is a small difference in the total number of weights they used: hers add up to 352, while Fred's add up to 350. If they are going to count their evaluations equally, they will have to "normalize" their scores. The easiest way to do this is simply to divide the total score each gave each option by the total number of weights they used. Adding up the normalized scores will give an overall, joint score for each option, as shown in table 18:

TABLE 18. JOINT SCORES

	Full-time live-in care for Ginger's mother in new place	Move to new house with Granny suite
Ginger's score	2356	2961
Ginger's total weights	352	352
Ginger's normalized score (A)	6.69	8.47
Fred's score	2840	2610
Fred's total weights	350	350
Fred's normalized score (B)	8.11	7.46
Total joint score (A+B)	**14.81**	**15.93**

It turns out that the overall score favors Ginger's preferred option anyway, so she can embrace this purely democratic method of integrating the evaluations and avoid the hassle of arguing with Fred about whether he is taking his moral duties seriously enough, or about who knows better what is best for her mom.

Suppose, for the sake of argument, that the purely democratic method of integration had resulted in a tie, or had narrowly favored Fred's preferred option. What then? Ginger might reasonably have argued that Fred should defer to her scores for her mother's comfort and care, and that they should each defer to the other's scores for their own happiness. As appendix 3 demonstrates, these adjustments in this case would not only have made the second option even *more* attractive upon integration—they would also have reversed Fred's preferences! Both Fred and Ginger would have preferred moving to the new house with the

Granny suite over providing full-time live-in care for Ginger's mother in a new place of her own.

Finally, suppose Fred's weights and scores were so skewed toward his own material comfort and convenience that *any* attempt to integrate their evaluations would have forced Ginger to accept an extremely unattractive option. In this case, the exercise would still have had considerable value, because it would have clearly demonstrated that she should consider yet another option: "Leave Fred and move in with Mom." Given the new information the exercise would have given her about her good-for-nothing husband, she would probably reduce her weights for "Fred's happiness" and "My marriage," and this new option would score very highly indeed.

Now, this procedure is not foolproof. There are various ways in which it could lead you astray if you are not careful. One danger, which Fred and Ginger managed to avoid quite well, is over-weighting certain considerations by failing to notice that two or more apparently independent implicated values are, in fact, essentially the same thing. If Fred had insisted upon scoring individual amenities such as wine cellars and stereo systems separately, in addition to providing a general score for "Comfort of house," it is likely that his evaluation of the options would have been skewed, since the amenities themselves are a major part of what makes a house comfortable.

Another danger they managed to avoid quite well is under-weighting certain considerations by virtue simply of having too long a list of implicated values. Ginger clearly means to indicate that she cares deeply about her mother's care and comfort by giving them each a weight of 100, but if she had a longer list of implicated values to which she had assigned weights, then the sum total of those weights might have been (say) 600, not 352, in which case her duty to her mother might have borne less on her evaluation than she would ideally want. To guard against this, she performed a mental check by asking herself whether she meant everything else to count for just over half as much as her mother's care and comfort combined. And indeed she did.

Ginger and Fred also both appreciate that the numerical exercise they went through gives a somewhat false sense of precision to their decision-making process. They were quantifying things that have no natural units and about which their judgments were unavoidably somewhat impressionistic. They were also combining and integrating these numbers in a way that can amplify errors in the underlying structure of their deliberation, and in their original inputs. So at the end of the day they both take seriously the question, "Has this process of evaluation clarified things in my own mind, and has it resulted in a choice that both my gut and my head agree to be the right one?" For Ginger, the answer is clearly yes. Fred is not quite so sure on first glance, particularly since the seniors' home option fared so badly in his own evaluation. But on further reflection he decides that this option appeared more attractive to him when he was concentrating too much on certain implicated values (such as convenience), and not enough on the big picture. The numerical exercise, while somewhat artificial, provided a very helpful discipline that helped him both straighten out his preferences and avoid an unnecessary fight with his wife.

Now, from a philosophical perspective, the exercise is neither fish nor fowl. It does not simply evaluate the options according to their fit with some body of moral rules or principles, the way an orthodox deontological analysis would do. But neither is it purely consequentialist. It vaguely resembles Bentham's "hedonic calculus" in form, but it does not merely attempt to maximize the pleasure of the relevant parties. It very deliberately attempts to factor duties and principles into the equation, and it does so in a way that permits trade-offs with other duties and principles, and even with nonmoral considerations. This *is* a form of utility-maximization (Fred and Ginger, after all, were trying to optimize here); but "utility" in this case very expressly included the importance of fidelity to certain principles and duties.

This is something of a heresy, from a moral philosophy perspective, and by holding it out as an example to follow, I invite brickbats from my philosopher colleagues. But I would make two points in my defense, one practical and one principled. The practical point is that this method is the best available for doing what we all do most of the time anyway. We take seriously both rules and consequences. Morality *informs* our decisions, but not always to the complete exclusion of other considerations. We are not all of us Mother Teresa. If we are going to blend rules and consequences, and if we are going to factor both moral and nonmoral considerations into our decision making, we might as well do so as clearly and as systematically as we can, and this method fares well on this criterion.

The principled point is that there is something definitely wrong with an approach to moral reasoning that cannot accommodate normal (and powerful) intuitions and practices. Moral theory can be seen as an attempt to map our actual moral sensibility, much as the purpose of attempting to formulate rules of grammar is to map our actual sense of grammaticalness.[9] I faulted Kant and Bentham because of their inability to accommodate powerful moral intuitions. The method of moral deliberation I propose here cannot fail to accommodate them.

There is no compelling reason, then, to think of moral decision making as radically different from instrumental decision making. The chief difference is that a truly other-regarding person who takes her moral impulses seriously will simply be careful to give those impulses great weight in her deliberations. But problem solving is problem solving, whether or not the problem at hand is chiefly a moral one. If you are the kind of person who takes moral decision making seriously—as you should, for the sake of your self-respect and well-being, in view of the fact that it is part of human nature to do so and that stifling one's nature is a surefire recipe for misery—you should find that it pays to approach moral decisions in precisely the same way as you would approach nonmoral ones.

It is certainly *not* the case, at any rate, that purely instrumental decisions warrant *greater* attention to process than moral choices do. If anything, you should take greater care when attempting to do what is *right* than when merely attempting to get what you *want*.

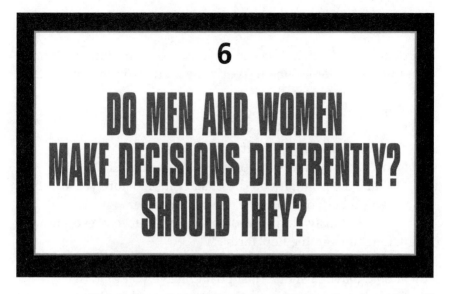

6

DO MEN AND WOMEN MAKE DECISIONS DIFFERENTLY? SHOULD THEY?

She's been on the team for three seasons now, but the males still don't trust her. They know that if she had to choose between catching a fly ball and saving an infant's life, deep in her soul, she would probably elect to save the infant's life, without even considering whether there were men on base.
                                    —Dave Barry, "Why Sports Is a Drag"
                                    (Dave Barry's Greatest Hits)

Jack and Jill enjoy each other's company. They go hiking in the mountains together. They like to rollerblade. They like to dine out and go to movies. They are deeply and profoundly in love. They are the very image of domestic bliss.

One evening, they go grocery shopping. The expedition begins pleasantly. They are both in a good mood. Halfway down aisle 2, however, things start to go awry. Jack sprints ahead, grabbing boxes, cans, and bottles from the shelves, tossing them haphazardly into the basket, then wheeling around for more. Jill asks him to wait, plucks things from the basket, checks the price, and scans the ingredients. "This is too expensive," she says. "The other brand is better." "This has too much sugar." "We have plenty of this at home already; we don't need any more."

At first, Jack is amused. Then he is irritated. Eventually he starts to fume. In aisle 4 he can no longer contain himself. "So, do you think we should plan to spend the night?" he snaps.

"What's your rush?"

"I'm not in a rush."

"It sure looks to me like you're in a rush."

"No, I'm not. Can we hurry up, please?"

"Don't you think it's important to shop carefully?"

"What's the point, if you die of starvation before you finish?"

"If you'd help me here, we'd get done faster."

"You obviously don't need my help. You veto everything I want. Oh, here are the Pop Tarts . . ."

"Those have too much fat."

"Look, maybe I should just go and leave you to it."

"Jack, it's important to do these things together. Besides, I want your company. And your help."

"There's precious little evidence for *that*!"

"Fine, I'll just do it myself!"

Things go from bad to worse. Every decision is a fresh irritant. By aisle 6 they are steaming mad at each other. By the time they get to the checkout, they are no longer on speaking terms. Jill reaches for her wallet. Jack loses his temper and insists on paying.

Here we see gender-based decision-making stereotypes. Many couples shop together in perfect harmony. Sometimes when they don't, it is the man, not the woman, who shops more slowly and more carefully. But was that a little smile of recognition I saw on your face just there? Come on, now, admit it.

It turns out that studies comparing the shopping habits of men and women reveal some interesting differences. Men do tend to shop more quickly than women, buy more on impulse, pay less attention to nutrition, and spend more money. The stereotypes, in short—while admittedly overdrawn cartoons—appear to have a grain of truth. They may also help explain why the decisions we sometimes make turn out badly, and why they sometimes generate conflict.

We operate with stereotypes all the time, and there are perhaps none so well developed and so familiar as gender stereotypes.

Indeed, folk wisdom has it that men and women behave in such radically different yet somehow predictable ways that it seems at times as if they simply came from different planets. This is the premise, at any rate, of John Gray's runaway best-seller, *Men Are from Mars, Women Are from Venus: A Practical Guide for Improving Communication and Getting What You Want in Your Relationships.*[1] This is a book that invoked, built on, reinforced, and perpetuated gender stereotypes. It was such a hit that it spawned sequels on dating, love, and sex, and inspired a television show. Some of the Mars/Venus books are available on audiocassettes and in Spanish translation. Apparently, there is even a board-game version, though I haven't seen it in my local toy store. There are even copycat books. My favorites are *Women May Be from Venus, but Men Are Really from Uranus* and *Women Are from Venus, Men Are from Hell.*[2]

Are men and women so very different? If so, do these differences translate into different decision-making styles? And if they do, is one style better than another? These are the topics I address in this chapter.

I would be unwise if I did not acknowledge at the outset that I tread on dangerous ground here. In the first place, it is clear that these are extremely difficult questions with complex, somewhat unclear answers. I will have to simplify a great deal, and skip over a great deal else, which will invite inaccuracies and misunderstandings. Second, these issues are normatively and politically charged. Whatever I say is bound to offend someone. Third, there are many people who would insist that I am not competent to discuss these questions because, as a male scholar who has not made gender a particular focus of my own research, I have no expertise. Perhaps most importantly, from the perspective of my likely critics, I cannot speak for women, not having experienced the world *as* a woman.

There is certainly merit in all of these objections, but I have three compensatory assets: (1) I can read; (2) I am sensible; and (3) I have expert female colleagues who kindly let me inflict drafts of this chapter upon them. Nothing that I say in this chapter has escaped the scrutiny of a competent, full-time, professional woman. This is simply another way of saying that I can always blame others for my errors.

SEX AND GENDER

To avoid confusion later, it is a good idea to begin by clearing up the meanings of some key terms and exploring the relationships between them. The two most important of these are *sex* and *gender*. By "sex" I mean not the activity but the biological attributes of those who engage in it. At the risk of stating the obvious, there are two sexes: male and female. Men are members of the male sex, and women are members of the female sex.

There are various possible ways of distinguishing men from women. The average person on the street does it all the time simply by looking for outward clues: height, build, hair pattern, voice tone, clothing, behavior, and so on. This is usually good enough, but it is neither scientific nor reliable. Men can easily look, dress, and act like women, and vice versa. We have all had the embarrassing experience of mistaking a male for a female or a female for a male.

Dogs have a more reliable technique: they check reproductive equipment. While this is more accurate, it is a practice polite society frowns upon.

A third way is to check chromosomes. Everyone gets at least one chromosome from each parent, and the vast majority of us get only one from each. If you have two X (female) chromosomes, you are a woman, and if you have one X (female) and one Y (male) chromosome, you are a man. Think of this as the genetic analogue to male dominance.

This may seem like an unnecessary rehashing of common knowledge, but, in fact, it turns out that more people are sexually ambiguous than you might think. Either they are neither clearly male nor clearly female, anatomically speaking (as a result of either genetic factors or fetal development), or they have an extra chromosome (XXY). The latter case is especially interesting. Since the Y chromosome contains the genes that tend to encourage strength and bulk, yet is outnumbered by two X chromosomes, someone with an XXY chromosomal makeup may resemble a woman anatomically yet more closely approximate a man's physical strength—like the former East German women's Olympic swimming team.

We feel a social compulsion to classify everyone as either male or female, and we exert enormous pressure—and sometimes even inflict surgery—upon people to make them outwardly unambiguous.[3] For this reason, it makes sense to think of sex not merely as a biological category, but also, at least partly, as a *social* one. But while the number of people who are biologically sexually ambiguous is almost certainly larger than you would guess, the fact remains that as a proportion of the human population as a whole, it is a very small group. To a first approximation, then, we can assume that everyone is either a man or a woman biologically.

Gender is quite different. Gender is largely (some would argue *entirely*) a socially constructed category. We use it as a shorthand to catalogue behavioral characteristics people display. There are two genders: *masculine* and *feminine*. If you asked two people to draw up a list of masculine and feminine traits, you wouldn't necessarily get identical lists, but there would at least be a family resemblance between them. To be "masculine," most people would say, is to be brave, courageous, independent, self-reliant, strong-willed, tough-minded, cool-headed, rational, logical, methodical, decisive, physically strong, and violent. To be "feminine," most would say, is to be quiet, demure, sweet, charming, thoughtful, caring, sensitive, passionate, creative, intuitive, emotional, dependent, physically weak, and squeamish. Hollywood icons of masculinity include Clint Eastwood, Arnold Schwarzenegger, and John Wayne. Hollywood icons of femininity include Ingrid Bergman, Audrey Hepburn, and Marilyn Monroe.

There are two things worth noting about masculinity and femininity. First, they are ideal-types. In the real world, everybody exhibits some mixture of both. Nobody exhibits purely masculine or purely feminine characteristics. The only question is the relative balance of the two. John Wayne was thoughtful, caring, and sensitive in *The Green Berets*. Audrey Hepburn was independent, self-reliant, and cool-headed in *Breakfast at Tiffany's*. It is hard to imagine a society more taken with masculine and feminine ideals than Georgian England, nor a literary genre that traded in them more energetically than romantic fiction, and yet even in Jane Austen's *Pride and Prejudice*—the archetype of the Georgian romance—the essentially feminine heroine Elizabeth Bennet is strong-willed and tough-minded, and the essentially masculine hero, Mr. Darcy, is passionate and emotional. Indeed, Darcy's inner struggle against his feminine side—which he regards as a character flaw (he thinks it unmanly that his mind cannot control his heart)—is what makes him an interesting and believable character instead of a cardboard cutout.

This leads directly to the second thing worth noting: society values masculinity more highly than femininity. (The technical social-scientific term for a social structure that systematically favors the masculine over the feminine is "patriarchy.") In saying this, I don't mean simply to imply that we think being masculine is good and being feminine is bad. Being called "masculine" can certainly be construed as an insult. I know a lot of women who wouldn't take it kindly. I know a lot of men who wouldn't take it kindly, either, for that matter. What I mean when I say that society values masculinity more highly than femininity is that the struggle for power, wealth, opportunity, and influence favors masculine virtues over feminine ones, and penalizes masculine vices (e.g., a propensity toward violence) far less harshly than feminine ones (e.g., a tendency to react to things emotionally). Being tough never hurt Margaret Thatcher. Ed Muskie's presidential hopes died the day he wept on national television.

While everyone displays some mixture of masculine and feminine attributes, there is a clear correlation between being a man and being masculine, and between being a woman and being feminine. There are feminine men and masculine women, but the average man is more masculine than the average woman. This much few people would dispute.

The debates get ugly, though, when you take the next step and ask, "Does this correlation have a biological basis?" In other words, are men biologically predisposed to exhibit more masculine traits, and women predisposed to exhibit more feminine ones? Or is the correlation purely an artifact of social norms and customary practices—for instance, the subtle and not-so-subtle ways in which we teach boys and girls from a very young age to behave?

The reason this is such a charged issue is that some people would seize upon "natural" differences between men and women to justify inequalities. Indeed, historically, this has been the norm. Women's imagined "inabilities" have been used as barriers to limit their social, economic, and political roles virtually everywhere. As recently as the last century in the so-called enlightened West, women were denied the vote in part because of their alleged inability to understand public issues and exercise responsible judgment.

Of course, some cultures and religions take great pains to pretend that sex roles grounded in natural differences between men and women are not "unequal," merely "different." But this smacks too much of the old racial doctrine of "separate but equal" for my tastes. Blacks were certainly kept separate from whites in the Jim Crow South and in apartheid South Africa, but anybody who thinks they enjoyed even a semblance of equality lives in cloud-cuckoo land. No matter where you look, you will find that women do not have the same opportunities as men. Women make up just over half of the world's population, but are responsible for two-thirds of all working hours, represent one-third of the world's paid labor force, receive one-tenth of the world's income, own less than 1 percent of the world's property, and are grossly underrepresented in politics, business, and the professions. In some places women do not enjoy equal protection of the laws. In a few places, they are completely at men's mercy.

It is easy to see why people who are committed to equality would see great danger even in entertaining the idea that there might be natural differences between the sexes. This is because a lot of people have trouble distinguishing between "different from" and "better than." As far as I can tell, there is no logical connection between natural differences between the sexes and social inequalities. What possible biological difference between the sexes could justify the fact that men own more than 99 percent of the world's property? If social inequality had roots in biology, why would inequalities between the sexes be so much more pronounced in Sierra Leone than in Sweden?[4] Aren't men more or less the same everywhere, biologically speaking? Women, too? It seems to me that it is *inequality* that is socially constructed.

Does biology predetermine gender? Certainly not in the strictest possible sense. The mere fact that there are feminine men and masculine women demonstrates this. And yet it is difficult to escape the conclusion that there is some connection. Exactly how much of a connection we will probably never know. If you wanted to gauge the relative strength of "nature" and "nurture" in shaping gender attributes, you would have to conduct an experiment. You would have to raise some large number of boys and girls in a completely gender-neutral environment and see whether the boys tended to display masculine characteristics and the girls feminine ones. We have no gender-neutral environment in which to conduct such an experiment, and it is hard to know how we would even design one. Even if we could, it would be illegal to try. Human-subject ethics codes do not permit this kind of research. So the best we can do is to try to draw inferences obliquely.

Natural scientists make fairly strong claims about the natural connection between sex and gender. Evolutionary biologists, for example, have shown that in other species, males are far more likely than females to compete for status and power, engage in violence, murder, rape, bond for instrumental as opposed to emotional reasons, or strike out on their own. Such patterns are very evident in our closest animal relatives, the chimpanzees.

Neurophysiologists tell us that there are some interesting structural differences between male and female brains that may have something to do with differences in behavior and skill. Different parts of the brain perform different tasks, and some parts of the brain are larger or more complex in men than in women and vice versa. Differences in the ways in which male and female brains are "wired up" may help explain why women tend to do better than men on verbal tasks while men tend to do better on spatial tasks, or why women seem more adept at doing many things at once, while men are more comfortable doing one thing at a time. Neurological differences may even help explain women's "intuition." Men's brains may be less adept at storing and processing subtle cues, and may make it harder for those parts of the brain responsible for the emotions or the subconscious to gain access to the conscious part of the brain. We don't know a great deal about this yet, but we know enough to suspect that neurological differences are real and important.

And then there are hormones. "Men and women differ biologically mainly because men produce 10 to 20 times as much testosterone as most women do," writes Andrew Sullivan, "and this chemical, no one seriously disputes, profoundly affects physique, behavior, mood, and self-understanding."[5] Sullivan should know. When he discovered that his natural testosterone levels had started to drop, he began a regimen of supplementary testosterone therapy. The results were dramatic, immediate, and far-reaching:

> Because the testosterone is injected every two weeks, and it quickly leaves the bloodstream, I can actually feel its power on almost a daily basis. Within hours, and at most a day, I feel a deep surge of energy. It is less edgy than a double espresso, but just as powerful. My attention span shortens. In two or three days after my shot, I find it harder to concentrate on writing and feel the need to exercise more. My wit is quicker, my mind faster, but my judgment is more impulsive. It is not unlike the kind of rush I get before talking in front of a large audience, or going on a first date, or getting on an airplane, but it suffuses me in a less abrupt and more consistent way. In a word, I feel braced. For what? It scarcely seems to matter.
>
> And then, after a few days, as the testosterone peaks and starts to decline, the feeling alters a little. I find myself less reserved than usual, and more garrulous. The same energy is there, but it seems less directed toward action than toward interaction, less toward pride than toward lust. . . .
>
> Then there's anger. I have always tended to bury or redirect my rage. I once thought this an inescapable part of my personality. It turns out I was wrong. Late last year, mere hours after a T shot, my dog ran off the leash to forage for a chicken bone left

in my local park. The more I chased her, the more she ran. By the time I retrieved her, the bone had been consumed, and I gave her a sharp tap on her rear end. "Don't smack your dog!" yelled a burly guy a few yards away. What I found myself yelling back at him is not printable . . . but I have never used that language in public before, let alone bellow it at the top of my voice. He shouted back and within seconds I was actually close to hitting him. He backed down and slunk off. I strutted home, chest puffed up, contrite beagle dragged sheepishly behind me. It wasn't until half an hour later that I realized I had been a complete jerk and had nearly gotten into the first public brawl of my life. I vowed to inject my testosterone at night in the future.[6]

Clearly, then, there is *some* link between biology and behavior. Nature does make a difference. But nurture is not powerless, either. If it were, how could we explain why some societies are more peaceful and more egalitarian than others? The nature-versus-nurture debate will continue.

FEMININITY, MASCULINITY, AND DECISION-MAKING MYTHS

Everything I've said to this point suggests that the title of the chapter is not quite right. The question is not whether men and women make decisions differently, but whether there is a masculine and a feminine decision-making style. A decision-making style is a behavioral trait, after all, not a physiological one, and if gender differences are evident in decision making, we should expect to find plenty of men who make decisions in a feminine way, and plenty of women who make decisions in a masculine way. Nevertheless, almost all of the literature on gender and behavior presents itself as exploring differences in the behavior of men and women, as though there were some near-perfect correlation between sex and gender.

You would think that gender and decision making would be a well-studied subject. It is not—at least, not in general. There are plenty of studies comparing the performance and behavior of males and females on specific mental tasks. There are lots of studies, too, about the effect of gender roles on personal and social choices. But the picture that emerges from this body of research is murky and incomplete. It's hard to look at it and say that we have a firm empirical grip on whether men and women tend to make decisions in systematically different ways.

There are, however, well-developed and familiar myths about how men and women make decisions. For the most part, these myths cohere with what psychologists, sociologists, and others tell us about gender and behavior. It is useful to explore these myths, because, just like masculinity and femininity themselves, these myths are stereotypes—simplified, exaggerated abstractions that define the extremes between which we all find ourselves. Understanding the stereotypes can help us understand ourselves, because they throw the subtle contours of our own personalities into bold relief, even if they aren't especially accurate.

The myths themselves are quite simple. Men are reputed to be cool-headed, rational, logical, efficient, and decisive. They listen to their heads, not to their hearts. Since they do not look back, they rarely feel regret. Women, on the other hand, are indecisive, intuitive, and illogical. They let emotions get in the way of their reason. They agonize before making a decision, and afterward they constantly fret that they have made the wrong one. Now, right away we can see that these myths are downright silly. If given the choice, a woman is much more likely than a man to buy a Volvo instead of an MG convertible. Who is being more rational and logical here? Who has let emotion get in the way of reason? Who is going to feel regret? But let's put this aside for the moment.

Also according to the stereotype, men approach decision making in a technical, instrumental way. Decision making, for a man, is nothing but a special case of problem solving. It represents an intellectual challenge. Solving the challenge is the material reward; solving it well is the psychic reward. Both are important. Taking too long and relying on others are evidence of incapacity, and hence unmanliness. This is why men never look at assembly instructions. Women, on the other hand, see in a decision an opportunity for relationship building. They will consult ad nauseam, and will subordinate their own preferences to those of others if this will make others happy or strengthen ties between them. Their hand-wringing over whether they have made the right decision is merely a poorly disguised request for affirmation and stroking.

Now, the odds are poor that anyone sees him-or herself perfectly reflected in either of these myths. But the odds are good that men will relate better to the masculine decision-making myth, and that women will relate better to the feminine one. What we know about other aspects of gender and behavior suggests why this is so.

In 1982, Carol Gilligan published a path-breaking study, *In a Different Voice: Psychological Theory and Women's Development*.[7] While this book did not explore decision making as such, it did have a great deal to say about how males and females approach an important *class* of decisions: moral decisions, which we looked at in the previous chapter. Gilligan found strong and systematic differences in the moral-psychological development of boys and girls, and of young men and young women. The males in her study gave strong evidence of reasoning in accordance with what she called an "ethic of justice," in which everyone is treated the same according to abstract universal principles of right. The females in her study, in contrast, gave strong evidence of reasoning in accordance with what she called an "ethic of care," in which the primary duty is to avoid hurting others. The females among Gilligan's subjects clearly identified themselves as members of networks of relationships in which the concerns and desires of others powerfully shaped their own preferences. The males, on the other hand, clearly valued independence and autonomy above all else, and were prepared to demand the greatest latitude in their choices consistent with a similar latitude for all. The males, in other words, tended to think deontologically, and the females tended to think consequentially. The point of Gilligan's study was to show that the prevailing theories of moral psychological development in children—those of Freud, Piaget, and Erikson, for example—unconsciously mistook a masculine style of moral reasoning for the "normal" style. Seen in this light, women's moral development seemed at best stunted and at worst deviant. But an unintended consequence of Gilligan's study was to highlight important differences in male and female social dynamics that are clearly reflected in stereotypes about masculine and feminine decision-making styles.

Gilligan's study (among others) suggested that certain gender-based differences in behavior have roots in deep psychological needs. A man's self-esteem relies not only on a sense of capability, but also on the admiration of others. Wealth, social status, and political power gratify a man's self-esteem because they are outward marks of accomplishment. You cannot be rich or powerful in any meaningful sense if everyone else is, too, and so a man's self-esteem depends to some extent on people comparing him favorably to others. In short, men must compete successfully with others to feel really good about themselves. So a man will feel good about himself if he is able to fix a broken radio. He will feel *very* good about himself if someone finds out he has fixed a broken radio and says, "My, aren't you handy!" He will feel *absolutely terrific* if someone says, "Wow! Joe spent a whole week trying to fix that radio and failed!"

A woman's self-esteem seems to depend more heavily on whether she can be brought to believe that she is doing something useful and important with her life. "Useful" and "important" are often other-regarding standards. It is in helping others that many women find the most ego gratification. Again, public recognition enhances the effect, but is not always necessary. In fact, often it is not even sufficient. Some women will always think themselves worthless human beings no matter how many people tell them they are wonderful, and no matter how much good they do for others.

Again, I want to stress that these are stereotypes. There are plenty of men who sustain their sense of self-worth by helping others and do not care whether they are rich, powerful, or noticed. Plenty of women need to climb the corporate ladder, stomping on others on their way up. I would also like to stress that the distinction I have drawn here is not a simple distinction between egocentrism and altruism. The fact that it is important for you to be recognized for your capacities—for who you are—does not mean that you do not care for other people, any more than the fact that it is important for you to be recognized for what you do for others means that you do not care about yourself. A recent study of why women chose nursing careers illustrates the point. While Gilligan's "ethic of care" featured prominently in the responses women gave when asked why they decided to become nurses, even more striking was the sense of personal empowerment.[8] There are many different ways of satisfying the basic human need for efficacy and control, and altruistic behavior is one of them.

It is in the study of communication between the sexes that these various differences between men and women, and between the masculine and the feminine, are most evident and most entertaining. No one has done a better job of exploring them than Deborah Tannen. Her 1990 best-seller, *You Just Don't Understand: Women and Men in Conversation*,[9] is a rich catalogue of stories and anecdotes illustrating the perils and pitfalls of men and women trying to communicate. The chief virtue of the book is that it enables us to see clearly how different styles of communication can lead men and women not merely to misunderstand each other, but to hurt one another, even when they have the best of intentions at heart.

Consider the following example:

> Eve had a lump removed from her breast. Shortly after the operation, talking to her sister, she said that she found it upsetting to have been cut into, and that looking at the stitches was distressing because they left a seam that had changed the contour of her breast. Her sister said, "I know. When I had my operation I felt the same way." Eve made the same observation to her friend Karen, who said, "I know. It's like your body has been violated." But when she told her husband, Mark, how she felt, he said, "You can have plastic surgery to cover up the scar and restore the shape of your breast."
>
> Eve had been comforted by her sister and her friend, but she was not comforted by Mark's comment. Quite the contrary, it upset her more. Not only didn't she hear what she wanted, that he understood her feelings, but, far worse, she felt he was asking her to undergo more surgery just when she was telling him how much this operation had upset her. "I'm not having any more surgery!" she protested. "I'm sorry you don't like the way it

looks." Mark was hurt and puzzled. "I don't care," he protested. "It doesn't bother me at all." She asked, "Then why are you telling me to have plastic surgery?" He answered, "Because you were saying you were upset about the way it looked."

Eve felt like a heel: Mark had been wonderfully supportive and concerned throughout her surgery. How could she snap at him because of what he said—"just words"—when what he had done was unassailable? And yet she had perceived in his words metamessages that cut to the core of their relationship. It was self-evident to him that his comment was a reaction to her complaint, but she heard it as an independent complaint of his. He thought he was reassuring her that she needn't feel bad about her scar because there was something she could do about it. She heard his suggestion that she do something about the scar as evidence that he was bothered by it. Furthermore, whereas she wanted reassurance that it was normal to feel bad in her situation, his telling her that the problem could easily be fixed implied she had no right to feel bad about it.

Eve wanted the gift of understanding, but Mark gave her the gift of advice. He was taking the role of problem solver, whereas she simply wanted confirmation for her feelings.[10]

The example nicely illustrates what is no doubt a common gendered dynamic, but it actually points to a weakness in Tannen's central thesis. Tannen argues that when men communicate they are marking status, trying to preserve independence, and trying to avoid failure. But when women communicate they are trying to establish and sustain networks of connections for mutual confirmation and support, or to reach consensus. I cannot speak to how well Tannen's interpretation fits the female experience, but as a man who has at one time or another exhibited *all* of Tannen's male communication pathologies, I was struck the first time I read the book many years ago, and again when I reread it recently, how poorly this interpretive lens fits some of her male examples. No doubt there are plenty of situations in which Tannen would be perfectly right to suggest that men's ulterior motive is to establish hierarchy or preserve autonomy—what she prefers to call a "metamessage" of control. This is, after all, what we would expect if recognition played an important role in maintaining male self-esteem. But not everything is a self-esteem game, and in any case trying to reassure one's spouse is a nice thing to do about which one is entitled to feel good. Mark wasn't negotiating hierarchy with Eve in this particular case. He was trying to be helpful. He is obviously not the kind of despicable cad who would use the occasion of his own wife's breast surgery to elevate himself at her expense.

What else might have been going on here? I think some of Tannen's other examples help provide the answer. I will quote one more, and then provide an anecdote of my own, before I suggest what I think may be a preferable way of interpreting some of the male behavior she describes.

Tannen reports a conversation between a couple in their car in which the woman had asked her husband whether he would like to stop for a drink. He answered "No," and they kept driving. Later, he learned that his wife was annoyed with him, because *she* had wanted to stop for a drink. Why didn't she just say so? he wondered. Why did she play games? "The wife, I explained," Tannen writes, "was annoyed not because she had not gotten her way, but because her preference had not been considered. From her point of view, she had shown concern for her husband's wishes, but he had shown no concern for hers."[11]

This anecdote is interesting because it shows us quite clearly how Tannen interpreted the husband's "no"—*he wanted to have his way*. I don't know whether he actually said that in the interview Tannen relates, but he certainly doesn't put it that way in her account of it. I'm sure we can all agree that he was insensitive, or simply too lazy to think about whether his wife's question was pregnant with significance. Perhaps these amount to the same thing. But I suspect he may just have taken her question at face value. The suggestion that he was actually using such an innocuous question as the occasion for asserting control or preserving independence seems a bit far-fetched.

The point emerges even more clearly from an experience a close friend of mine had in graduate school. He was a well-meaning, honest, upright character whose long-standing girlfriend had just dumped him. He was lonely and missed female companionship. He dated several women, most of whom were not especially good matches for him. At one point, though, he struck up a relationship that seemed quite promising. Before long, however, it became clear that she began to doubt that the relationship had a future. They liked each other very much, but she decided that she had to move on. He thought things were going fairly well and wanted to work to keep the relationship going, but he sensed the end was near. He tried to hide his disappointment, but we could all see that he was going to be hurt when the axe fell.

She finally called him up and explained as carefully and as compassionately as she could that, much as she liked him and enjoyed his company, it was clear to her that they had no long-term future together, and she "just wanted to be friends." (These, by the way, are the most painful words anybody can inflict upon a young man. If you're thinking of dumping your boyfriend, be kind and simply say, "You're history, Jack.") She then said that she considered them both free to date others. "Well, I'm very disappointed," my friend said. "I'm sorry to hear that you feel that way. Obviously I have to respect your wishes. Do you think you could introduce me to some of your friends?"

She slammed down the receiver so hard that his eardrum almost burst. Seconds later she called back and let forth a torrent of indignant abuse. She was barely able to breathe between her screams and her tears. "How can you be such an insensitive pig?" she demanded to know. "What did I do?" he protested. "You just broke up with me! You just finished saying that we were both free to date others!"

We all had a good laugh about this after the fact, though the men laughed harder than the women did. Without exception, the women who heard the story were appalled at what he had done and sympathized with her completely. The men understood at an intellectual level the mistake he had made. They agreed that he had been insensitive. But the men also felt obliged to console him—with precisely the kind of backslapping "That's women for ya; who can figure 'em?" demeanor that you would expect from males in their early twenties—by congratulating him on his unimpeachable logic. He wanted to date a woman; she liked him but no longer wanted to date him; she knew other women who might want to date him; she could help him by introducing him to others. This is exactly what the eponymous hero of Anthony Trollope's *Phineas Finn* had asked of Lady Laura when she refused him in favor of Mr. Kennedy—and *she* had been man enough to oblige![12]

Here is a case where it is clearly wrong to interpret male speech as status marking and seeking to preserve autonomy. My friend was the one who wanted to maintain the connection; *she* was the one seeking independence.

All three of these examples have a common theme: men have a tendency to be literal. They pay attention to text, and are less adept at reading subtext. Why this is so is unclear. It may have a physiological basis. Perhaps male brains are just wired badly for picking up and processing subtle messages. Perhaps there is an evolutionary explanation: it may be that women, having had to survive in patriarchal societies in which displeasing the powerful could be disastrous, found it advantageous to cultivate empathy; to try to anticipate the needs, desires, and anger of others; and to pick up subliminal cues. They may have passed these skills on to their daughters through socialization, through natural selection, or both. Neither I nor anyone else really knows. But I think it is safe to say that the average man interprets things more literally than does the average woman.

Apparently this is true also of Martians and Venusians. Gray provides the following helpful table of examples:[13]

Women say things like this	Men respond like this
"We never go out."	"That's not true. We went out last week."
"Everyone ignores me."	"I'm sure some people notice you."
"I am so tired, I can't do anything."	"That's ridiculous. You are not helpless."
"I want to forget everything."	"If you don't like your job, then quit."
"The house is always a mess."	"It's not always a mess."
"No one listens to me anymore."	"But I am listening to you right now."
"Nothing is working."	"Are you saying it is my fault?"
"You don't love me anymore."	"Of course I do. That's why I'm here."
"We are always in a hurry."	"We are not. Friday we were relaxed."
"I want more romance."	"Are you saying I am not romantic?"

In most of these cases, men evaluate what women say for their literal truth and respond accordingly. Gray writes: "You can see how a 'literal' translation of a woman's words could easily mislead a man who is used to using speech as a means of conveying only facts and information. We can also see how a man's responses might lead to an argument. . . . The number one complaint women have in relationships is: 'I don't feel heard.' Even this complaint is misunderstood and misinterpreted!"[14]

When men do pay attention to subtext, they often misread it. In Gray's list, the subtext to "Nothing is working" is not "You are an incompetent loser," and the response "Are you saying it is my fault?" is inappropriate. The man here is being overly defensive. But at least he is trying to read subtext. If he were merely being literal, he would have replied, "That's not true; the doorbell still rings." More successful is the response to "I want more romance." The subtext here almost certainly *is* "You are not romantic enough."

Tannen herself is sensitive to the difference between text and subtext. She distinguishes, for example, between "rapport-talk," in which women tend to engage, and "report-talk," which is more common among men. Rapport-talk is "a way of establishing connections and negotiating relationships." It provides an opportunity for establishing trust, creating intimacy, strengthening the bonds of friendship, legitimizing one's concerns, validating one's feelings, addressing insecurities, or building self-esteem. Report-talk conveys information. Tannen suggests that rapport-talk can be thought of as "private speaking"—the kind of communication that takes place in the intimacy of the home, for example—while report-talk can be thought of as "public speaking"—the kind of thing one could comfortably engage in with strangers. Yet Tannen still insists that we can best make sense of this difference by looking at it through an interpretive lens contrasting women's search for connection with men's search for status. "For most men," Tannen writes, "talk is primarily a means to preserve independence and negotiate and maintain status in a hierarchical social order. This is done by exhibiting knowledge and skill, and by holding center stage through verbal performance such as story-telling, joking, or imparting information. From childhood, men learn to use talking as a way to get and keep attention."[15]

No doubt the average man is more comfortable speaking in public than is the average woman, and public speaking can be both competitive and ego-gratifying. But Tannen mistakes a special case of report talk—competitive report-talk—for the general category. Very often men's conversations simply convey information. Men sometimes mean nothing more and nothing less than what they say. Consider the following snippet of humor recently circulating on the Internet:

MEN AND WOMEN ON HAIRCUTS

(1) Women:

> "Oh my God, I love your haircut!"
> "You really like it?"
> "Oh, it's fabulous! What a great color!"
> "You think it's okay? I wasn't sure about it. I'm thinking I should have stuck with my natural color, but it's so dull. . . . "
> "Are you kidding? I'd *die* for your natural color. But red really suits you, too! And I *love* the way you cut it just above the shoulder. I could never do that; I've got these two-by-fours for shoulders. . . ."
> "What are you talking about? You have great shoulders. I always wondered why you hid them—not that long hair doesn't look great on you or anything, but you never even tie it back."
> "Oh, I couldn't do that! I'd look like a water buffalo with my hair tied back."
> "No you wouldn't, you've got great shoulders; you should try it."
> "You really think so?"
> "Sure. It'd be great! I can't do it, because my hair has a mind of its own. If I grow it out and tie it back it just finds some way to escape, and then I look like an Afghan caught in a tornado. I've thought about growing it out and trying a perm, but I don't know; what do you think?"
> "A perm could work. You've got such great hair. But I like this cut; it suits you."

"Thanks."
"I should get my hair cut, too."
"Your hair looks great."

(2) Men:

"Haircut?"
"Yeah."

Rapport-talk is not always such a benign connection-building activity, either. This is a point made particularly well by Eric Berne in his 1964 best-selling book on transactional analysis, *Games People Play: The Psychology of Human Relationships*.[16] Berne presents and examines a number of "games" in which people adopt certain roles and play out particular kinds of scripts, essentially for ulterior (Berne says "dishonest") purposes. One of these games is "Why Don't You—Yes But," a game, Berne writes, that "occupies a special place in game analysis, because it was the original stimulus for the concept of games. It was the first game to be dissected out of its social context, and since it is the oldest subject of game analysis, it is one of the best understood."[17]

Berne provides the following example from a group therapy session:

> White: "My husband always insists on doing our own repairs, and he never builds anything right."
> Black: "Why doesn't he take a course in carpentry?"
> White: "Yes, but he doesn't have time."
> Blue: "Why don't you buy him some good tools?"
> White: "Yes, but he doesn't know how to use them."
> Red: "Why don't you have your building done by a carpenter?"
> White: "Yes, but that would cost too much."
> Brown: "Why don't you just accept what he does the way he does it?"
> White: "Yes, but the whole thing might fall down."

"Such an exchange," Berne writes, "is typically followed by a silence. It is eventually broken by Green, who may say something like, 'That's men for you, always trying to show how efficient they are.' "

Berne notes that the purpose of the game is not to solicit suggestions for solving the problem, but to reject them: "A good player can stand off the others indefinitely until they all give up, whereupon White wins." The game is ego-gratifying. Rejecting each move "brings its own little pleasure," but "the real payoff is the silence or masked silence which ensues when all the others have racked their brains and grown tired of trying to think of acceptable solutions. This signifies to White and to them that she has won by demonstrating it is they who are inadequate. If the silence is not masked, it may persist for several minutes. In the paradigm, Green cut White's triumph short because of her eagerness to start a game of her own, and that was what kept her from participating in White's game. Later on in the session, White demonstrated her resentment against Green for having abridged her moment of victory." The game Green tried to start Berne characterizes as "PTA, Delinquent Husband Type," but it also resembles the opening move of "Ain't It Awful."

Here an exercise in rapport-talk more closely resembles competitive status marking than connection building. White elevates herself by lowering everyone else. Note that in the example, and in Berne's presentation of the game more generally, all of the characters are female. Nowhere does Berne explain why this is the case. This is interesting because, at the very beginning of the book, Berne writes: "For conciseness, the games are described primarily from the male point of view unless they are clearly feminine."[18] Evidently Berne thought "Why Don't You—Yes But" is played primarily by women. But I have no difficulty imagining men playing such a game. In fact, I play it myself from time to time. Nor do I have difficulty imagining men engaging in constructive rapport-talk in which they cultivate intimacy and connection (this is the real purpose, after all, of Poker Night and Fishing With the Boys). For that matter, I have no difficulty imagining that one and the same conversation could be *both* rapport-talk *and* report-talk. I have been told that in the locker room, for example, women are brutally explicit about their sex lives—*and that they never lie.*

What are we to make of male and female conversational styles, then? On the one hand, it seems that there are different styles and that men and women exhibit different tendencies. However, it is equally clear that there are no hard and fast rules, and it is easy to overdraw the differences. It is also easy to oversimplify the motivations behind male and female styles. We purvey stereotypes not only when we *describe* behavior, but when we *analyze* it as well. We must always remind ourselves that stereotypes are, by definition, inaccurate. We may see more of ourselves in one and less of ourselves in another, but if we see ourselves perfectly reflected in any, then we are in very big trouble—for stereotypes are never entirely complimentary. More often than not they are, on balance, negative. They define the kind of person we would rather *not* be, not the kind of person we aspire to become.

So let us stick with the stereotypes, but recognize them as such. We know that there are differences in the ways in which the average man and the average woman behave. We know that men tend to exhibit masculine behavior and that women tend to exhibit feminine behavior. We know that men and women tend to exhibit different conversational styles. Everything we know about these things suggests that myths about how men and women make decisions have some basis in reality. Yet we know that these differences are overdrawn. Real people exhibit a combination of masculine and feminine attributes, and fall somewhere between the poles that the stereotypes define. We also know that people are capable of changing their behavior, at least on the margin. The next question is obvious: given that men and women *tend* to make decisions differently, *should* they?

NO, THEY SHOULD NOT

Most of what I have said in this book about how one should make a decision has addressed *process*, not *substance*. I have said relatively little about what you ought to want. My chief purpose has been to help you understand *how* to get what you want no matter *what* you want.

Stereotypically gendered decision making differs both in process and in substance. According to the myths, men like to make decisions themselves, with as little help as possible, and as quickly as possible, so as to demonstrate their independence, their autonomy, their efficacy, and their decision-making prowess. Women, on the other hand, often treat decisions as opportunities for building connections with others. This is the antithesis of the masculine style, because you cannot build connections with others by rushing through decisions and refusing to consult. In both cases there are interesting ego dynamics at work. While decision making is an opportunity for buttressing self-esteem in both instances, men and women gratify their self-esteem in different ways.

By the same token, men are likely to pursue goals and goods that will promote their differentiation from others, demonstrate their skills and capacities, and signify their mastery of nature. This is why men like to buy power tools. Women are more likely to pursue goals and goods that will make it possible for them to believe they are pursuing a useful and important life. This is why women like to buy self-improvement books.

My view is that we should try to be as agnostic as possible about any gendered *goals* men and women pursue; we should try to highlight and encourage awareness of any gendered differences in the *implicated values* of a decision; and we should try to combat any gendered pathologies in the decision-making *process*. In other words, from a procedural standpoint, men and women should make decisions in precisely the same way. Both the masculine stereotype and the feminine stereotype are flawed. Neither is likely to yield a good outcome very often. But the flaws are different. In a sense, they complement each other. The way to fix an overly masculine decision-making process is to try to be a little more feminine about it, and vice versa. There is a gender-neutral procedural ideal, and in this final section my primary goal is to unpack it.

Is it possible to eliminate *all* gender differences in decision making? No. Would it be desirable? Again, I think the answer is no. The world would be a boring place if it were populated only

by the androgynous, much as it would be if there were but one culture, or if Baskin-Robbins had but one flavor of ice cream. People
come in flavors, too. The masculine flavor and the feminine flavor
both have their intrinsic aesthetic value. The trick is to celebrate
and enjoy each without putting the other down. This is hard to do
in a politically charged context. No one ever objects to an Irish folk
festival, for example, because Irish culture as such oppresses and
threatens no one. But there are good reasons why people object to
an Orange Order march through a Catholic neighborhood in
Portadown. The Protestant revelers may certainly enjoy celebrating their history and their identity, but by its very nature the celebration is hurtful to others.

We are still a long way from the point where we can celebrate
gender differences without triggering the brickbats. Many feminists, for example, are *pro-feminine*, in the sense that in addition to
seeking to reduce economic, social, and political inequalities
between the sexes, they would like to see society validate and promote the virtues and values of caring, connection, empathy,
mutual empowerment, and nonviolence. They see society as
overtly and unhealthily masculine. Free enterprise, small government, deregulation, and a bill of rights define a masculine utopia
of autonomy, separation, and self-reliance. This is why feminism
provokes such a hostile reaction among some men. Few men disagree anymore that women should have equal rights and opportunities in society, but some sense in feminism an acute threat to
masculine virtues and values. Hence they react defensively and
derisively to man-hating "FemiNazis"—a reaction catalogued in
minute and careful detail by Susan Faludi in *Backlash: The Undeclared War against American Women*,[19] a book unfairly but perhaps
inevitably criticized for being antimale.

Just as interesting was the reaction of feminists to the publica-
tion of Robert Bly's *Iron John: A Book About Men*[20]—the book credited with spurring the so-called Men's Movement. Bly's critics
were savage. They accused him of belittling women and scorned
him as an apologist for male domination. They mocked the image
of men gathering in small groups in the wilderness, wearing

nothing but loincloths and hunting only with spears, arrows, and their bare hands, grunting and sweating together around open-pit fires, to discover their true "masculine" selves. I am convinced that most of Bly's critics never read the book. It is a thoughtful and engaging discussion of how it is important for men to be in touch with both their masculine *and* their feminine sides. There is no grunting or sweating whatsoever. Bly is in any case an unlikely hero for masculinism. He's a rumpled poet who doesn't look anything like the Burt Reynolds character in *Deliverance*. But Bly is concerned that men in modern Western society are losing touch with their masculinity and deliberately trying to suppress it. It is easy to understand why this concern would provoke a backlash from feminists who think neither that men are becoming feminine, nor that it would be a bad thing if they were.

We are not concerned in this book with reengineering society, however. We are concerned merely with effective decision making. And to make decisions effectively, one must indulge one's masculinity or femininity in the appropriate way. If you are a man (or woman, for that matter) who values privacy, independence, autonomy, and self-reliance, you should know this, and you should not pretend that you do not. You should explore your masculinity and its role in your sense of self. You should freely admit that it is important to your sense of well-being. Every once in a while, when you must decide what to do on your vacation, you should choose backpacking solo in the mountains over visiting the relations back on the farm. The health of your psyche depends upon it. You should not ignore this need. You certainly should not attempt to suppress it every time simply because it is not the "family" thing to do. Likewise, if you are a woman (or a man) whose psychic satisfaction depends upon periodic intense intimacy with your close friends, every once in a while, instead of spending a week in a cabin in Tahoe with your spouse, you should vacation with your friends in Myrtle Beach. If your feminine side is important to you, you should indulge it from time to time.

What you should *not* do is let your gender run away with your common sense. The characteristic flaws of a masculine decision-making process are (a) that it is rushed, and (b) that it is based on insufficient information about the likely outcomes of the various possible choices (very often because of a failure to gauge the preferences of others and to anticipate their reactions). The characteristic flaws of a feminine decision-making process are (a) that it drags on far longer than is necessary, and (b) that it involves grossly disproportionate costs.

Bob and Carol are going to a party in a strange part of town late at night. It is raining. Just before they leave, Carol asks Bob whether he has directions. Bob says that he has an address, and that's enough. She asks whether he at least has a map. There is one in the car, he replies. They head out, and before long become hopelessly lost. Carol suggests to Bob that he stop and check the map. Bob replies that there is no need. He got his platoon to Khe San without a map, so he can figure out how to get to a party. An hour later they find themselves retracing their steps. Carol is now angry. She complains that the party will be half over by the time they get there. She insists that Bob stop and look at the map. Grudgingly, he obliges. The map is nowhere to be found. "You said you had a map!" she shouts. "I thought I did!" he shouts back. "Pull into that gas station, then, and ask directions," she commands. "I don't need directions," he maintains, in the face of all reason and evidence. "Well, then *I'm* going to ask directions!" she says, and promptly opens the door and trudges across the road in the pouring rain to ask for help.

Bob was being pigheaded. He let his masculine drive for self-reliance run amok. He refused to take the time to get directions before he left, and he could not be bothered to check to make sure that he had a map in case he got lost. He wanted to do everything as efficiently as possible, and he wanted to do it all himself, with the result that they were late, Carol got wet, they both got mad at each other, he suffered the public embarrassment of having his wife ask directions for him at a gas station, and when they finally arrived at the party, they were both in a foul mood and had no prospect of enjoying themselves.

Was this smart? Of course not. Navigating to a party in a

strange part of town is not an acid test of one's manhood. If Bob had given the problem three seconds' thought at the outset, he would have realized that the costs of getting directions, checking to see whether he had a map, and anticipating his wife's reaction just in case he *did* get lost without having taken the precautions she suggested were all very low. The payoff was very high. Even if he had been the most talented navigator in the world, this would still have been the SEU-maximizing thing to do. All he needed was to put slightly more effort into his decision making, and to factor in his wife's preferences and likely reactions to the one seriously negative possible outcome (getting lost).

Alice gets a flyer in the mail advertising a self-defense course for women that meets three hours every Tuesday night for six weeks and costs $150. She has been thinking that she has been getting out of shape. Her regular routine is also getting a bit monotonous. The idea of a new challenge and an opportunity to meet new people appeals to her. So does the idea that she could defend herself better if attacked late at night in a park by some mugger disguised as a priest. But she is not sure whether she would learn anything very useful; she is not sure that she is up to the challenge; and she is not sure how much she would *like* learning a martial art, because she does not think of herself as a violent person. Taking the course would also leave her husband, Ted, alone with the kids on Tuesday nights. She worries that that would be unfair. She worries that she does not see her kids enough during the weekdays as it is, since she works and they are in school. She is not sure whether $150 is a good price for a martial arts course, and she wonders whether that would put an unfair burden on the monthly budget.

Alice calls her best friend and explains all of her concerns. Her friend listens attentively, and affirms Alice's concerns. Alice asks whether her friend would do it with her. She replies that she's not sure; she might; she would have to think about it.

Alice's sister calls. She goes through the whole thing again—as she does with everyone else on her block over the next week and a half. Finally, about two weeks after receiving the flyer, she asks Ted what he thinks. How would he feel about being left alone with the kids for a few hours every Tuesday night? That's fine with him, no problem. What does he think of the cost? Seems reasonable, he replies. What about the monthly budget? "You look after the finances," he replies, "you should know whether there is room in the budget." Does he think she ought to do it? "It's up to you," he says, glancing at his watch. Does he think she would get anything out of it? "Probably," he says. Alice replies that she will think about it, convinced that his failure to raise any objections is a tacit signal of disapproval.

Alice asks her kids what they think. They couldn't care less. This bothers her. What does that say about her mothering? She calls her best friend again. Is she a lousy mother? Therapy follows. An hour later, Alice is reassured. She genuinely half-believes that she is not the world's worst mother. She hangs up the phone and goes back to her husband. Is it really all right with him if she does this? He observes that they have already had this conversation. She checks one more time the next day with her best friend, who, after much consultation, has decided that she will do it also. She calls the number on the flyer. The course is fully booked.

Alice was being far too indecisive. She agonized far more than the decision warranted. She consulted too many people. She read too much into what her family said. The whole thing took so long that it became moot. She turned a fairly simple choice about how to spend her Tuesday nights into a life-defining dilemma. The whole process served only to confirm her sense of failure and inefficacy. She should have given herself twenty-four hours to think about it, and she should have consulted her husband, her kids, her sister, and her best friend at most once each (maybe her best friend twice, if she really wanted her to join her in the course). Had she done this, she would have had her black belt in no time.

Now, it is true that there was a silver lining: Alice's agonizing did give her an opportunity to build connections and negotiate relationships. This was an important value implicated in the decision. Her best friend, her sister, and her neighbors all rose to the occasion, though her husband and kids did not. She certainly did gain something from the agonizing. This justifies budgeting a little more time and effort for the decision. But not *that* much more. After all, she may have missed out on an opportunity to make several new friends at the judo academy, and the excess time she spent building connections on this particular problem she might have been able to spend building connections on more important and more constructive decisions.

It is easy to see from these two examples that there is a golden mean between the stereotypical masculine and feminine decision-making styles. Bob should have taken more time and made greater effort to take account of the judgments and preferences of others. Alice should have taken less time and paid relatively more attention to what *she* wanted. A proper budgeting of time and energy early in the decision-making process would have served both of them well. Putting a little bit more effort into thinking about how to make the decision would have paid off. The decisions would have been less expensive, and their outcomes more gratifying.

To see why men and women should not make decisions differently, it is useful to do the thought experiment of switching around the characters. Let us have Alice drive to the party, and Bob decide whether to take up martial arts. We will have to make the additional assumption either that Alice's husband, Ted, is not stereotypically masculine, or that he is out of town. Otherwise he would insist on driving.

Now, since women do not invest their sense of self-worth in their automobiles or in instrumental tasks such as navigation, Alice will naturally leave the house armed with directions and a map. If Ted is with her, she will naturally ask whether he minds that she drive. She will be both prepared and considerate, and she will get them to the party on time and in good humor. She will do everything the way Bob should have done. Since she does not suffer from testosterone poisoning in a context that is uniquely pathological for males, her decision making will be flawless.

Similarly, as Bob thinks about whether to take a martial arts course on Tuesday nights, he will reflect on what he might get out of it himself; he will reflect on the cost; and he will ask his wife and kids what they think, since he takes his responsibilities as a husband and father seriously. Whatever he decides to do, he will make up his mind in plenty of time to secure a place in the course if he wants one. Well-supplied with testosterone, he is unlikely to exhibit the pathology of allowing a simple temporary lifestyle choice to bear heavily on his sense of self-worth. He faces only one real danger: too readily interpreting his wife literally if she says, "You do whatever you want, dear, I want you to be happy." This *might* really mean: "I will take your abandoning me on Tuesday nights as a personal rejection and as a repudiation of our relationship." Bob must practice looking for the cues in posture, voice tone, and expression that would tip him off to this.

As Aristotle so wisely said, even too much of a good thing can be bad.[21] Efficiency is a valuable trait, but if you pursue efficiency too vigorously, you can make ill-informed and ill-considered judgments. Paradoxically, your decision making can even become grossly *in*efficient. Self-reliance is often a good thing, too. But there are times when too much self-reliance is stupidity. It is often very wise to consult others before you make a decision, but you can consult too much. It is also good to be able to read subtext, but you can try so hard to read subtext that you miss utterly what someone is really trying to tell you. As with most things, effective decision making requires a sense of proportion and balance.

Now, some might object that my entire discussion of decision making in this book has been irretrievably masculine. After all, I have presented decision making as a technical skill best approached in a linear, methodical way that leaves little room for—and that clearly undervalues—the less formal, more intuitive, more impressionistic, less linear, less individualistic style of deliberation that more closely resembles the feminine ideal and that resonates better with women's experience. I, like so many others, have exalted a masculine style of deliberation and confused it for an ideal.

If you have had this impression, you have misunderstood me, and you need to read the book again. (There will be a test.) Start with the introduction, where I take great pains to make clear that I do not consider decision making a narrow technical task, but rather an art in the Aristotelian sense of a skill or talent informed by science. Look again at my exhortations to tailor your decision making to suit your particular strengths and to accommodate your particular weaknesses. Ask yourself whether there is any real harm done, and whether there might not be some advantage, in trying to think more explicitly about the decisions that you will otherwise make haphazardly anyway.

I believe you will find that the tools and resources covered in this book are equally useful to men and women, and equally applicable to people who relate better to the masculine stereotype and to people who relate better to the feminine stereotype. If the stereotypes have any validity, then we should find that masculine decision makers will have an easier time relating to the admittedly fairly linear information-processing skills that I believe everyone should try to cultivate. But feminine decision makers will have an easier time carrying out the information-gathering tasks that are equally important to effective decision making. Introspection is a crucial decision-making skill, and self-knowledge a crucial decision-making asset. According to the stereotypes, women enjoy advantages over men on both of these dimensions. Intuition and the ability to read subtext are both foreign and mysterious to the masculine experience, but they are no more—and no less—than highly developed sensitivities to subtle cues that enable feminine decision makers more accurately to judge and anticipate the preferences and reactions of others upon which the likely outcomes of one's choices often so heavily depend.

The approach to decision making that I advocate in this book, in short, is gender neutral in the best sense, because there is no obstacle in principle to a man or woman using it equally effectively, no matter how masculine or feminine he or she may be.

CONCLUSION

GETTING INTO THE HABIT

Virtue, then, being of two kinds, intellectual and moral, intellectual virtue in the main owes both its birth and its growth to teaching (for which reason it requires experience and time), while moral virtue comes about as a result of habit. . . .

— Aristotle, *Nicomachean Ethics* 2.1

We have all heard the expression "Practice Makes Perfect." Nonsense. We are human beings. No matter how hard we practice, we will never attain perfection. Perfection is true flawlessness. A perfect decision maker would never make mistakes. What a dull place the world would be! What striving would remain? What would we do for a good lament? How could we have a decent laugh at ourselves? What stories would we tell our children? Perfection is vastly overrated.

Sometimes things will turn out badly even when our decision making is beyond reproach. We can count on fate to step in from time to time to thwart us, to humble us, to remind us of our humanity—and thus to keep us in line.

But while perfection is both impossible and overrated, most of us would like to make as few mistakes as possible. In the best of all possible worlds, this is exactly what would happen. If we cannot have and do not want perfection, at least we can strive for excellence. Excellence is well within reach.

What *is* excellence, anyway? The ancients thought about this notion a great deal and took it rather more seriously than we do today. The Greek word for excellence was *aretê*. It connoted a striving to attain perfection, and coming as close to it as is humanly possible. The word did double-duty in ancient Greek, meaning "virtue" as well as "excellence," because the Greeks understood these two terms to be related. Today we don't, really. We would readily say that Mother Teresa was a virtuous nun and Michael Jordan an excellent basketball player, but it would sound odd to a modern ear to call Michael Jordan a virtuous basketball player and Mother Teresa an excellent nun. To an ancient Greek ear, this would not sound odd at all. Or perhaps I should say, only "nun" and "basketball player" would sound odd.

In the ancient Greek worldview, everything had its characteristic place, purpose, or function. This is what we would call its natural end or characteristic good. A doctor's purpose, for example, is to heal the sick. A doctor who does this well does so with excellence or virtue. How does a doctor learn to heal? Partly through study and experience, which gives her knowledge of diseases and treatments. This is intellectual virtue. Cultivating it takes time. But a good doctor has some native talent, too, which cannot be taught. In addition, she has another kind of virtue—moral virtue. This is a habit of acting in a certain way—acting rightly—which is acquired and sustained through repetition. To coin an accurate if somewhat infelicitous phrase: Practice Makes Excellent.

It is part of the tragedy of the human condition that even an excellent doctor will be unable to heal everyone. But this is not through neglect or lack of trying. It is because things simply don't work out sometimes. Were it otherwise, it would be possible to be a perfect doctor, and not merely an excellent one.

Why am I dwelling on this? At the beginning of the book, I described decision making as a skill in the sense of an art informed by science—what the Greeks called *technê*. The medical art is such a skill. So is rhetoric and oratory, as the Greeks understood them (and the Greeks took rhetoric and oratory *much* more seriously than we do today, as anyone who has read Thucydides or Plato and watched a modern U.S. presidential debate will know and bemoan). An excellent speaker understands the principles of rhetoric and oratory—how to persuade an audience through reason, and how to move an audience through passion. But he also has certain natural capacities that cannot be taught. These include the ability to read an audience, to sense its mood, to know when one style of argument will be more effective than another, and to apply the abstract principles of rhetoric and oratory to concrete circumstances that vary from case to case. A good speaker also knows his own strengths and weaknesses as an orator. He will play to his strengths, and finesse his weaknesses. By combining a systematic study of theory with thoughtful introspection—self-study—and endless hours of practice, an excellent orator can cultivate almost an instinctive ability to know how to perform in any given circumstance. This is the true mark of an effective speaker. Sadly, it is something of a lost art nowadays.

Decision making is a skill in precisely this sense. It is a *technê* for which one can seek *aretê*. Effective decision making requires understanding a certain amount of theory. It requires understanding an ideal. It requires a familiarity with various principles and strategies. It requires an understanding of money and probability. It requires some familiarity with things as diverse as psychology, philosophy, and sociology. But it also requires sensitivity to the important differences between decision making in theory and decision making in practice. It requires an ability to judge when and how to deviate from the ideal. A skilled decision maker is familiar with method, and is attentive to it, but she is also attentive to a great deal besides—for example, her own needs and wants; her own strengths and weaknesses as a decision maker; the needs and wants of others; and their likely reactions to her choices.

To some extent, decision-making skill is a function of raw talent. Some of us are born better able than others to perform crucial tasks. But even talented decision makers benefit enormously from study and practice. If you have found this book useful, it is probably largely because of the information and techniques it has introduced you to (or reminded you of). This is the sense in which the book can be seen as a resource. Working through the puzzles and problems in it has, I hope, helped you become familiar with this information and these techniques. As a result, you will become adept at spotting others' misunderstandings of money or chance. You will catch people making invalid inferences and estimates by leaning on inappropriate heuristics or invoking bad rules of thumb. You will see well-meaning people paralyzed by their inability even to know how to go about resolving moral dilemmas where duties conflict with other duties, or where rules and consequences point toward different courses of action. You will see people stumble because of a misplaced conscious or unconscious concern to live up to gender stereotypes. As you become more sensitive to decision-making pathologies in others, you will, with luck, become less and less susceptible to them yourself.

But what this book *cannot* do is tell you about yourself. I have stressed the importance of self-knowledge and have suggested that it is a crucial decision-making asset. But only you can know who you are, who you would like to be, and whether it is feasible to move from one to the other. Introspection can be very hard and very painful, but it is absolutely essential if you want to become an effective decision maker. You need to ask yourself what you want; what you need; what and whom you care about; what you do and do not understand; why you can or cannot read others; whether you are good or bad with numbers; which things you find easy and do well, and which you find hard; and whether you tend to make certain characteristic mistakes. Perhaps most importantly, introspection is not something you can ever finish. It is important to revisit these questions from time to time, because you change. You do not want to work with an outdated and inaccurate image of yourself.

And this points us back to the crucial issue of *habits*. Being an effective decision maker requires cultivating certain habits. Introspection should be one of these, and it is probably the single most important. But it is worthwhile cultivating other habits as well. The nine steps can become second nature, for instance, if you simply cultivate the habit of working through them explicitly any time you face a decision difficult or important enough to warrant serious attention to process. Thinking explicitly about which strategies are appropriate to which circumstances will enable you, over time, to become so familiar with them that you will almost instinctively know when to invoke one rather than another. Training yourself to spot crucial judgments and estimates, to ask yourself what assumptions they must presuppose, or to reflect on what shortcuts might have led to them, will help you improve the quality of the information on the basis of which you make decisions, and can help you help others improve *their* decision making as well. Making a habit of reflecting on whether there are different ways of framing a problem and of representing options can help you develop a sixth sense for how best to persuade others. Looking for clever marketing tricks will sensitize you to the attempts of others to manipulate your decision making. And so forth and so on.

Effective decision makers know the value of *routines*. A routine is a regular, scripted procedure for performing a certain task. Routines have something of a bad name nowadays. We laugh at Kant, for instance, for taking a walk at precisely the same time every day, and for following precisely the same route. In my field—international politics—cataloguing the unfortunate effects of soldiers or bureaucrats mindlessly following routines has become something of a cottage industry. There are plenty of good stories. Some are tragic. Some are comic. Some are a bit of both.[1] But we easily forget that no complex organization could function without routines. We hear a small number of stories every year about the terrible consequences of people mindlessly following routines, but we never hear about the millions of cases of people profitably following them every day.

Kant's attitude toward routines may not fit well with modern self-expressive "Just Do It" Generation-Y iconoclasm, but it is worth reflecting on why such a smart guy was so uptight about them. A routine, for Kant, was not merely a way of accomplishing a regular task: it was also a form of self-discipline. All of us resist doing certain things that we know are good for us, because they are hard, unpleasant, or distract us from things we would otherwise rather be doing. No doubt Kant would have preferred reading and writing to walking the same route around Königsberg every day. If he had been inclined to be lazy, building a regular walk into his daily routine would have been an effective way of making himself do something healthy without requiring—or even permitting—an agonizing daily deliberation. Moreover, his self-discipline would have contributed to his self-respect. And the more one exercises self-discipline, the easier it becomes to exercise self-discipline in other cases. Willpower is like a muscle. It gets stronger with exercise.

I, too, laughed when a philosophy professor of mine first told me some of the anecdotes from Kant's unusually rigid life. And I confess to having a natural inclination toward laziness, too. In my twenties my doctor began to lobby me to eat better, lose some weight, and get regular exercise, especially in view of my father's early death from heart disease. I hate exercise. It's hard. It's unpleasant. I have never experienced the euphoria that dedicated runners claim they get after just a few miles' jog (either they are lying, or I have been ripped off, biochemically). But I also discovered that it was unpleasant eating poorly, being overweight, and leading a sedentary life. I felt tired all the time. My back hurt. Even moderate exertion was hard. When I finally realized that I really should do something about my lifestyle, I would agonize every time I faced a decision between doing something I wanted to do (sit and read a book, for instance, or eat a doughnut) and doing what I knew I ought to do (go for a run, or eat an apple). The agonizing was itself unpleasant, and I would only choose what was good for me sporadically and unreliably. I made no real progress toward improving my health and fitness, and was on the verge of giving up trying.

Finally, one day I was thinking about Kant and his rigid habits, and for some reason my reaction this time was one of admiration, not mirth. I realized that Kant was on to something. If I could cultivate his dedication to routine, my problem would be solved. I resolved then and there that I would establish a regular exercise routine and follow it religiously. I also resolved to establish different shopping and eating habits. I made these decisions once. I did not permit myself to revisit them. I did not allow myself to forsake them. And in no time I started to feel better, not only physically, but also psychologically. I started to feel better about myself. And the more established the routines became, the easier I found maintaining them. Establishing new routines and habits became easier and easier, too.

Of course, it is possible to overdo everything in life. You can have, or do, too much of a good thing.[2] I discovered this myself late one summer when I rather pigheadedly insisted on adhering to my morning routine of swimming in the lake despite coming down with a rather nasty cold. Before long I had a serious case of bronchitis, and my doctor, who had otherwise admired the turn-around in my lifestyle, wondered out loud in my presence how such a smart guy could be such an idiot. She was quite right. I ought to have known better. I *did* know better. I was just overly concerned with following the routine and had lost sight of the purpose of the routine in the first place.

GIVING FATE HER DUE—
BUT NOT MORE THAN HER DUE

It is not always easy to know when to stick to a routine and when to abandon it. Routines exist for the purpose of helping us do certain things efficiently. But sometimes a situation arises where sticking to the routine might do more harm than good. What do you do, for example, if you are a pilot, and you smell smoke in the cockpit? Do you follow the prescribed routine, going through a checklist to try to isolate the cause of the smoke? Or do you throw the handbook out the window (metaphorically speaking, of course) and try to land your plane at the nearest airfield as quickly as you possibly can?

This was precisely the dilemma faced by the crew of Swissair Flight 111 on the evening of September 2, 1998, as they flew their wide-body MD-11 jet from New York to Geneva. About an hour into the flight, as the cabin crew was busily serving dinner to the passengers, the cockpit crew noticed an unusual smell. Copilot Stephan Loew, who was flying the plane, turned the controls over to Captain Urs Zimmermann, and left his seat to investigate. But the source of the smell proved elusive, and the cockpit began to fill with smoke. The crew declared a midlevel emergency ("Pan Pan Pan") and requested permission to land. Initially inclined to turn back to Boston, where Swissair had a maintenance facility, the crew quickly accepted air traffic controllers' suggestion to divert to Halifax, Nova Scotia, which was much closer, and for whose runway 06 the aircraft was very nearly lined up already. As the plane descended, the flight crew, wearing oxygen masks, continued to try to isolate the cause of the smoke while the flight attendants collected trays and began preparing the cabin for landing. But the captain decided that the plane was too high and too heavy for a straight-in approach to Halifax, and requested permission to turn, lose some altitude, and dump fuel, while they went through the prescribed checklist to try to isolate the source of the smoke. Suddenly, in the middle of their turn, the crew declared a full emergency and announced that they had to land immediately. At 10:26 local time, air traffic controllers lost contact with the plane. Residents of Peggy's Cove, Nova Scotia, reported hearing the sound of jet engines passing overhead, followed by silence and then an explosion as the plane dove headlong into the sea, killing all 229 people on board.

Did the crew of Swissair 111 err in deciding to follow their routines? Should they have abandoned the smoke checklist and tried to land quickly, with a nearly full load of fuel, even if this would have violated the standard operating parameters for an MD-11? Given the result, we may be tempted to say yes. But from what we know at the moment, it is very difficult to find fault with their judgment. First of all, it is clear from the transcript of the radio communications between the flight crew and ground controllers that the pilots did not realize that their situation was dire until very late.* Second, while smoke in the cockpit is not common, it is not unusual, either. Every day, in the United States, one commer-

---

*I present and analyze the transcript in greater detail in appendix 4. As I write, the Transportation Safety Board of Canada, which has jurisdiction over the investigation of the accident, has not determined its precise cause, nor has it released the full transcript of the cockpit voice data recorder.

cial jet crew (on average) requests permission to divert and land because of smoke. It is literally a daily occurrence. Yet it seldom results in disaster.[3] In most cases the flight crew is able to find the source of the smoke and to stop it, or land without incident and well within operational guidelines. Third, these guidelines, and the smoke checklists, are designed to ensure the safety of the aircraft. Smoke is something that all pilots take very seriously, of course—and more seriously now than they used to, thanks to the fate of Swissair 111—but there are risks to trying to land quickly, just as there are risks to trying to land cautiously with a cockpit full of smoke. While it is true that some pilots have successfully landed aircraft at excessive speeds and weights, clearly the faster and heavier an aircraft lands, the greater the danger of a fatal accident on the ground. Those who criticize the flight crew's by-the-book approach would surely have been equally critical of their recklessness if they had attempted to bring the plane straight down, resulting in a massive fireball and the deaths not only of all those on board, but of some additional number of people on the ground as well.

Could the pilots have landed the plane straight-in from a high altitude and with a heavy load of fuel? Perhaps so. Pilots have managed the feat in a flight simulator—though I for one would be more impressed if they did it in a simulator filled with smoke, and with flight control systems switching on and off or failing one by one. But the key question in any case is whether the crew of Swissair 111 had any reason to believe that they were more likely to land the plane safely by engaging in what they surely knew to be some risky flying than by following standard procedures. It seems that they did not. They were not aware of any base rate information suggesting that following standard procedures when dealing with smoke in the cockpit is a worse gamble than trying to land quickly with a full load of fuel. As far as I can tell, no such information exists.

The press has been quick to compare the tragic outcome in this case, however, with happier outcomes in other cases. Three years before the Swissair disaster, for example, the crew of a Federal

Express DC-10—a forerunner of the MD-11—successfully landed their aircraft at an unfamiliar airport shortly after they smelled smoke in the cockpit on a flight from Memphis to Boston:

> The FedEx crew—two pilots and a flight engineer—quickly assessed the situation as serious, asked air-traffic control for an immediate diversion to the nearest airport, began a high-speed emergency descent and landed at Stewart International Airport at Newburgh, N.Y., 17 minutes after a warning light first indicated there might be smoke in the cabin of the DC-10 cargo aircraft. . . .
>
> A review of the cockpit voice recording, which was published in the United States by the National Transportation Safety Board a month before the Swissair crash, showed that the FedEx captain was determined to land the aircraft as soon as possible, even if that meant disregarding standard procedures.
>
> The review showed that a number of items on the smoke checklist were omitted by the FedEx crew in their haste to land.
>
> At one point the FedEx captain tells the co-pilot: "Keep the speed up; don't slow down to 250 [knots, the advised speed for conducting the smoke checklist]; we're in an emergency situation here."
>
> Earlier, he had told air-traffic control: "We need to get it on the ground. We need to get it to Stewart. Give us the vectors."
>
> The FedEx DC-10 was only 40 kilometres from Stewart on a flight from Memphis, Tenn., to Boston when the pilot radioed air-traffic control to report "smoke in the cockpit. . . . We're at 33 [thousand feet] and like to proceed direct [to the nearest airport] and we need to descend at this time," but the airport was directly behind the aircraft and the crew needed to make a 180-degree turn as well as an emergency descent. The flight path, including the turn, was about 100 kilometres.
>
> FedEx Flight 1406 landed 14 minutes after it reported smoke to air-traffic control.[4]

Unlike someone who has not read this book, you will appreciate that the happy story of FedEx Flight 1406 provides no basis whatsoever for criticizing the performance of the crew of Swissair Flight 111. You can't generalize from a single case. Only someone completely oblivious to the availability heuristic would think otherwise.

Now, even though it seems to be hard to fault the Swissair pilots' fidelity to routines, it may be possible to find fault with the routines themselves. Did the pilots' manual specify operational parameters for emergency landings too conservatively? Was the smoke checklist flawed? Possibly. Indeed, some critics have suggested that the very procedures the Swissair crew used to try to isolate the source of the smoke may actually have made their situation worse. The argument is that by switching circuits on and off in which frayed wires were arcing, the crew actually succeeded in sparking or exacerbating a fire in the cockpit.[5] This argument depends, of course, on whether frayed wiring is to blame. If so, no doubt we will see it meticulously presented and critiqued by those seeking to establish or escape liability for the disaster. But it will be interesting to see whether a court will assign liability for the disaster by faulting a procedure generally recognized as effective for isolating the source of cockpit smoke. That would seem illogical, at the very least.

From what we know at the moment, then, it would appear that we should simply regard the ill-fated flight of Swissair 111 as a reminder that things do not always work out perfectly in this world. Sometimes even well-meaning, well-trained, and highly-skilled people acting as best they can on the basis of the information available to them at the time will simply fail to avert tragedy. This is, after all, why we use words such as "ill-fated" and "tragic" to describe circumstances of this kind. Bad outcomes, in short, are not necessarily indictments of routines.

We must not forget, too, what can happen when people *fail* to follow routines. The Chernobyl nuclear disaster provides perhaps the most shocking example of this. On April 25, 1985, technicians at Chernobyl Reactor Unit 4, not far from Kiev, decided to conduct an experiment. Deliberately contravening established procedures, they shut down the reactor's power-regulating and emergency safety systems and withdrew most of the control rods from the reactor core—just to see what would happen. In the early hours of the morning on April 26, the reactor went critical. There were several explosions. An enormous fireball blew the steel and concrete lid off the containment building. The reactor's graphite core caught fire and partially melted down. An enormous cloud of radioactive material spewed into the atmosphere, where air currents carried it as far away as Scandinavia. Thirty-two people died in the immediate aftermath of the incident. Dozens of others, some of whom later died, suffered serious radiation sickness. The plant released somewhere between 50 and 185 million curies of radionuclides into the air—many more times the radioactivity released by the atomic bombings of Hiroshima and Nagasaki at the end of the Second World War. Millions of acres of forest and farmland were contaminated. Nobody knows exactly how many people will suffer or die from radiation-induced cancers over the long term.[6]

DECISION MAKING IN PERSPECTIVE

I do not mean to misuse the availability heuristic myself here by suggesting that a single illustration justifies the generalization that most breakdowns of routines have catastrophic consequences. But it requires not very much reflection to realize that our lives are so complex that they would become utterly unmanageable if we were not to script various tasks and activities. Habits and routines are as useful for decision-making tasks as they are for anything else. It is always a challenge to know when to follow them, when to modify them, and when to abandon them—but there is no denying the general utility of cultivating them. They will not always serve you well; but they will serve you well more often than not.

To make good use of the theory, techniques, and insights I have covered in this book, then, it is necessary to try to embed them in your daily practices. Practice will never make perfect, but it can certainly encourage the kind of excellence that consists in understanding the *science* of decision making and appreciating the *art* required to apply the science to the concrete and varying situations that you face in the light of your particular values, goals, strengths, and weaknesses. An excellent musician, an excellent doctor, and an excellent speaker must all know something about theory; they must all have a firm grasp of a range of facts relevant to their endeavors; they must understand the nature and the limitations of their particular talents; and they must constantly work to maintain (or, if possible, to improve) their skills. Habits enable them to do this. There is no interesting or important difference between decision making, in this respect, and music, medicine, or oratory.

It is this perspective on decision making that I have sought to present and to justify in this book. There is a great deal we can learn and benefit from the science of decision, and I have delved into what I consider to be some of the more interesting and more useful bodies of research that bear on decision making from a wide variety of angles. Sound decision making, I am convinced, rests upon a certain familiarity with the theory of decision; its various methods; its real-world limitations; strategies and principles of choice; numbers; probability; psychology; moral reasoning; and gender dynamics. But just as no one could possibly become an excellent musician, doctor, or speaker just by reading books, neither this book nor any other could possibly make you an excellent decision maker. Only you can do that. I hope that this book can help by serving as a resource—a store, as it were, of useful tips and insights—but I believe it can help you most of all by putting decision making in a perspective that helps you understand precisely why decision making cannot be treated as a purely mechanical exercise.

In sum, we must be philosophical about decision making—in the broadest possible sense of the word.

And on that note, we are done.

APPENDIX 1

The following is a detailed analysis of the SEU calculation in the hypothetical World Series example from chapter 1.

Let us suppose that your three potential hitters have all performed as follows against this particular closer in the past:

TABLE 19. PAST PERFORMANCE

	Slugger	Pinch hitter	On-deck hitter
Appearances	95	78	48
Singles	9	12	7
Doubles	3	2	0
Triples	0	1	1
Home runs	6	4	2
Hit-by-pitch	3	0	0
Walks	11	1	8
Strikeouts	24	12	14

You convert these to percentages (this is the same as table 4):

TABLE 20. PERCENTAGES

	Slugger	Pinch hitter	On-deck hitter
Singles	.095	.154	.146
Doubles	.032	.026	.000
Triples	.000	.013	.021
Home runs	.063	.051	.042
Hit-by-pitch	.032	.000	.000
Walks	.116	.013	.167
Strikeouts	.253	.154	.292

These probabilities may also be represented as follows:

TABLE 21. PERCENTAGES AGAIN

	Slugger	Pinch hitter	On-deck hitter
Probability of getting a hit (single, double, triple, or home run)	.189	.244	.208
Probability of drawing a walk or getting hit by a pitch	.147	.013	.167
Probability of getting on base (add the above two probabilities)	.336	.257	.375
Probability of making an out (1.000 minus the probability of getting on base)	.664	.743	.625

This yields the following probabilities of winning the game various different ways:

TABLE 22. PROBABILITIES OF THE VARIOUS WAYS OF WINNING

Event	Comment	Probability of this if you let your slugger bat	Probability of this if you pinch-hit
(A) You win the game this inning at bat.	Your batter has to get a hit.	.189	.244
(B) Your on-deck batter wins the game for you this inning.	Your batter has to draw a walk or get hit by a pitch, and the on-deck batter then has to get on base.	.055	.005
(D) You win the game this inning	Either (A) or (B) happens. Add these two probabilities to get the probability of winning this inning.	.244	.249
(E) The game goes into extra innings.	Your batter has to draw a walk (or get hit by a pitch) and the on-deck batter has to make an out.	.092	.008
(F) You win the game if it goes into extra innings.	By assumption, the odds of this are fifty-fifty.	.500	.500
(G) You win the game in extra innings.	This is the probability of the game going into extra innings if you let this batter bat (E) times the probability of your winning the game if it goes into extra innings (F)	.046	.004
(H) You win the game in this inning or in extra innings	This is the sum of the probabilities of the various ways you have of winning the game (A+B+G)	.290	.253

It may be easier to visualize this diagrammatically, to see all of the various pathways to victory or defeat. Add up all of the probabilities of various ways of winning, and you can see why you should let your slugger hit:

FIG. 6. SLUGGER'S PATHWAYS TO VICTORY AND DEFEAT

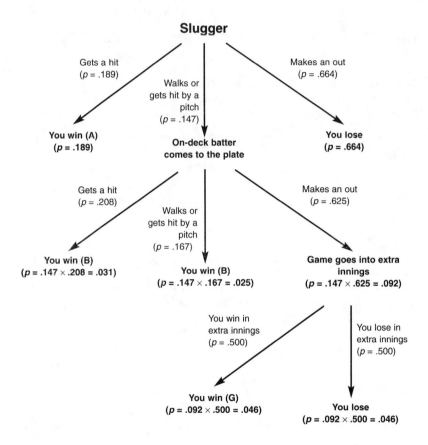

FIG. 7. PINCH HITTER'S PATHWAYS TO VICTORY AND DEFEAT

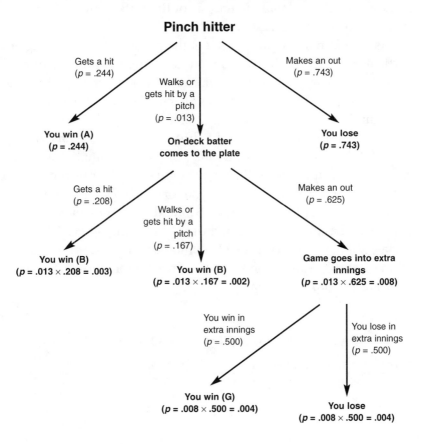

APPENDIX 2

The following is a detailed analysis of the Kafkaesque game show example in chapter 2. Recall table 7.

As I explain in chapter 3, we get the probabilities of rolling any particular number with two dice by counting the number of combinations that will yield that number as a proportion of the total number of possible combinations. Each die has six faces, so the total number of possible combinations is $6 \times 6 = 36$. There is only one combination that will yield a throw of 2: each die has to come up "1." Likewise, there is only one possible combination that will yield a throw of 12: each die has to come up "6." Thus the odds of rolling either a 2 or a 12 are 1-in-36, or 0.027778. There are more possible combinations for intermediate throws, however. You can roll a 3 by having one die come up "1" and the other "2" or vice versa—so there are two possible combinations. You can roll a 4 by rolling 1 and 3, 2 and 2, or 3 and 1—three combinations, and so on. Here are the probabilities:

TABLE 23. DIE ROLL PROBABILITIES

Roll	Number of combinations	Odds	Probability
2	1	1 in 36	0.027778
3	2	2 in 36	0.055556
4	3	3 in 36	0.083333
5	4	4 in 36	0.111111
6	5	5 in 36	0.138889
7	6	6 in 36	0.166667
8	5	5 in 36	0.138889
9	4	4 in 36	0.111111
10	3	3 in 36	0.083333
11	2	2 in 36	0.055556
12	1	1 in 36	0.027778

Thus we can cross-reference the probability of any particular outcome for each game:

TABLE 24. PROBABILITIES OF INDIVIDUAL OUTCOMES

Probability	Game A	Game B	Game C	Game D	Game E	Game F
0.027778	$1,000,000	$50	$2,000,000	$1,000	$40	$50
0.055556	$100,000	$25	$0	$100	$35	$40
0.083333	$10,000	$10	$0	–$10	$30	$30
0.111111	$1,000	$5	$0	–$25	$25	$20
0.138889	$100	$0	$0	–$50	$20	$10
0.166667	$10	–$2	$0	–$100	$15	$0
0.138889	–$10	–$5	–$100	–$200	–$5	$0
0.111111	–$100	–$10	–$1,000	–$300	–$5	$0
0.083333	–$1,000	–$25	–$10,000	–$400	–$5	–$100
0.055556	–$10,000	–$1,500	–$100,000	–$500	–$2,000	–$1,500
0.027778	–$100,000	–$2,000	–$1,000,000	–$3,000	–$2,500	–$3,500

The expected utility of each game is the sum of all the possible outcomes multiplied by their respective probabilities. We calculate the expected utility of game A as follows:

TABLE 25. EXPECTED UTILITY OF GAME A

Probability	Outcome	Probability times outcome
0.027778	$1,000,000	$27,777.78
0.055556	$100,000	$5,555.56
0.083333	$10,000	$833.33
0.111111	$1,000	$111.11
0.138889	$100	$13.89
0.166667	$10	$1.67
0.138889	–$10	–$1.39
0.111111	–$100	–$11.11
0.083333	–$1,000	–$83.33
0.055556	–$10,000	–$555.56
0.027778	–$100,000	–$2,777.78
GRAND TOTAL		**$30,864.17**

We can read the minimum and maximum outcomes for each game right off the first table, but the probabilities of a disastrous outcome, an acceptable outcome, and a loss are a little trickier to calculate. To calculate the probability of a disastrous outcome, we sum the product only of losses $1,000 or greater with their respective probabilities. To calculate the probability of an acceptable outcome, we sum the product only of outcomes that represent a $10 loss or better and their respective probabilities. To calculate the probability of a loss, we sum the product only of negative outcomes and their respective probabilities. Again taking game A as our example:

TABLE 26. PROBABILITIES OF DISASTER, ACCEPTABLE OUTCOME, AND LOSS (GAME A)

p	Outcome	Disaster?	p	Acceptable outcome?	p	Loss?	p
0.028	$1,000,000	No		Yes	0.028	No	
0.056	$100,000	No		Yes	0.056	No	
0.083	$10,000	No		Yes	0.083	No	
0.111	$1,000	No		Yes	0.111	No	
0.139	$100	No		Yes	0.139	No	
0.167	$10	No		Yes	0.167	No	
0.139	–$10	No		Yes	0.139	Yes	0.139
0.111	–$100	No		No		Yes	0.111
0.083	–$1,000	Yes	0.083	No		Yes	0.083
0.056	–$10,000	Yes	0.056	No		Yes	0.056
0.028	–$100,000	Yes	0.028	No		Yes	0.028
TOTAL			0.167		0.722		0.417

Table 27, then, gives the master list of the features of each game relevant to the various decision rules, with the best outcome on each criterion in boldface.

TABLE 27. PREFERABLE GAME BY DECISION RULE

	Game A	Game B	Game C	Game D	Game E	Game F
Expected utility (SEU): Higher is better	**$30,864.17**	–$138.94	$21,263.89	–$199.44	–$168.61	–$179.17
Worst possible outcome (Minimax): Higher is better	–$100,000	**–$2,000**	–$1,000,000	–$3,000	–$2,500	–$3,500
Best possible out come (Maximax): Higher is better	$1,000,000	$50	**$2,000,000**	$1,000	$40	$50
Probability of disaster (Disaster Avoidance Principle): Lower is better	0.166667	0.083333	0.277778	**0.027778**	0.083333	0.083333
Probability of acceptable outcome (Risk Minimization Principle): Higher is better	0.583333	0.722222	0.583333	0.083333	**0.916667**	0.833333
Probability of a loss (Loss Avoidance Principle): Lower is better	0.416667	0.583333	0.416667	0.916667	0.416667	**0.166667**

APPENDIX 3

The following are the results of an alternative method of integrating Fred and Ginger's evaluation of Ginger's mother's care options from chapter 5.

Recall table 16, simplified to consider the two remaining options on the table. Let us replace Ginger's estimates of Fred's happiness with Fred's own estimates (in bold):

TABLE 28. GINGER'S SCORES (MODIFIED)

Consideration	Weight	Full-time live-in care for Mom in new place	Move to new house with Granny suite
Mom's comfort	100	2	10
Mom's care	100	9	9
Fred's happiness	40	**10**	8
My sanity	30	2	7
My marriage	60	10	8
Cost	0	2	4
Comfort of house	10	8	8
Quality of neighborhood	5	10	8
Proximity to friends	5	10	3
Convenience	2	8	8
Total score	**352**	**2356**	**3061**

Let us also replace on table 17 Fred's estimates of Ginger's happiness with Ginger's own estimates, and also substitute Ginger's estimates of her mother's comfort and care for Fred's, since she knows her mother better than Fred does (also in bold):

TABLE 29. FRED'S SCORES (MODIFIED)

Consideration	Weight	Full-time live-in care for Ginger's mother in new place	Move to new house with Granny suite
Ginger's mother's comfort	10	2	10
Ginger's mother's care	10	9	9
My [Fred's] happiness	80	10	8
Ginger's happiness	60	2	7
Our marriage	60	8	9
Cost	20	3	5
Comfort of house	70	8	7
Quality of neighborhood	20	10	8
Proximity to friends	10	10	4
Convenience	10	10	6
TOTAL SCORE	**350**	**2530**	**2640**

This now yields the following joint evaluation:

TABLE 30. MODIFIED JOINT SCORES

	Full-time live-in care for Ginger's mother in new place	Move to new house with Granny suite
Ginger's score	2356	3061
Ginger's total weights	352	352
Ginger's normalized score (A)	6.69	8.70
Fred's score	2530	2640
Fred's total weights	350	350
Fred's normalized score (B)	7.23	7.54
Total joint score (A+B)	13.92	16.24

APPENDIX 4

Here is the transcript of radio communications between Swissair 111 and air traffic controllers, with commentary.

My original source for this transcript was http://www.bst-tsb.gc.ca/french/about/emergency/background/furgent_atc_prelim_transcript.html. The Transportation Safety Board of Canada has since removed the transcript from its Web site as a result of a reinterpretation of Canadian law. As I write, however, a version of the transcript may still be found at http://aviation-safety.net/cvr/atc_sr111.htm.

I have modified speaker designations and some typography for clarity and correctness (leaving Canadian spellings in the original, however), and I have converted universal coordinated time (UTC) to local time. The transcript refers to Swissair 111 "heavy" because the MD-11 is a wide-body aircraft.

> SWISSAIR 111 (9:58:15.8 Atlantic Daylight Time): Moncton Centre, Swissair one eleven heavy; good, uh, evening; level three three zero [33,000 feet].
>
> MONCTON ATC (9:58:20.4): Swissair one eleven heavy, Moncton Centre. Good evening. Reports of, uh, occasional light turbulence at all levels.
>
> SWISSAIR 111 (9:58:26.1): Moncton Swissair. . . .

The plane has just entered airspace controlled by Moncton ATC. This is a routine contact and acknowledgement. Everything is fine.

> SWISSAIR 111 (10:14:18.0): Swissair one eleven heavy is declaring Pan Pan Pan. We have, uh, smoke in the cockpit, uh, request [deviate?], immediate return, uh, to a convenient place, I guess, uh, Boston [unintelligible].
>
> MONCTON ATC (10:14:33.2): Swissair one eleven roger . . . turn right proceed . . . uh . . . you say to Boston you want to go?
>
> SWISSAIR 111 (10:14:33.2): I guess Boston . . . we need first the

weather so, uh, we start a right turn here. Swissair one one one heavy.

MONCTON ATC (10:14:45.2): Swissair one eleven roger and a descent to flight level three one zero [31,000 feet]. Is that okay?

SWISSAIR 111 (10:14:50.3): Three one zero [Unintelligible words obscured by a noise, possibly the noise associated with donning oxygen masks.] Three one zero [unintelligible] one one heavy.

MONCTON ATC (10:15:03.1): Swissair one eleven Centre.

SWISSAIR 111 (10:15:06.6): Swissair one eleven heavy; go ahead.

MONCTON ATC (10:15:08.6): Uh, Would you prefer to go into Halifax?

SWISSAIR 111 (10:15:11.6): Uh, Standby. . . .

SWISSAIR 111 (10:15:38.4): Affirmative for Swissair one eleven heavy. We prefer Halifax from our position.

MONCTON ATC (10:15:43.8): Swissair one eleven roger, proceed direct to Halifax, descend now to flight level two niner zero [29,000 feet].

SWISSAIR 111 (10:15:48.7): Level two niner zero to Halifax, Swissair one eleven heavy. . . .

The crew just made their first important decision: preparing to land in Halifax, which is ahead of them, rather than turning back to Boston. The plane starts to descend.

MONCTON ATC (10:16:36.5): Swissair one eleven, you're cleared to ten thousand feet and the Hal . . . altimeter is two nine eight zero.

SWISSAIR 111 (10:16:41.7): Two niner eight zero, ten thousand feet, Swissair one eleven heavy.

MONCTON ATC (10:16:52.5): And Swissair one eleven, uh, can you tell me what your fuel on board is and the number of passengers?

SWISSAIR 111 (10:16:58.3): Uh, roger, standby for this. . . .

MONCTON ATC (10:18:19.3): Swissair one eleven, you can contact Moncton Centre now one one niner decimal two [a new radio frequency].

SWISSAIR 111 (10:18:24.4): One one niner point two for the Swissair one one one heavy.

MONCTON ATC (10:18:31.0): Roger.

SWISSAIR 111 (10:18:34.3): Moncton Centre, good evening. Swissair one eleven heavy flight level two five four [25,400 feet] descending flight level two five zero [25,000 feet] on course Halifax. We are flying at the time on track zero five zero.

HALIFAX ATC (10:18:46.8): Swissair one eleven good evening; descend to three thousand, the altimeter is two nine seven nine [29.79, a local barometric setting for the altimeter].

SWISSAIR 111 (10:18:51.8): Ah, we would prefer at the time around, uh, eight thousand feet, two nine eight zero [29.80, a local barometric setting for the altimeter], until the cabin is ready for the landing.

HALIFAX ATC (10:19:00.9): Swissair one eleven, uh, you can descend to three, level off at an intermediate altitude if you wish. Just advise.

SWISSAIR 111 (10:19:07.2): Roger. At the time we descend to eight thousand feet. We are anytime clear to three thousand. I keep you advised.

Here is a second decision. The air traffic controllers have cleared the plane to descend to 3,000 feet, but the cockpit crew prefers to descend slowly so that the cabin crew can collect and stow dinner trays. If the plane descended more quickly at this point, it would be a little less risky later to try a straight-in approach to Halifax. But the crew has no reason yet to think that the plane is in serious danger. They are simply dealing with smoke in the cockpit—something that could be caused by a variety of things, and which most of the time turns out to be something quite minor.

HALIFAX ATC (10:19:14.5): Okay. Can I vector you, uh, to set up for runway zero six at Halifax?

SWISSAIR 111 (10:19:19.4): Ah, say again latest wind, please?

HALIFAX ATC (10:19:22.1): Okay, active runway Halifax zero six. Should I start you on a vector for six?

SWISSAIR 111 (10:19:26.3): Yes, uh, vectors for six will be fine; Swissair one eleven heavy.

HALIFAX ATC (10:19:31.0): Swissair one eleven roger, turn left heading of, ah, zero three zero.

SWISSAIR 111 (10:19:35.1): Left, ah, heading zero three zero for the Swissair one eleven.

HALIFAX ATC (10:19:39.5): Okay, it's a back course approach for runway zero six. The localizer frequency one zero niner decimal niner. You've got thirty miles to fly to the threshold.

SWISSAIR 111 (10:19:53.3): Uh, we need more than thirty miles; please, ah, say me again the frequency of the back beam.

The cockpit crew thinks the plane is too high for a straight-in approach. It is descending, but less than a minute and a half ago, it was at 25,400 feet, and four minutes before that it was at 33,000 feet. So if the rate of descent is roughly constant thus far (just over 2,100 feet per minute), presumably the aircraft is still above 21,000 feet.

HALIFAX ATC (10:19:59.5): Swissair one eleven roger, you can turn left heading three six zero to lose some altitude; the frequency is one zero niner decimal niner for the localizer, it's a back course approach.

SWISSAIR 111 (10:20:09.5): One zero niner point niner roger, and we are turning left to heading, ah, north. Swissair one eleven heavy.

There is still nothing to indicate that the plane is in serious danger. The decision to turn and lose more altitude gradually eliminates the option of a straight-in approach. Once the plane is part-way into its turn, it will no longer be lined up with runway 06.

HALIFAX ATC (10:21:23.1): Swissair one eleven, when you have time could I have the number of souls on board and your fuel on board, please, for emergency services?

SWISSAIR 111 (10:21:30.1): Roger, at the time, uh, fuel on board is, uh, two three zero tonnes. We must, uh, dump some fuel. May we do that in this area during descent?*

HALIFAX ATC (10:21:40.9): Uh, okay, I am going to take you. . . Are you able to take a turn back to the south or do you want to stay closer to the airport?

SWISSAIR 111 (10:21:47.0): Uh, standby short, standby short.

SWISSAIR 111 (10:21:59.1): Okay we are able for a left or right turn towards the south to dump.

HALIFAX ATC (10:22:04.2): Swissair one-eleven, uh, roger, uh, turn to the, ah, left heading of, ah, two zero zero degrees and, ah, advise me when you are ready to dump. It will be about ten miles before you are off the coast. You are still within about twenty-five miles of the airport.

SWISSAIR 111 (10:22:20.3): Roger, we are turning left and, ah, in that case we're descending at the time only to ten thousand feet to dump the fuel.

HALIFAX ATC (10:22:29.6): Okay, maintain one zero thousand. I'll advise you when you are over the water. It will be very shortly.

SWISSAIR 111 (10:22:34.4): Roger.

SWISSAIR 111 (10:22:36.2): [In German: You are in the emergency checklist for air conditioning smoke?]

HALIFAX ATC (10:22:42.9): Uh, Swissair one eleven say again, please?

---

*Two hundred thirty tonnes is the current gross weight of the aircraft, not the amount of fuel on board.

SWISSAIR 111 (10:22:45.3): Ah, sorry it was not for you. Swissair one eleven was asking internally. It was my fault, sorry about.

HALIFAX ATC (10:22:50.8): Okay.

The crew is still trying to isolate the cause of the smoke.

HALIFAX ATC (10:23:33.1): Swissair one-eleven continue left heading one-eight zero; you'll be, ah, off the coast in about, ah, fifteen miles.

SWISSAIR 111 (10:23:39.2): Roger, left heading one eight zero. Swissair one eleven, ah, and maintaining at ten thousand feet.

HALIFAX ATC (10:23:46.3): Roger.

HALIFAX ATC (10:23:55.7): You will, ah, be staying within about, ah, thirty-five, forty miles of the airport if you have to get to the airport in a hurry.

SWISSAIR 111 (10:24:03.9): Okay, that's fine for us. Please tell me when we can start, ah, to dump the fuel.

HALIFAX ATC (10:24:08.8): Okay.

SWISSAIR 111 (10:24:28.1): [Background tone] Ah, Swissair one eleven. At the time we must fly, ah, manually. Are we cleared to fly between, ah, ten thou—eleven thousand and niner thousand feet? [Sound of Autopilot disconnect warbler]

HALIFAX ATC (10:24:38.7): Swissair one eleven you can block between, ah, five thousand and twelve thousand if you wish.

SWISSAIR 111 (10:24:45.1): Swissair one eleven heavy is declaring emergency.

Something serious and unexpected has happened.

SWISSAIR 111 (10:24:46.4): [Second voice overlap:] [Roger?] we are between, uh, twelve and five thousand feet; we are declaring emergency now at, ah, time, ah, zero one two four. [Possible intercom sound toward the end of the transmission.]

HALIFAX ATC (10:24:56.0): Roger.

SWISSAIR 111 (10:24:56.5): ... Eleven heavy we starting dump now; we have to land immediate.

For the first time, the crew is aware that the situation is dire. But the plane is no longer lined up with the runway.

HALIFAX ATC (10:25:00.7): Swissair one eleven just a couple of miles I'll be right with you.

SWISSAIR 111 (10:25:04.1): Roger. [Sound: probable Autopilot disconnect warbler.]

SWISSAIR 111 (10:25:05.4): And we are declaring emergency now Swissair one eleven.

HALIFAX ATC (10:25:08.6): Copy that.

HALIFAX ATC (10:25:19.2): Swissair one eleven you are cleared to, ah, commence your fuel dump on that track and advise me, ah, when the dump is complete.

HALIFAX ATC (10:25:43.0): Swissair one eleven, check; you're cleared to start the fuel dump.

SWISSAIR 111 (10:25:49.3): [Unintelligible.]

Just over a minute has passed between the crew's realization that their situation was dire and the loss of radio contact.

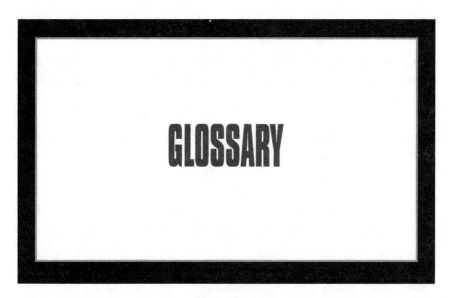

GLOSSARY

ACT UTILITARIANISM. The ethical doctrine that one should always act so as to maximize social utility (see also "utility"; "social utility"; and "Greatest Happiness Principle," below. Cf. "rule utilitarianism," also below).

ANCHORING AND ADJUSTMENT HEURISTIC. The tendency to make judgments of value, magnitude, likelihood, or degree relative to some "anchor," or initial available value.

ARETÊ. An ancient Greek word meaning "excellence" or "virtue."

AVAILABILITY HEURISTIC. The tendency for estimates of frequency or likelihood of a phenomenon to be influenced by the ease of recall of examples.

BELL CURVE. See "normal frequency distribution," below.

BIAS. A systematic distortion of judgment, estimation, or perception.

BOLSTERING. The tendency to defend one's beliefs against discrepant information by seeking out countervailing supporting information.

CERTAINTY EFFECT. The tendency to give too much weight to outcomes one considers certain (compared to outcomes one merely sees as probable).

CONJUNCTION FALLACY. The error of thinking two events occurring (or two conditions obtaining) more likely than one of them alone.

CONSEQUENTIALISM. The view that one should judge the morality of an action solely by its consequences.

CONSTRAINED OPTIMIZATION. A strategy of attempting to find the best option from among some subset of the complete set of all options.

DEONTOLOGY. The view that one should judge the morality of an action solely by assessing its fit with a body of authoritative rules or principles.

DESCRIPTIVE ETHICAL RELATIVISM. The empirical claim that moral judgments differ from person to person, group to group, or culture to culture.

DISASTER AVOIDANCE PRINCIPLE. A principle of choice prescribing the option with the smallest chance of disaster.

DOMINANCE. An attribute of an option that is at least as good as all other options on every dimension, and better than all others on at least one.

EGOCENTRIC BIAS. The tendency to exaggerate one's own role as a determinant of the behavior of others.

ELIMINATION BY ASPECT. Rejection of an option because of its failure to satisfy some minimum specific requirement.

ENDOWMENT EFFECT. The propensity to demand more to give something up than one would be willing to pay for it.

EXPECTED UTILITY. "Utility" (see below) weighted by probability (also see below).

FEMININE. One of two genders (the other being "masculine"—see below) denoting a set of characteristics, dispositions, or behaviors commonly thought of as belonging properly to women.

FEMINISM. Advocacy of the rights of women based upon the doctrine of equality of the sexes.

FREQUENCY DISTRIBUTION. A count of the number of elements of a set having each value, or falling within each value range, of a particular variable (typically presented as a table or chart).

FUNDAMENTAL ATTRIBUTION ERROR. The tendency to attribute to personal dispositions (rather than situational constraints) the bad behavior of people we dislike or the good behavior of people we like, and the tendency to attribute to situational constraints (rather than personal dispositions) the good behavior of people we dislike or the bad behavior of people we like.

GENDER. A social or cultural characterization of attributes, dispositions, and behaviors thought properly to apply either to men ("masculine") or to women ("feminine").

GENDERED. Denoting a witting or unwitting characterization of a concept as having, or privileging, masculine or feminine traits.

GREATEST HAPPINESS PRINCIPLE. The ethical principle that one should always seek to promote the greatest happiness of the greatest number, i.e., to maximize "social utility" (see below).

HEDONIC CALCULUS. A method invented by Jeremy Bentham for determining which of two or more options maximizes "social utility" (see below).

HEURISTIC. A shortcut to judgment or estimation.

HYPERVIGILANCE. Dysfunctionally heightened alertness and sensitivity, combined with exaggerated intensity of behavior, intended to detect threats.

IMAGE. A collection of beliefs about people's motivations, intentions, attitudes, and dispositions.

ISOLATION EFFECT. The tendency to ignore the components of risk that two or more options share, concentrating solely on their differences.

LOSS AVOIDANCE PRINCIPLE. A principle of choice prescribing the option that carries the smallest chance of loss.

MARTINGALE SYSTEM. A system of betting involving doubling the stake after a loss so as to recoup oneself eventually.

MASCULINE. One of two genders (the other being "feminine"—see above) denoting a set of characteristics, dispositions, or behaviors commonly thought of as belonging properly to men.

MASCULINISM. Celebration or privileging of manliness or masculinity (usually derogatory).

MAXIMAX. A principle of choice prescribing the option that has the best possible outcome in the domain of gains (*maximizing a maximum*).

MAXIMIN. A principle of choice prescribing the option whose smallest possible gain is larger than that of any other option (*max-*

*imi*zing a *mini*mum). Functionally equivalent to prescribing the option with the best worst outcome in the domain of gains (see also "Minimax," below).

MEAN. The average value of a frequency distribution (see "frequency distribution," above).

MEDIAN. The value in a frequency distribution that divides all elements into two equal-size groups with higher and lower values (see "frequency distribution," above).

METAMESSAGE. An underlying meaning or hidden message.

METASTRATEGY. A strategy for choosing a strategy.

MINIMAX. A principle of choice prescribing the option whose largest possible loss is smaller than that of any other option (minimizing a maximum). Functionally equivalent to prescribing the option with the best worst outcome in the domain of losses (see also "Maximin," above).

MONTE CARLO FALLACY. The error of believing that the probability of any particular forthcoming outcome in a series of repeated but independent events changes as a result of the outcomes of past events in the series.

MOTIVATED BIAS. A systematic distortion of judgment, estimation, or perception caused by a subconscious desire to gratify deep psychological needs.

MULTI-ATTRIBUTE UTILITY MAXIMIZATION. A method of determining the best option among two or more when each option may be ranked or scored on two or more dimensions of value.

NORMAL DISTRIBUTION. A symmetrical frequency distribution (see "frequency distribution," above) whose mean and median have the same value (see "mean" and "median," above) and whose shape resembles a bell (see "bell curve," above); technically, a Gaussian distribution described (with variable x) by the expression $(-x^2/2\pi\sigma^2)/\sqrt{(2^2)}$.

NORMATIVE ETHICAL RELATIVISM. The claim that what is right or wrong for one person, group, or culture may not be right or wrong for another person, group, or culture.

OPPORTUNITY COST. The value of the best foregone alternative.

OPTIMIZE. A strategy whose goal is to find the best possible option.

p. Probability—variable from 0 ("no chance") to 1 ("certain"). See "probability," below.

PRESELECTION. A strategy whereby one chooses directly a known specific option from among the available set.

PRIMING. The phenomenon by which concepts, concerns, or experiences already present to consciousness render a specific interpretation of ambiguous information more likely.

PROBABILITY. A measurable likelihood of a particular event based upon the relative frequencies of the elements of a set of events (see "p," above).

PROPORTIONALITY BIAS. The tendency to infer other people's intentions from the apparent costs and consequences of their actions.

RANDOM CHOICE. A strategy for making a choice prior to the evaluation of options, or a principle for choosing among evaluated options, whereby the specific outcome can only be predicted with probabilistic confidence.

REPRESENTATIVENESS HEURISTIC. The tendency to use a characteristic (or set of characteristics) of something which we believe to be typical of a larger group or class as the basis for judging frequency or likelihood.

RISK MINIMIZATION PRINCIPLE. A principle of choice prescribing the option that carries the highest chance of an acceptable outcome.

RULE OF THUMB. A rough and ready measure; a rule or guideline derived from practice, experience, or folk wisdom.

RULE UTILITARIANISM. The ethical doctrine that one should always act according to that body of rules compliance with which would maximize social utility (see also "utility" and "social utility," below, and "Greatest Happiness Principle," above. Cf. "Act utilitarianism," also above).

SATISFICE. A strategy that prescribes the choice of the first acceptable option.

SEU. See "Subjective expected utility" and "Subjective expected utility maximization," below.

SEX. Either of the two divisions of a species distinguished biologically as male and female respectively.

SOCIAL UTILITY. The happiness, pleasure, or satisfaction of society as a whole.

STANDARD DEVIATION. A measure of dispersion in a frequency distribution (see "frequency distribution," above) equal to the square root of the mean of the squares of the deviations from the average.

SUBJECTIVE EXPECTED UTILITY. The happiness, pleasure, or satisfaction one can expect to realize from any given option.

SUBJECTIVE EXPECTED UTILITY MAXIMIZATION. The attempt to realize the greatest possible happiness, pleasure, or satisfaction one can expect from the available options.

TECHNÊ. An ancient Greek word denoting an art informed by science, in contrast to a narrow technical skill.

TRANSACTION COST. A cost of doing business.

UNMOTIVATED BIAS. A systematic distortion of judgment, estimation, or perception caused by normal human information processing.

UTILITARIANISIM. The ethical doctrine that the Greatest Happiness Principle (see above) should guide human conduct. See also "act utilitarianism," "rule utilitarianism," and "social utility,"above; and "utility," below.

UTILITY. Happiness, pleasure, or satisfaction.

INTRODUCTION

1. See, e.g., Graham T. Allison, Albert Carnesale, and Joseph S. Nye Jr., eds., *Hawks, Doves, and Owls: An Agenda for Avoiding Nuclear War* (New York: Norton, 1985); Joseph S. Nye, Graham T. Allison, and Albert Carnesale, eds., *Fateful Visions: Avoiding Nuclear Catastrophe* (Cambridge, Mass.: Ballinger, 1988).

2. James G. Blight and David A. Welch, *On the Brink: Americans and Soviets Reexamine the Cuban Missile Crisis*, 2d ed. (New York: Noonday, 1990); James G. Blight, Bruce J. Allyn, and David A. Welch, *Cuba on the Brink: Castro, The Missile Crisis, and the Soviet Collapse* (New York: Pantheon, 1993); James G. Blight and David A. Welch, eds., *Intelligence and the Cuban Missile Crisis* (London: Frank Cass, 1998); James G. Blight and David A. Welch, "Risking 'The Destruction of Nations': Lessons of the Cuban Missile Crisis for New and Aspiring Nuclear States," *Security Studies* 4, no. 4 (summer 1994): 811–50.

3. E.g., David A. Welch, "The 'Clash of Civilizations' Thesis as an Argument and as a Phenomenon," *Security Studies* 6, no. 4 (summer 1997): 185–204.

4. Author's interview; Blight and Welch, *On the Brink*, p. 183.

5. See, e.g., David A. Welch, *Justice and the Genesis of War* (Cambridge: Cambridge University Press, 1993); David A. Welch, "Remember the Falklands? Missed Lessons of a Misunderstood War," *International Journal* 52, no. 3 (summer 1997): 483–507.

6. The Greek word *technê* is often mistranslated as "technical skill"

in the latter sense. A fundamental misunderstanding of this concept lies at the heart of Robert Pirsig's otherwise engrossing best-seller, *Zen and the Art of Motorcycle Maintenance: An Inquiry into Values* (New York: Morrow, 1974).

CHAPTER 1: HOW TO MAKE DECISIONS IN THE IDEAL WORLD

1. John Rawls, *A Theory of Justice* (Cambridge, Mass.: Belknap, 1971), p. 62.

2. David A. Welch, "The Politics and Psychology of Restraint: Israeli Decision-Making in the Gulf War," in *Choosing to Co-operate: How States Avoid Loss*, ed. Janice Gross Stein and Louis W. Pauly (Baltimore: Johns Hopkins University Press, 1993), pp. 128–69.

3. Ingrid Peretz, "Lottery Windfall Dragged Woman 'Through Hell'," *Globe and Mail (Toronto)*, 4 March 2000, p. A3.

CHAPTER 2: STRATEGIES, RULES OF THUMB, AND PRINCIPLES OF CHOICE

1. See Duncan Grinnell-Milne, *Mad, Is He? The Character and Achievement of James Wolfe* (London: Bodley Head, 1963), esp. pp. 82, 207, 257. Grinnell-Milne's highly entertaining hagiography manages to make Wolfe's scheme seem risk-free, but on this point he is in the minority. Cf., e.g., C. P. Stacey, *Quebec, 1759: The Siege and the Battle* (Toronto: Macmillan, 1959); W. T. Waugh, *James Wolfe: A Man and Soldier* (Montreal: L. Carrier & Co., 1928).

2. *Webster's Encyclopedic Unabridged Dictionary of the English Language* (New York: Gramercy Books, 1989).

3. See http://lawlibrary.ucdavis.edu/LAWLIB/Oct97/0639.html, especially Fred Shapiro's posting, citing the *Los Angeles Times*, 13 August 1994, and the *Washington Post*, 25 January 1995.

4. Edward Wallerstein, "Circumcision: The Uniquely American Medical Enigma," *Urological Clinics of North America* 12, no. 1 (February 1985): 123–32.

5. United States Bureau of Justice Statistics, *Violent Crime* (Washington, D.C.: U.S. Dept. of Justice Bureau of Justice Statistics, 1994); United States Bureau of Justice Statistics, *Violent Crime by Strangers* (Washington, D.C.: U.S. Dept. of Justice Bureau of Justice Statistics, 1982); L. Kellermann Arthur and A. Mercy James, "Men, Women, and Murder:

Gender-Specific Differences in Rates of Fatal Violence and Victimization," *Journal of Trauma* 33, no. 1 (1992): 1–5.

6. Alice H. Eagly, Richard D. Ashmore, Mona G. Makhijani, and Laura C. Longo, "What Is Beautiful Is Good, But . . . : A Meta-Analytic Review of Research on the Physical Attractiveness Stereotype," *Psychological Bulletin* 110, no. 1 (July 1991): 109–28.

7. For a technical discussion of dominance, see Paul Weirich, *Equilibrium and Rationality: Game Theory Revised by Decision Rules* (Cambridge: Cambridge University Press, 1998), pp. 116 ff.

8. If you enjoy academic blood sport, compare Gregory M. Herek, Irving L. Janis, and Paul Huth, "Decision Making During International Crises: Is Quality of Process Related to Outcome?" *Journal of Conflict Resolution* 31, no. 2 (June 1987): 203–26; David A. Welch, "Crisis Decision-Making Reconsidered," *Journal of Conflict Resolution* 33, no. 3 (September 1989): 430–45; Gregory M. Herek, Irving L. Janis, and Paul Huth, "Quality of U.S. Decision Making During the Cuban Missile Crisis: Major Errors in Welch's Reassessment," *Journal of Conflict Resolution* 33, no. 3 (September 1989): 446–59.

CHAPTER 3: BY THE NUMBERS: MONEY AND CHANCE

1. Hannum was a Syracuse banker, and a competitor to Barnum, best known as the owner of the Cardiff Giant, a popular 1869 attraction.

2. See, e.g., http://www.publicdebt.treas.gov/opd/opd.htm; http://sat-nd. com/topics/iridium.htm.

3. There is also a small cottage industry of financial self-help books of varying quality. A particularly readable one for people whose personal finances are a mess is Suze Orman, *The 9 Steps to Financial Freedom: Practical & Spiritual Steps So You Can Stop Worrying* (New York: Crown, 1997).

4. Let's assume no one was born on February 29 (which only appears in leap years) and that one is just as likely to be born on one day of the year as on any other. That leaves 365 possible birthdays. The probability that two people in a group share a birthday is 1.0 minus the probability that they do not. If your birthday is January 1, then I don't share a birthday with you if mine is any of the other 364 days in the year. So the probability that I share your birthday is 1 − (364/365), or roughly .27 percent. With three people, the probability that at least two of them share a birthday is 1 − ([364/365] × [363/365]), or roughly .8 percent, and with four it is 1 − ([364/365] × [363/365] × [362/365]), or roughly 1.6 percent. As you add people, the probability rises, as you can see. Lo! and behold,

once you get to twenty-three people, the probability cracks the 50 percent barrier for the first time (50.7 percent). You have more than a 99 percent chance of a shared birthday with fifty-seven people in the group. In a group of 365 people, it is mathematically possible that no two people will share a birthday (every day of the year would be someone's birthday, but no two people would share one): but the odds are *overwhelmingly* against this. The probability would be 1.5×10^{-157} (a decimal point followed by 156 zeroes, and then, finally, a one and a five!) Once you have a group of 366 people, however, it is no longer possible *not* to have a common birthday. There aren't enough days in the year.

5. This kind of "common mode failure" is often responsible for serious accidents. Safety systems that designers believe to be independent are, in fact, sometimes susceptible to simultaneous failures because of some hidden mutual dependency. For a good scare, see Scott Sagan, *The Limits of Safety: Organizations, Accidents, and Nuclear Weapons* (Princeton, N.J.: Princeton University Press, 1993).

6. See the Bill Gates Net Worth Page, http://www.quuxuum.org/~evan/bgnw.html. Much of Bill Gates's worth consists of shares in Microsoft, of course, which, like many technology stocks, is quite volatile. If you check this site today, you may discover that the current estimate of his net worth differs quite a bit from the $85 billion figure I found there at the time of writing.

7. Based on the period 1982–1998; see http://www.ntsb.gov/aviation/Table3.csv.

8. See, e.g., Edward W. Packel, *The Mathematics of Games and Gambling* (Washington, D.C.: Mathematical Association of America, 1981).

9. See, e.g., , Stanley Milgram, "The Small World Problem," *Psychology Today* 1 (May 1967): 60–61.

10. For a sobering view, see George Soros, *The Crisis of Global Capitalism: Open Society Endangered* (New York: Public Affairs, 1998).

CHAPTER 4: JUDGMENT, PERCEPTION, AND CHOICE: THE QUIRKS AND TRAPS OF HUMAN PSYCHOLOGY

1. These are all situations where people evince quite different preferences between two options, even though there is no real monetary difference between them. For discussion of these and other examples, see Amos Tversky and Daniel Kahneman, "The Framing of Decisions and the Psychology of Choice," *Science*, no. 211 (30 January 1981): 453–58.

2. Readers who wish to explore the topics I cover in this chapter in

more detail may wish to begin with two unusually readable and accessible treatments: Scott Plous, *The Psychology of Judgment and Decision Making* (New York: McGraw-Hill, 1993); and Stuart Sutherland, *Irrationality: Why We Don't Think Straight!* (New Brunswick, N.J.: Rutgers University Press, 1992).

3. Daniel Kahneman and Amos Tversky, "Prospect Theory: An Analysis of Decisions under Risk," *Econometrica* 47, no. 2 (March 1979): 26.

4. Tversky and Kahneman, "The Framing of Decisions and the Psychology of Choice," p. 453.

5. Ibid.

6. See, e.g., Glen Whyte, "Escalating Commitment to a Course of Action: A Reinterpretation," *Academy of Management Review* 11, no. 2 (April 1986): 311–21.

7. The literature on behavioral decision theory is enormous and growing rapidly. It tends to be presented in a fairly technical way, but those interested in exploring further may wish to begin with Richard H. Thaler, *The Winner's Curse: Paradoxes and Anomalies of Economic Life* (New York: Free Press, 1992). A shorter piece that repays close study is Amos Tversky and Daniel Kahneman, "Rational Choice and the Framing of Decisions," *Journal of Business* 59, no. 4 (1986): S251–S77. For a broader recent treatment, see William Mark Goldstein and Robin M. Hogarth, eds., *Research on Judgment and Decision Making: Currents, Connections, and Controversies* (New York: Cambridge University Press, 1997).

8. The examples in this paragraph and the following three are drawn from Kahneman and Tversky, "Prospect Theory."

9. See, e.g., Daniel Kahneman, Paul Slovic, and Amos Tversky, eds., *Judgment under Uncertainty: Heuristics and Biases* (Cambridge: Cambridge University Press, 1982); and Plous, *The Psychology of Judgment and Decision Making*, pp. 107–88.

10. Fritz Redlick, *Hitler: Diagnosis of a Destructive Prophet* (New York: Oxford University Press, 1999).

11. Alexander L. George and Juliette L. George, *Woodrow Wilson and Colonel House* (New York: John Day Co., 1956).

12. The best analysis is Richard Ned Lebow, *Between Peace and War: The Nature of International Crisis* (Baltimore: Johns Hopkins University Press, 1981), pp. 119–47.

CHAPTER 5: DOING THE RIGHT THING: MAKING MORAL CHOICES

1. For a useful summary of religious positions, see http://www.religioustolerance.org/euthanas.htm.

2. "An action done from duty has its moral worth, not in the purpose that is to be attained by it, but in the maxim according to which the action is determined." Immanuel Kant, *Grounding for the Metaphysics of Morals*, 3d ed., trans. James W. Ellington (Indianapolis: Hackett, 1993), pp. 12–13.

3. Reprinted in ibid., pp. 63–67. Kant quotes Constant's objection in the first paragraph of the essay cited immediately below.

4. Ibid.

5. Jeremy Bentham, *The Rationale of Reward* (London: John and H. L. Hunt, 1825), p. 206.

6. From *BreakPoint*, September 29, 1999, copyright 1999; reprinted with permission of Prison Fellowship, P.O. Box 17500, Washington, D.C., 20041-0500.

7. This was an insight first noted by Karl Duncker more than sixty years ago; see "Ethical Relativity? (An Enquiry into the Psychology of Ethics)," *Mind*, n.s., 48, no. 189 (January 1939): 39–57.

8. Based on U.S. Bureau of the Census data, March 1996; http://www.census.gov/population/www/projections/natproj.html.

9. John Rawls, *A Theory of Justice* (Cambridge, Mass.: Belknap, 1971), pp. 46–47.

CHAPTER 6: DO MEN AND WOMEN MAKE DECISIONS DIFFERENTLY? SHOULD THEY?

1. John Gray, *Men Are from Mars, Women Are from Venus: A Practical Guide for Improving Communication and Getting What You Want in Your Relationships* (New York: HarperCollins, 1992).

2. By Katherine Black (Los Angeles: Oak Tree, 1998) and Amanda Newman (Holbrook, Mass.: Adams Media Corp., 1999) respectively.

3. Suzanne Kessler, "Creating Good-Looking Genitals in the Service of Gender," in *A Queer World: The Center for Lesbian and Gay Studies Reader*, ed. Martin Duberman (New York: New York University Press, 1997); Kathryn Morgan, "Sexuality as a Metaphysical Dimension," in *Philosophy and Women*, ed. Sharon Bishop and Marjorie Weinzweig (Belmont, Mass.: Wadsworth, 1979).

4. See http://www.undp.org/hdro/98gem.htm.

5. Andrew Sullivan, "The He Hormone," *New York Times Magazine,* 2 April 2000, pp. 46ff.

6. Ibid., p. 48.

7. Carol Gilligan, *In a Different Voice: Psychological Theory and Women's Development* (Cambridge, Mass.: Harvard University Press, 1982).

8. S. Boughn and A. Lentini, "Why Do Women Choose Nursing?" *Journal of Nursing Education* 38, no. 4 (April 1999): 156–61.

9. Deborah Tannen, *You Just Don't Understand: Women and Men in Conversation* (New York: Ballantine, 1990).

10. Ibid., pp. 49–50.

11. Ibid., p. 15.

12. Anthony Trollope, *Phineas Finn, The Irish Member,* new ed. (London: Chapman and Hall, 1877).

13. Gray, *Men Are from Mars, Women Are from Venus,* pp. 60–61.

14. Ibid., p. 61.

15. Tannen, *You Just Don't Understand,* p. 77.

16. Eric Berne, *Games People Play: The Psychology of Human Relationships* (New York: Grove Press, 1964).

17. Ibid., p. 116. The full presentation of the game is on pp. 116–22.

18. Ibid., p. 12.

19. Susan Faludi, *Backlash: The Undeclared War against American Women* (New York: Crown, 1991).

20. Robert Bly, *Iron John: A Book About Men* (Reading, Mass.: Addison-Wesley, 1990).

21. Aristotle, *Nicomachean Ethics,* bk. 2, secs. 2, 6–7; bk. 4.

CONCLUSION: GETTING INTO THE HABIT

1. I survey a few such stories and attempt to put them in context in "The Organizational Process and Bureaucratic Politics Paradigms: Retrospect and Prospect," *International Security* 17, no. 2 (fall 1992): 112–46.

2. As I mentioned in chapter 6, Aristotle stressed this, too; *Nicomachean Ethics,* bk. 2, secs. 6–7; bk. 4. Aristotle was an especially wise and insightful thinker. It's a shame his writing is so dull.

3. Paul Koring, "Swissair: Pilot Tactics Queried," *Globe and Mail (Toronto),* 2 September 2000; http://www.theglobeandmail.com/gam/TopNational/20000902/USWISN.html.

4. Paul Koring, "Human Factors, Different Rules Separate Two Airline Emergencies," *Globe and Mail (Toronto),* 2 September 1999, pp. A1, A3.

5. See, e.g., Stephen Thorne's Canadian Press article, "Swissair Checklist Suspect, Say Experts," 8 October 1998; http://www.canoe.ca/CNEWSSwissairCrash/oct8_swissair2.html.

6. Grigorii Medvedev and Andrei Sakharov, *The Truth about Chernobyl* (New York: Basic Books, 1991).

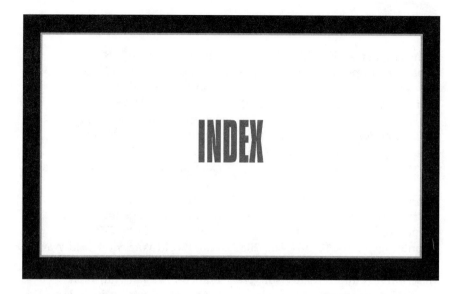

INDEX